Ahead in the Cloud

Ahead in the Cloud

BEST PRACTICES FOR NAVIGATING THE FUTURE OF ENTERPRISE IT

◆ ◆ ◆

Stephen Orban

Global Head of Enterprise Strategy at Amazon Web Services

"Culture eats strategy for breakfast"—Peter Drucker

ISBN: 1981924310
ISBN 13: 9781981924318
Library of Congress Control Number: 2017919575
CreateSpace Independent Publishing Platform
North Charleston, South Carolina

Table of Contents

Foreword

Andy Jassy, CEO, Amazon Web Services

◆ ◆ ◆

In 2003, when we decided to build Amazon Web Services (AWS), none of us had the audacity to predict it would grow as fast as it did or that it would be as big as it is now.[1] But a few factors led us to believe it could be a meaningful business for us.

First, we'd become good at running deep infrastructure services (e.g., compute, storage, and database) and highly reliable and cost-effective data centers to grow Amazon's retail business as fast as we did for the first eight years of Amazon's history. We had a strong competency in running very scalable infrastructure.

Second, in the early part of the 2000s, Amazon was building a business called Merchant.com, where Amazon provided e-commerce technology that fueled external companies' e-commerce websites. To deliver that capability, we had to decouple all of our technology components and make them accessible via Application Programming Interfaces (APIs). This turned out to be a lot harder and more time-consuming than we'd anticipated. And when we realized how much easier and faster it was for teams inside and outside of Amazon to access our technology if they had access to it via well-documented, hardened APIs, we developed religion about building in this loosely coupled, service-oriented architecture fashion.

Third, as we were adding lots of software developers at Amazon in 2002 and 2003, we noticed that projects were still taking us the same amount of

1 At the end of 2017, AWS had a $20 billion annual run rate and is growing 45% year over year.

time to complete as when we had fewer resources. This was surprising to us, and counter to what teams predicted. When we investigated, we found that virtually every team was spending several months and people resources re-creating the same infrastructure software pieces (compute, storage, database, analytics, machine learning, etc.). It turned out that teams were spending 80% of their time on the undifferentiated heavy lifting of infrastructure and just 20% of their time on what differentiated their ideas. We wanted to flip that equation on its head to let Amazon teams invent and experiment more quickly. And we figured if a strong technology company like Amazon had this challenge, it was likely that a lot of other builders at small and large companies (and governments!) would, too.

This led to our pursuing the mission that remains AWS's mission today: to enable any company, government, or developer to build and run any technology application on AWS's infrastructure platform. We launched our first service (Amazon Simple Storage Service—Amazon S3) in early 2006, and the cloud was effectively born.

While it wasn't always the case, the benefits of the cloud are now reasonably well known. The conversation starter is almost always cost savings. For most companies, if they can trade the old model of heavy capex outlay (where you have to commit to the capital for datacenters and servers up front) for variable expense (where you pay as you consume), it's quite attractive. On top of that, the variable expense for customers is less on AWS than what they could procure themselves on-premises because AWS has such large scale and passes this on to its customers in the form of lower prices (we've lowered our prices on over 60 different occasions in the last 10 years!). And then, in the cloud you get real elasticity. You don't have to provision for the peak and then sit on wasted capital when you settle into your normal traffic pattern. With the cloud, you provision what you need, scale up seamlessly when needed, and shed resources and costs when it's not needed.

Cost savings are compelling for most companies; however, the number one reason enterprises are moving to the cloud so quickly is speed and agility. And this agility isn't just being able to get a server in minutes in the cloud, versus the 10 to 18 weeks it takes on-premises. It's because when you have 100+ technology services at your disposal, turning ideas into products and services becomes much, much easier. You don't have to build all of the underlying software. You don't have to build the large compute or virtualization clusters. You don't have to build and tune databases. You don't have to build the storage solution or constantly try to manage the capacity. Instead, you can allow what might be your scarcest resource—your software developers—to focus on building their ideas.

We now see every imaginable vertical segment using AWS in a meaningful way. Financial services organizations like Capital One, Intuit, FINRA, and NASDAQ; healthcare companies like Johnson & Johnson, Bristol Myers Squibb, Novartis, and Merck; media players like Netflix, Disney, HBO, Turner, and Fox; consumer packaged goods companies like Kellogg's, Coca Cola, and Nestle; manufacturing companies like General Electric (GE), Siemens, and Phillips—all of them are benefiting from the cloud, and many are reinventing themselves in the process.

And it's not just private sector companies—government agencies, educational institutions, and non-profit organizations are using the cloud to deliver on their missions as well. NASA's Jet Propulsion Laboratory used AWS to stream images of the Mars Curiosity Rover's landing, and the Singapore Land Transport Authority uses AWS to improve the commuting experience for Singapore's residents. The American Heart Association is creating a big data platform for cardiovascular research on AWS. And, the US Intelligence Community chose AWS as its infrastructure provider for the critical work they do. Nearly 3,000 government agencies worldwide, 8,000 academic institutions, and over 22,000 nonprofits are using AWS today.[2]

The move to the cloud is happening at an incredibly fast pace, and enterprises that don't learn to move fast risk being left behind. To survive in the current business environment, you have to be able to take advantage of evolving technology trends, and the one thing that's been constant the last 10

2 As of February, 2018.

years—and I believe will continue to be constant the next 20 or 30 years—is that technology is going to continue to change at a rapid pace.

The cloud is the biggest technology shift of our lifetimes. But at the same time, there are a number of enterprises who need help making this shift. That's where Stephen's book comes in. This book includes learnings from many that have gone before you, and shares those best practices and key changes required to leverage this transformational technology.

Some of the most compelling lessons I've learned in my time managing AWS are shared in Stephen's book. In my opinion, the single biggest differentiator between those who talk a lot about the cloud and those who have actual success is the senior leadership team's conviction that they want to take the organization to the cloud. It's not enough to think it's a good idea. It's not enough to talk about it. It's not enough to get a few of your leaders to agree with you. Inertia is a very powerful blocker in large organizations. Senior leaders need to present the vision of why they want to move to the cloud, get their entire leadership team aligned and committed to making the move, set an aggressive top-down goal to push the organization to move faster than they would otherwise, and have mechanisms to see the actual progress and avoid the pocket vetoing that sometimes transpires in large organizations.

One of my favorite examples of commitment came from GE, a large company that has been on the leading edge of cloud adoption. A few years ago, then-CIO Jamie Miller decided she wanted to move GE to the cloud. She got much of her staff in a room and said that GE was going to move 50 applications to AWS in the next 30 days. This set off a 45-minute discussion with the consensus that it was a dumb idea, it couldn't happen, and it wouldn't happen. Jamie listened to the discussion and then said, "I heard everything you just said, but we are going to do it." GE didn't quite get to 50 in 30 days (they got to about 40), but in the process, they demystified the cloud, figured out the cloud security and compliance model, had successes that built momentum, and developed ideas on what else to migrate. GE has since migrated several thousand applications to AWS.

We've also seen how important it is for teams to think holistically about their application estate without trying to boil the ocean. Most of our enterprise customers segment their applications into tranches: those that are easy to move to the cloud, those that are medium hard, and those that are hardest. They also segment applications into those that can easily be lifted and shifted into the cloud and those that need to be re-architected before moving to the cloud. A common mistake I've seen is when companies paralyze themselves if they can't figure out how to move every application. The reality is that since many can be moved to the cloud rather easily, you get to enjoy all the benefits I mentioned above, and this early experience helps inform how to move the harder applications.

I could rattle off many more of these lessons, but you're better off reading Stephen's book, which more eloquently details these learnings.

The world is moving fast. Being two to three years behind competitors (some of whom may not even be hatched yet) is a tough place to be. I hope this book gives you the motivation, tools, and guidance you need to help you invent on behalf of your customers, build a sustainable and long-term business, and make your company an inspiring and fun place for builders to work.

Giddy up!

Foreword

Adrian Cockcroft

◆ ◆ ◆

WHERE DO THE BEST PRACTICES for enterprise IT come from? Why do we need new ones? Technology changes all the time, but every few years the change reaches a fundamental level and disrupts the industry. As a result, both suppliers and customers have to question assumptions and figure out from first principles what new patterns and opportunities appear.

This is actually the third time I've been part of a global movement to fundamentally retool enterprise IT. The first time was when I joined Sun Microsystems in 1988. In those days, the new, radical technologies were open standards like Unix, NFS, TCP/IP, and Ethernet, and we were up against proprietary operating systems and networking standards like DEC's VAX/VMS or standalone PCs and minicomputers. I was a solutions architect in Sun's UK sales operation, and met several customers every day. It was fun working with customers and some of the best talent in the industry at a fast-growing company that was changing the world, and that's what I still enjoy most about my current role at AWS.

Sun moved me to Silicon Valley in 1993—just in time to get involved in the early days of the World Wide Web and the commercial internet, and its adoption by startups and enterprise IT. This was my second "movement." I spent a lot of time with customers, helping them build new kinds of applications, scale their web sites, and keep them up and running. By the early 2000s, I was working on an internal proposal for Sun to rent centrally located computers to customers over the internet, but we couldn't find any IT executives who liked the idea! Sun didn't have a consumer-oriented business model or experience running its own web services, so in the end it was Amazon who put together the web services, direct-to-consumer/developer business model. This did an end run around the IT executives, who still didn't like the idea, but couldn't stop it.

I joined Netflix in 2007—just as they launched streaming—to manage a team of developers working on personalization algorithms, and to use my previous experiences to help make the service more scalable and available. It was soon clear we needed to make a radical change to our architecture and a large investment in infrastructure to cope with the rapid growth in streaming. By 2009, we'd decided to avoid trying to build a global network of large datacenters, and instead to leverage AWS by migrating to cloud. Several teams were formed to work on the migration, and I led the cloud migration of the personalization platform before becoming the overall cloud architect for Netflix. I started to document the "cloud native" architecture and present it at conferences, and as people saw proof that it provided agility, scalability, and high availability, we got more and more interest. The interest wasn't just from startups though, we started to get requests to talk to large enterprises and government departments globally. Some of the IT executives had finally decided that cloud was interesting! Eventually it made sense for me to leave Netflix and focus on helping everyone else with their cloud migration, as the third big "movement" in my career.

As Stephen quotes up front, "Culture eats strategy for breakfast." I agree. My time at Netflix was like living on the inside an MBA case study in company culture, and Amazon also has a big focus on culture to tie together a large and diverse organization. However, culture is hard to change and curate, and I'd like to add my own counter-quote "You get the culture you pay for." As we work on technology migration with enterprises, it's usually people and processes that are the blockers, not technology problems. Getting to cloud effectively means you need to figure out DevOps, but DevOps is often a re-org, not adding or re-naming a team. The whole organization needs to be recruited and compensated with an aligned strategy and rewards to get the culture right. In other words, you won't get long-term strategic results like Amazon or Netflix without a culture that is supported by a long-term, focused compensation structure. In some enterprises, the best answer to "Can you help us move to cloud?" could be "Sure, can I start by meeting your board of directors to talk about your culture and compensation policy?" The right culture also unlocks internal talent, because you don't add innovation to a company—you get out of its way. An executive once told me "We can't copy Netflix because we don't have the people." My response was "Where do you think they used to work? We hired them from you and got out of their way..."

When I joined AWS in 2016, Stephen Orban was a key contact for me, and we work together on the same team. I met him a few years before and heard about his focus on enterprise IT for AWS. My complementary focus is the startup world, large-scale web companies, and open source, but there's a big overlap as everyone learns from each other. Stephen has hired an exceptionally experienced team, and captured his experiences along with theirs in this book. It's packed full of good advice, techniques, patterns, and processes. We all learn something new from every customer we meet, and look forward to getting your feedback on this book at an Executive Briefing Center meeting one day.

Foreword

Mark Schwartz

◆ ◆ ◆

ENTERPRISES TODAY ARE IN A peculiar position. On one hand, they recognize that their industries are being disrupted and the pace of change has increased. On the other hand, they have put a lot of effort into creating their status quo—that is, what has worked for them in the past—and establishing controls to maintain that status quo. They've built for the present, but the future is upon them.

This is why we talk so much about "digital transformation." Startups have no need to transform; they are what they are. Enterprises, however, have to break free from what they have been.

In my book, *The Art of Business Value*, I showed how enterprises, over time, learn how to succeed given their circumstances and assets, and how the techniques that lead to success become embedded in their cultures, rules, and processes. In other words, deeply embedded in a company's culture is everything that has worked well for them *in the past*.

When I became CIO of US Citizenship and Immigration Services, for example, I discovered a culture of extreme caution and risk aversion. We often talked about the need to avoid appearing on the front page of the Washington Post. Why? Well, we had learned that being mentioned negatively in the press made it difficult to get our work done. It would lead to calls for explanation from Congressional Committees. It would cause new rules to be slammed into place reactively, rules that would get in the way of our everyday work. That's organizational culture: the norms that arise to reinforce behavior that has led to success.

Similarly, companies create rules—bureaucracy, essentially—based on activities that have worked for them in the past. Standard operating procedures, for example. These aren't just made up *in vacuo*; they are procedures that have worked, and therefore get memorialized in writing. Both culture and bureaucracy are forms of institutional memory: ***this*** is what works for us.

Things are going well for the enterprise and then—WHOOSH—a new player enters the market, a technology changes, a new law is passed, a competitor introduces a surprise innovation—and suddenly things start changing at a frantic pace. What worked yesterday is not going to work anymore. The enterprise's culture and formal processes no longer apply. What has made them successful in the past will make them unsuccessful in the future.

So they need to transform. But here's the thing. They don't just need to transform to be successful ***now***: the reality of our environment is that change will continue. We are not talking about a one-time change, we are talking about a change to continuous change. In my second book, *A Seat at the Table*, I talk about continuous transformation and the kind of adjustment it requires in how we think about IT.

The only way we can keep up with future change is to build agility into our enterprises. I mean that in both the everyday and the technical senses of agility. I mean, simply. that enterprises need to invest in being able to change quickly and constantly. I faced precisely this challenge at USCIS. For many years now—since well before I started at USCIS—there have been rumors that "comprehensive immigration reform" was imminent. Unfortunately, no one could say when it would happen. Still less could anyone say what exactly it would look like when it happened. I was told that if Congress did get around to it, there would be lots of last-minute horse trading, so we wouldn't know until the last minute what the new rules would be. But without a doubt we would be told we had to roll out the changes immediately. When President Obama introduced DACA, for example, we had only 60 days to make all of the IT changes to accommodate it. And comprehensive reform would be vastly more disruptive.

What does a CIO do in such a case? We couldn't get a head start building for immigration reform, because we didn't know what it would look like. All that we could do, I realized, was build agility and flexibility into our systems, our underlying technology, our people, and our organization. That agility would mitigate our risks and let us be responsive to whatever happened.

Most enterprises have not optimized for agility. If anything, they have optimized for efficiency – for doing what they do at the lowest cost. This is the dilemma. An enterprise must transform by changing its culture, changing its bureaucracy, changing its organization, changing its technical architecture—and making them agile.

There is one indispensable tool available to help them do so. That is the cloud. Yes, there is all that agile development stuff—but the truth is that today's agile best practices—DevOps, microservices, containerization, and so on—all rely heavily on the cloud. I suppose they can be done without the cloud, in theory—just as you can dig the foundation for a building by using a spoon. But the cloud changes everything, when it comes to agility.

With the cloud, you can get rid of physical assets, while making their virtual equivalents appear and disappear instantaneously at your command. In the old days, you had to order hardware, wait for it to be shipped, mount it in racks and weave a tangle of cables, and set it up and configure it. All that took time. Then what if you decided you didn't need it? Tough luck. You'd already paid. In the cloud, you spin up the infrastructure right when you need it, you dispose of it when you no longer need it, and you pay only for the time you used it. ***That*** is agility.

It gets better. The cloud lets you implement the best practices of DevOps, a lean IT process. Two important characteristics of lean processes: they eliminate waste and they reduce cycle time. In IT delivery terms, that means that you can quickly and inexpensively get new IT capabilities into the hands of users. ***That*** is agility.

One more thing. In the cloud there are many high-level services available for you to use as building blocks. If you want to create something quickly (and securely and reliably) chances are that AWS offers services that you can incorporate into your IT systems in no time. There are powerful features for artificial intelligence and machine learning, for example. Analytics, security, identity management, mobility … you name it. ***That*** is agility.

So – enterprises need to transform, they need to transform to continuous transformation, and the cloud is the key to continuous transformation. It follows therefore that all they need to do is change the culture, rules, and practices that they have spent years building and that have always made them successful in the past. Yeesh.

It's no surprise that enterprise executives feel a bit of vertigo as they look down into the abyss that awaits when they start undoing the culture and processes they have worked so hard to create.

That is where Stephen Orban and his enterprise strategy team come in. This book, and the collection of blog posts on which it is based, is the guidebook that enterprise leaders need to pull off this mini-revolution. Stephen's is the voice of calm, at once a reassuring goldmine of best practices and stories about how organizations have pulled this off successfully—and, at the same time—a playful voice of passionate enthusiasm for what the cloud can do. His excitement is palpable.

Ahead in the Cloud assembles the best ideas Stephen has found for moving to the cloud and making the most of it – specifically for enterprises. It is the voice whispering reassuringly in the enterprise executive's ear, saying "Don't worry. I've been there before. Take it one step at a time and it will all work out." And it is the voice coaxing and coaching the executive forward into the future and saying, "Look at what you will be able to do! Amazing, isn't it?"

We need a book like this, because transformation is hard. But not quite as hard as you'd think.

Preface

◆ ◆ ◆

"I say luck is when an opportunity comes along and you're prepared for it"
-Denzel Washington

I've been the Global Head of Enterprise Strategy for Amazon Web Services (AWS) since September of 2014, and am grateful to have a front-row seat to the largest technology shift in my lifetime. AWS is widely regarded as the founder of cloud computing as we know it today. Over the last 12 years, AWS has changed the paradigm by which IT infrastructure is delivered and consumed by listening to customers, not being afraid to challenge the status quo, and taking a long-term view. One of my favorite quotes from Jeff Bezos, Amazon's founder and CEO, is that "we are willing to be misunderstood for long periods of time." Using this approach, AWS has built one of the most feature-full and disruptive technology platforms that's existed in my lifetime, used by millions of customers from over 190 countries. Today, AWS offers more than 100 services across compute, networking, storage, databases, DevOps, serverless computing, big data, analytics, IoT (internet of things), artificial intelligence, machine learning, and more.

Since I started in this role, I have had the opportunity to meet with thousands of executives from hundreds of companies, all of whom are trying to understand how they can harness the power of this platform so that they can push more of their time, resources, and attention onto the things that make their business different rather than the things that don't (like managing datacenters). Some of the largest and most well-known brands in the world are using AWS to transform their business, including GE, Capital One, News Corp, Verizon, Airbnb, Netflix, Pinterest, Coca-Cola, to name just a few that you would probably recognize.

I consider myself very lucky. I have a loving wife (Meghan) and two healthy, inspiring, and intelligent daughters (Harper and Finley), all of whom have been supportive and understanding of my career ambitions, which often have me away from home for days and weeks on end. Without that support, the experiences that led to this book would not have been possible.

My family has allowed me to work hard, remain passionate about my work, and capitalize on a number of lucky breaks that landed me in the right place at the right time. Adding to my luck, I've been blessed with the gift of always knowing what I wanted to do when I grow up.

My attraction to software began at the age of 7, when I received my first Nintendo Entertainment System for Christmas. I played video games as though it was a full-time job from that moment until I graduated college and started my professional career. I can still beat *Contra* without dying (who needs up, up, down, down, left, right, left, right, b, a, b, a, start?), and still remember where every heart container, secret staircase, flammable tree, and bombable cave is in *The Legend of Zelda*.

My journey toward creating software started the following year when (again, in the right place at the right time) I found a TI-99[3] and a book on BASIC in my uncle's attic. I laboriously typed the book's example programs into the TI-99 console, and then spent countless hours making trial-and-error code modifications to see what I could make change on the screen. If that sounds impressive, it shouldn't, because I fed my technology obsession by starving myself in other subject areas. I am lucky to have graduated high school with awful-to-failing marks in any subject outside of math, science, and gym. I'm now married to a brilliant high school history teacher, and deeply regret this missed learning opportunity. I've spent the last 10 years trying to read everything Meghan suggests, in an effort to catch up on what's happened in the world for the last several thousand years. It turns out history

3 https://en.wikipedia.org/wiki/Texas_Instruments_TI-99/4A

is full of insightful lessons for today's corporate executive—but that missed opportunity is for another time.

Lucky to have been admitted to college, I majored computer science so I could fill my schedule with topics I was interested in, and my marks improved dramatically. I once even dropped a social sciences class because I was going to have to write a 10-page paper on modern Western civilization. I didn't yet appreciate how important writing would be in my professional life (particularly at Amazon, where writing is deeply ingrained in our culture and decision-making process), a point which held me back for much of my early career.

Since entering the workforce, I've had the opportunity to create software, new businesses, strategy, and (hopefully) some ongoing value for three well-known companies—Bloomberg, Dow Jones, and Amazon. I've watched the internet, then mobile, and now cloud change the role technology plays in business… each of these innovations spreading faster than the one before it.

In 2011, when I was the CTO of Web Infrastructure at Bloomberg LP, I learned how hard (and futile, as I'll later explain) it is to build an on-premises "private cloud." Not wanting to make the same mistake again, I spent the next three years using the cloud to transform how Dow Jones leveraged technology as their CIO. In 2014, I became the Global Head of Enterprise Strategy for Amazon Web Services (AWS), and in that role I help executives from large companies gain value from the cloud.

And I've learned that, as with any significant change, a move to the cloud can be hard for those who haven't done it before.

In this book, I will try to give you a perspective, based on my experiences, of the challenges large companies face as they move, and how they overcome those challenges. I have included personal experiences from myself and other executives who've "done it," and I hope that one day we'll be able to discuss a possible contribution from you as well! If this sounds interesting, please reach out to me at stephen.orban@gmail.com.

Introduction

◆ ◆ ◆

As I WAS PUTTING THIS book together, one (of the many) decisions I wrestled with was what to call it. My first thought was to choose a title that might stir up some controversy...something like *Digital Transformation Is Bullshit!* Part of me does believe that "digital transformation" is nothing more than a buzzword that helps management consultants secure large retainers with companies that don't fully appreciate the role technology plays in their business (more on this later), but the other part of me now understands that thousands of large businesses are, in fact, trying to transform into digital companies.

After contemplating a number of titles, I decided on *Ahead in the Cloud: Best Practices for Navigating the Future of Enterprise IT* because it's both fun and describes what this book contains.

WHY SHOULD YOU CARE ABOUT THE CLOUD?

While it may seem self-serving given my current role as the Global Head of Enterprise Strategy for AWS, I genuinely believe that cloud computing is the single most meaningful technology advancement in my lifetime, and that we are still in the early stages of discovering how the cloud will transform the world of business.

At AWS, we define cloud computing as the on-demand delivery of information technology (IT) resources via the internet with pay-as-you-go pricing. Instead of buying, owning, and maintaining their own datacenters and servers at significant cost, organizations can acquire technology such as compute power, storage, databases, and other services as they need them, and only pay for what they use.

The cloud has made countless new businesses possible, and has likely touched each of us in some way. Airbnb, Pinterest, and Netflix streaming, for example, didn't even exist 11 years ago (Netflix streaming launched in May 2007). These companies have the ability to move so fast because they are no longer constrained by how quickly they can provision servers, storage, and datacenters, and they have institutionalized their ability to take advantage of modern technology as a strategic competitive advantage.

Airbnb, for example—which runs all of its technology in the cloud today—has had well over 80 million guests use their service since 2008. Two million homes, 190 countries. Coupled with their current valuation of more than $30 billion, it's hard to argue against Airbnb being an amazing hyper-growth business. Netflix, another great example of a company that migrated their technology capabilities to the cloud, is completely redefining the way people consume television, and Netflix streaming was recently estimated to account for 36.5 percent[4] of all U.S. evening internet traffic.

So, now that the cloud has leveled the playing field for any aspiring young company by providing ubiquitous access to IT infrastructure on a global scale, what happens to the large enterprises that have historically used their access to capital and global IT resources as a competitive advantage?

They need to adapt—or die.

This statement isn't hyperbole. We all know the stories of formerly high-flying companies that failed to adapt to fast-changing market conditions and have either disappeared or become a shell of their former selves. Eastman Kodak invented the digital camera, yet they were put out of business by companies selling—digital cameras. Video rental giant Blockbuster had thriving brick-and-mortar stores all over the United States (I happily served as an assistant manager of one while I was in college), until Netflix ate their lunch by making it more convenient for customers to consume content and turned the Blockbuster stores into an expensive liability.

4 https://www.sandvine.com/downloads/general/global-internet-phenomena/2015/global-internet-phenomena-report-latin-america-and-north-america.pdf

I don't believe Kodak and Blockbuster's fate was intentional. I'm sure they tried to adapt. But, like many of the companies I speak to today tell me, change is really hard. The good news is that it is ***not*** impossible. To prove this, we need to look no further than General Electric.

General Electric is the *only* company left that was among the original Dow Jones Industrial Index, created in 1896. I believe that GE's resilience is largely—if not solely—due to their ability to always adapt to the changing conditions of business. You've probably seen GE's latest television ads where several different engineers from the company talk about how they're implementing digital technology across many GE business lines. After working with the company on its public cloud strategy, I can confirm that they are *very* serious about their digital transformation.

Your organization may not consider itself a technology company today, but the disruptors in your industry do consider themselves to be, and it's only a matter of time before these disruptors find a way to improve on (or even eliminate) what you do.

The good news is that you *can* avoid being disrupted, and the bigger your organization, the larger the benefit cloud and culture change can bring.

Who this book is for

If you are an executive at a large enterprise, then this book is for you. Regardless of how far you may be on your cloud journey, you will likely face many of the same challenges that other executives have faced, and this book will help you learn from their experiences. And the stories are not just useful for IT executives – there is a lot here for the leaders of marketing, finance, sales, and operations as well.

If you are an IT leader, then the contents of this book will help you lead and reorganize your teams, influence your peers, and (ideally) rebrand "enterprise IT" from a cost-center to a revenue generator. Moving to the cloud is not just about changing your infrastructure – cloud-native companies also adopt many of the related practices like DevOps, microservices, containerization, and so on. This book will tie all of these things together and add the experiences of leaders who have been there before. You will also find solutions to common situations, like migrating ERP systems or training your employees on cloud-related skills.

Finally, if you are simply interested in the cloud and the impact it is having, there is plenty here for you. Did you know that the American Red Cross was able to handle the huge volume of phone calls after Hurricane Harvey partly because it spun up a new cloud-based call center in just 48 hours? That FINRA is able to analyze petabytes of data – that is, over one quadrillion bytes, enough to fit on millions of CDs or billions of floppy disks – every day in order to spot patterns of financial fraud, by using AWS?

How this book is organized

In the first chapter of this book, I briefly describe my own journey with technology and how it brought me to the cloud. I'll touch upon my experiences leading teams at Bloomberg, Dow Jones, and now Amazon, and how these experiences shaped my views on just how essential cloud computing is to a modern-day enterprise. My hope is that some of the lessons I've learned over the years will be valuable to those leading transformations in their organizations.

In part one of this book, I describe how I've seen large organizations transform their culture using the cloud. There is no one-size-fits-all blueprint for this, but I outline the pattern I've observed as I've led or watched organizations transform using modern technology and the cloud.

In part two of this book, I explore some of the best practices that seem to commonly appear in organizations that are transforming. Much of the content in part two will be familiar to those who have read my blog, although I have made some purpose-fit changes to suit this book.

In the third part of this book, I turn it over to some of the most forward-thinking executives I know, all of whom are leading or have led digital transformations in their organizations.

In this section, you'll hear from (among others):

- **Bryan Landerman**, CTO, Cox Automotive, who talks about Cox Automotive's journey to the cloud.

- **Paul Hannan**, CTO of SGN, who explains how European utility provider SGN is modernizing its IT using the cloud.
- **Terren Peterson**, Vice President, Platform Engineering - Retail & Direct Bank at Capital One, who puts Capital One's journey to the cloud in terms of the Stages of Adoption.
- **Jay Haque**, who helped create a culture of experimentation as he led the New York Public Library on its cloud journey.
- **Jonathan Allen**, Enterprise Strategist covering Europe at AWS—and former CTO of Capital One UK—who details some lessons learned from Capital One's transformation.
- **Joe Chung**, Enterprise Strategist, AWS—and former Managing Director of IT at Accenture—who explores how tenets provide essential guidance on the cloud journey, and driving change and managing innovation in a cloud-first business reinvention.

I hope you enjoy this book as much as I've enjoyed the experiences that have led up to it. I'm looking forward to your feedback, and I would love to hear about your own experiences as you embark on your cloud or transformation journey—what's worked for you, and what hasn't. Not only will I post a selection of these contributions on my blog and in future editions of this book, but you'll have the opportunity to spotlight the efforts of your organization to transform, and hopefully gain some well-deserved recognized from your industry peers. If that sounds even the slightest bit interesting to you, please send me a note at stephen.orban@gmail.com.

CHAPTER 1

My Journey to the Cloud

"Luck is where opportunity meets preparation."

-Seneca

My journey toward cloud computing started long before I (or the industry) really knew what cloud computing was.

Before the cloud

I started my career as a developer at Bloomberg in 2001, and spent my first seven years there building software to help equity market professionals better understand companies and influence their investment decisions. I also built (and rebuilt) much of Bloomberg's messaging platform, which can be thought of as the cardiovascular system that allows Wall Street professionals to communicate and share information with one another.

As you are no doubt aware, in 2008, the market took a turn for the worse. Some of Bloomberg's biggest customers (remember Bear Stearns and Lehman Brothers?) went out of business, and many others started to experience significant challenges. For the first time in Bloomberg's history, the company was facing the prospect of negative growth. This was a shock to Bloomberg, after more than 20 years of growth. Rather than just retreat and accept their fate, Bloomberg's (then) president, Dan Doctoroff, came up with a financial incentive plan aptly named "10B" that we rolled out across the company. The goal he set was to get the company to go from $6 billion in revenue, which is where we were at the time, to $10 billion in revenue as quickly as possible.

Instead of relying on—or hoping for—the next wave of growth from the financial services industry, we would take Bloomberg's core competencies in data, analytics, software, and customer service, and find ways to apply them to new industries to grow the company while also diversifying revenue streams and not having all our eggs in the Wall Street basket.

This was one of those times in my career where I was in the right place at the right time. Being a big sports fan, I had often felt that a lot of the things that we'd developed for the equity market would be interesting to apply to professional sports. I joined forces with some like-minded colleagues and together we formulated our hypothesis as a simple question:

What if we treated a professional athlete like an equity and a professional sports team like a portfolio?

Then, if we took the data being generated and collected in professional sports and applied the same sort of analytics that we had made ubiquitous on Wall Street, we could potentially help professional sports teams manage their operations more effectively. If you're familiar with Michael Lewis's book *Moneyball*—about the use of statistician Bill James's idea of sabermetrics by Oakland Athletics general manager, Billy Beane—our idea was to make this thinking available to everyone in professional sports and to create a business out of it.

We spent the next four years building what became known as Bloomberg Sports. We first developed analytics offerings aimed at helping teams decide where to put their fielders based on the pitcher/hitter matchup ("the shift"), how a pitcher should approach a particular batter and vice versa, and how to compare the relative value of players. It turns out many teams thought this information was useful—28 of the 30 MLB teams bought at least one subscription our first year—but it wasn't until we married the analytics with an automated scouting system that we had something a few teams would be willing to pay decent money for.

In addition to the professional business, we built a variety of web and mobile analytics offerings for fantasy baseball and football players. All these tools were useful, though, in hindsight, we got the business model wrong. We tried to build the business by charging fantasy players a yearly subscription fee, but fantasy players aren't inclined to pay for information, so we should have attempted an ad-supported (or at least free-mium) model. The outcome of this business was less than spectacular—Bloomberg Sports was ultimately spun off, sold, and merged with Stats Inc.—but I learned a lot and had a lot of fun on the inside of baseball for a few years.

You may be wondering by now what any of this experience has to do with cloud computing. During the time we were building Bloomberg Sports, between 2008 and 2011, Bloomberg made investments in other ("off-Terminal") businesses in pursuit of 10B. Bloomberg Law, Bloomberg Government, Bloomberg Wealth, Bloomberg Talent, and other products were based on the same idea—that we could collect data relevant to a particular industry vertical, build some analytics on top of it, and sell it back to the professionals and decision makers in that industry to help them make better decisions.

But by 2011, we found that many of these businesses did not appear to be viable investments, largely because we were wasting a lot of money building the infrastructure to run these systems on. We were using the same IT infrastructure techniques we had become accustomed to while building the Bloomberg Terminal, which is a robust, latency-sensitive piece of technology that had matured over more than 30 years. It turns out that's not the right way to build infrastructure for a bunch of startup businesses. As someone who had experience working on both the Bloomberg Terminal and our off-Terminal businesses, I was "voluntold," as they say, to try and solve this problem.

Learning about the cloud....

Fortuitously, I had begun to familiarize myself with cloud technology while we built Bloomberg Sports. I became fascinated by AWS, in particular, and attended several of their conferences and meetups. The prospect of being able to provision servers on demand, rather than waiting the several months I'd become accustomed to, and most importantly, spin them down when we weren't using them, seemed like a much more effective way to quickly launch products and keep costs down. The primary reason our costs were so high was that we built infrastructure based on the maximum capacity we thought our applications would grow to need ("build for peak," as they say), and we were always wrong. We always overbuilt…which meant we always overspent.

This would be the first of many times I would build a case for using public cloud technology. Unfortunately, I didn't have enough tenacity or political influence to win everyone over, and the organization was not ready to entertain the idea that someone could do infrastructure better than us (a sentiment that many large and mature IT organizations still struggle with—if that sounds like you, this book may help).

Instead, we ended up building our own on-premises private cloud, and within a few months we stood up some very modest virtualization capabilities. These capabilities enabled our off-Terminal businesses to quickly deploy a handful of different types of servers on demand with some very basic configurations. Our costs quickly became much more manageable, and we went from waiting a few months to rack, stack, and deploy a server, to having one available in a few minutes.

From at least a few angles, this was a very successful strategy. First, everyone's P&L was no longer weighed down by infrastructure costs, so each business now had to justify its own performance. Second, the time it took to provision servers and get a business up and running—which was arguably our biggest problem—began to trend in the right direction. But, it didn't take long before we realized that provisioning servers is just table stakes for the technology capabilities our businesses needed. Each business needed to be able to send emails to their customers. Each business needed to have a CDN (content delivery network) to speed up response time for customers. Each business needed to send push notifications to its mobile applications. Each business needed APIs to access data from the Bloomberg Terminal. And each business needed to meter those APIs to know what data was going where, and when, and by whom.

Anyone who's worked in a large IT organization will probably recognize what happened next. We "taxed" each line of business so that we could fund the development of "shared services" to solve each of these problems, and my team quickly became viewed as a resource drain and bottleneck that held these businesses back from accomplishing their goals. As I continued to educate myself on the public cloud, I realized we could achieve these outcomes for a fraction of what it cost us to do it ourselves. I came to realize that a private cloud is not really a cloud at all, and it certainly is not a good use of company resources.

So, when I had the opportunity to help Dow Jones transform its business in 2012, I knew not to make the same mistake.

Starting a cloud journey

Dow Jones is a 125-year-old business that has done some very innovative things over the years. Among other things, they deliver more than two million *Wall Street Journal* hardcopy, physical newspapers to subscribers around the world six days a week. While most would agree that the internet is one of the most amazing inventions ever, optimizing a printing press and the logistics that drive the production and delivery of newspapers in such mass quantities is equally impressive.[5]

Dow Jones also invented a number of technologies to deliver low-latency news at a massive scale through products such as Dow Jones Newswires and Factiva, two of their flagship Professional Information Businesses (or "PIB" as Dow Jones refers to them).

Like many industries, however, the internet changed the news business forever. The proliferation of free content online made it increasingly difficult for many to justify spending $30-40 a month on a *Wall Street Journal* subscription, and advertising revenue for the newspaper started to shift toward Google, Facebook, and other online-native media companies.

The financial crisis that began in 2008 took a toll on their Professional Information Businesses, the same way as it did for Bloomberg. As with many storied companies, this disruption forced a variety of cost-cutting measures aimed at maintaining a healthy P&L, and the company outsourced much of its IT operations and product development offshore to India.

I don't have a strong position for or against IT outsourcing. But, if you are trying to remain competitive in an increasingly digital world, you probably need to maintain your ability to quickly and effectively build, enhance, and

5 Dow Jones gives customers tours of the print plants, which I used to frequent. If you ever get a chance to take one, I highly recommend it.

optimize your digital products based on customer feedback. Dow Jones found that their outsourcing arrangements made this more difficult.

On top of these challenges, the IT department was struggling to keep up with the ongoing maintenance of its existing infrastructure. Depreciation cycles were elongated to help keep costs down, which led to longer hardware refresh cycles. Aging systems break more often, can sometimes be hard to retain skills for, and can become more expensive to operate—particularly when coupled with processes requiring multiple handoffs in a largely outsourced model.

My first role at Dow Jones was as part of a small R&D team dedicated to helping the company think differently about how it developed products. Lex Fenwick—then-CEO of Dow Jones and former CEO of Bloomberg—asked us to think differently about how the company deployed technology, and not to be constrained by the existing Dow Jones architecture or processes. Lex had the idea that the subscribers to the *Wall Street Journal* **had** a lot of the world's wealth, and the subscribers to our Professional Information Business products (Factiva, Dow Jones Newswires) **managed** a lot of the world's wealth. If we could build a chat platform that would allow these users to communicate and do business with one another, we might be on to something. For all of us who had worked on the Bloomberg Message system, this was a familiar concept.

After my frustrating experiences building shared services at Bloomberg, and because we were given the freedom to think differently, I finally had the opportunity to demonstrate that the public cloud could actually deliver results. Within just two months—using a handful of AWS services and some open-source technology—we put together an application worth showing to our executive stakeholders and customers.

Our rapid progress started to get our executive team and leadership excited about our direction, and many were eager to see what else we could apply these lessons to. And, while some of the existing IT team were also becoming excited to work on something new, some were becoming a bit nervous because they weren't sure what to make of our team, our approach, and how the technologies we were using would impact their roles.

Building a cloud foundation

A few months later, I was offered the opportunity to lead Dow Jones's IT department as the CIO. Again, I was in the right place at the right time—this time with just enough ambition and naiveté to think that I might be able to help the company address some of the issues I highlight above, and transform the role IT played in the company.

To bring about change, we came up with a three-pronged strategy that we called "People, Process, and Platforms," or "3P" (I simply hadn't heard of People, Process, and Technology yet). Our goal was to change the role the IT department played in the organization by making it a much more formidable force in digital product development—which is, at the end of the day, what I think all top IT executives should be striving to achieve.

The *people* prong focused on insourcing and investing in our own talent. This meant hiring more developers, building a university recruiting program, and training our existing people in the skills they needed to transition to different roles. This included obvious things like vendor-led training, but also included setting aside time and budget for people to go to conferences, contribute to open-source projects, and attend lunch and learns with other companies we wanted to learn from. The overarching theme was that we were going to invest in everyone's abilities so that they could take more ownership and accountability over their respective areas, and have a greater impact on the business.

I used everything I had learned about university recruiting at Bloomberg—which hires more than 100 college graduates in software engineering roles each year—to build our own campus recruitment program with more than a dozen universities in the Northeast, London, and Hong Kong. I am amazed at how much more capable college graduates are each year, as each graduating class tends to start using technology earlier and earlier, and I love that they don't come with years of "how they did it elsewhere" baggage. Scaling this up over time allowed us to shrink our outsourcing contracts and reduce our dependency on our third-party outsourcing partners.

The *process* prong focused on giving each line of business more freedom to experiment and to react more quickly to shifting customer demands. To do this, we adopted continuous delivery practices and streamlined our project approval process. In place of a laborious "capital committee" process—where business owners would request multiple millions of dollars for projects that were going to last multiple years with an unclear (in my view, completely fabricated in many cases) return on investment—we established a different approach. We gave a fixed amount of resources to each line of business and held them accountable to key performance indicators (KPIs) that they set for themselves. Each technology and business owner overseeing a line of business had the ability to move resources around as their customer demand shifted, and we (the leadership team) reviewed KPIs and allocations quarterly to make any necessary changes.

Finally, for the *platform* prong, I had a real opportunity to avoid making the same mistake I had made building my own infrastructure at Bloomberg. We knew we were not going to be able to move fast enough and remain competitive if we continued to run our own infrastructure, which we didn't do terribly well to begin with. We needed to have our people laser focused on building product, and remove anything else that was a distraction.

Creating a dedicated team

I had experienced enough (good and bad) change management programs during my tenure at Bloomberg to know that any organization-wide change is much easier to implement when there is a team of people dedicated to driving the change, and constantly improving based on what they learn. (Amazon, I later learned, is composed of thousands of teams that have ownership of the product or service they deliver in what we call a "Two Pizza Team," meaning a team small enough that it can be fed by two pizzas. More on this in upcoming chapters.)

I also came to believe that the cloud paradigm combines several technology disciplines that were traditionally considered distinct. Building and managing applications that scale up and down automatically through code requires skills that cross the boundaries of software development, system administration, database administration, and network engineering (and probably others).

Managing applications *at scale* requires enterprise architects to think about managing fleets of disposable IT resources rather than racks of physical servers with static names, addresses, and locations.

While there were still plenty of people in the organization skeptical of both my leadership and our strategy, there were also a handful of people spread throughout various disciplines who were excited with the direction. These were the people we brought together to be part of the dedicated team, and we tasked them with codifying, professing, and scaling all the best practices, reference architectures, governance, and controls needed to run an increasing number of our applications on the cloud.

It was around this time that the DevOps movement began to gain traction in the industry, and while I was reluctant to accept that it had invented anything new, I appreciated how the movement had created language and awareness for best practices inside many software companies. If you haven't heard of it before, DevOps essentially refers to the commonsense best practices aimed at combining software development (Dev) with production operations (Ops). Bloomberg, for example, had been practicing "run what you build" and "know your customer" long before I started working there in 2001, and it was the only production software environment to which I had been exposed. Mark Schwartz, who you'll hear from later, summed up my feelings on the novelty of DevOps nicely as we debated some of the points made in this chapter: "The idea of dev and ops working together is really a throwback to when we weren't all so specialized and everyone just did what needed to get done."

So, while I realize that DevOps is more of cultural way of being than it is a specific group of people, we intentionally conflated the team with the movement by naming it the "DevOps team." This was our way of emphasizing the role this team would play in changing our culture. The primary role of the DevOps team would be to enable all teams to DevOps themselves and to provide them the tools and capabilities to make that easier.

We then came up with and communicated three tenets for the team, all of which were inspired by the DevOps movement.

The first tenet was that DevOps_had to treat the application teams as paying customers. My experience has been that infrastructure and application teams don't always get along with one another. The infrastructure teams think the app teams are cowboys, willing to sacrifice long-term operations to meet a short-term deliverable. The application teams think the infrastructure teams move too slowly and don't understand the pressure of their deadlines and commitments. I had already begun to get a whiff of the resulting finger pointing while triaging a few outages and missed deadlines, and I was eager to do what I could to eradicate it. We were all the same team, and would succeed or fail together. While we never came up with an adequate way to measure success, we reiterated this tenet so much that many other teams started to treat their end customers as paying customers as well.

The second tenet was that DevOps had to automate *everything*. Our view at the time was that if you were going to deploy anything in the cloud, you should do it "right" by leveraging a cloud-native architecture. We wanted to automate the deployment and scaling of our applications so that we could quickly iterate on product and not have to worry about capacity planning. As I'll explain shortly, we later learned that the "right" approach is more nuanced than this, and backed off this requirement once we saw a business case to lift-and-shift much of our legacy. I cover this in Chapter 7, Cloud Native or Lift-and-Shift.

The third tenet was that DevOps was not going to be responsible for the ongoing operations of the applications that the lines of business deployed to the cloud. We were going to become a "run what you build" culture, and each line of business would leverage the best practices, reference architectures, and non-negotiables from the DevOps team, but otherwise be accountable for the ongoing operations and change management of their applications. Once a line of business deployed something, it was on them to own and maintain it from then on. This allowed application teams to innovate and prevent DevOps from becoming yet another command-and-control bottleneck.

The DevOps team started small, with few capabilities or opinions on how things should work. As we gained experience, we became more opinionated—particularly around areas like security and change management. We always tried to create the right balance of non-negotiables that every line of business had to implement for their projects while maintaining their ability to innovate using new tools, services, and open-source technologies.

Expanding our cloud capabilities

As our teams began to move faster, we naturally wanted to increase the scope of the DevOps team and accelerate the rate at which we were changing. We used my monthly town hall meetings to evangelize the changes we were proud of, while drumming up interest in those who wanted to "lean in" to the change. Near the end of each of my quarterly town halls, I would ask if anyone was interested in joining the DevOps team. Each time, we found a few more people excited about the opportunity, and transitioned them into the DevOps team. More often than not, we intentionally didn't backfill their old roles. So, if a system administrator or network engineer supporting Dow Jones Newswires, for example, moved from their traditional role into the DevOps team, our DevOps capacity increased at the same rate as our capacity to operate in the status quo decreased.

This was an effective way to get application teams to work more with DevOps, where the resources were growing, but it was admittedly sometimes a messy process. I only recommend this approach if you are willing to make some mistakes to create change quickly. There were several escalations and small outages that we had to deal with, but we learned a lot and used every judgment call as an opportunity to strengthen our resolve.

We didn't (yet) have a concrete plan to migrate all our legacy systems to the cloud, and we were operating in what people now refer to as a hybrid mode. All new features were being deployed on the cloud using the reference architectures that the DevOps team was building while they were still, when necessary, communicating with the on-premises system.

The DevOps team was responsible for developing the best practices and building the capabilities that made this hybrid architecture work well, and these capabilities became more sophisticated over time as our needs matured. While we wanted to limit the line of business applications that the DevOps team had operational ownership over (because application teams should own them), they owned and operated our hybrid architecture, as well as some custom tools we built to manage costs and make sure our running cloud resources remained compliant with our non-negotiables.

One of the most impactful things Milin Patel[6], who led the DevOps team, did was build a curriculum he called "DevOps Days." This two-day curriculum started with a half day of AWS basics. It continued with another day and a half about how all the reference architectures, best practices, and governance that the DevOps team had built should be used. In addition to being a great way to educate our teams, it was a great way to get feedback from those that were already using those practices.

I would have never predicted it at the time, but this was a major turning point in our journey. A lot of our internal resistance started to fade once there were well-tenured Dow Jones people teaching other Dow Jones people. It was no longer about what some outside, ivory-tower executive was professing—it was a set of capabilities that the team had built up *themselves*. It was our shared agenda, and we were all in it together. I only wish we had done it sooner.

After the team made a number of improvements through the first iteration, we decided to make DevOps Days the mechanism by which we onboarded new employees. Each summer we hired a few dozen college graduates through our university recruiting program, and DevOps Days gave them exposure to how we worked, what tools and techniques we used, and a little bit of information about each line of business. This process made it a lot easier for them to become acclimated and learn which line of business might be best suited for their skills and aspirations. It also made it easier for each hiring group, because they could expect some baseline set of capabilities from each new hire that joined their group.

Migrating a single datacenter

Roughly a year into our journey, we were faced with another opportunity to think differently about our transformation. The real estate that housed our datacenter in Hong Kong was going to be used for something else, and we were given two months to vacate it. I really wanted to use this as an opportunity

6 Milin outlines his experience in Chapter 48

to accelerate our cloud migration, but the team quickly exposed a number of risks.

First, no one felt that two months was enough time to re-architect everything in that datacenter to be cloud-native (in other words, there wasn't time to rewrite our applications to take advantage of features only available in the public cloud, like auto-scaling). This was the first time we considered relaxing our "automate everything" tenet, and we began to entertain a lift-and-shift approach. This caused a lot of debate, because we assumed that this approach would inevitably be more expensive. But because the datacenter was small enough (a few hundred servers), and datacenters weren't in our long-term future, we decided to consider this approach anyway.

The remaining risks were technical. We were running a hardware load balancer and a hardware WAN (wide-area network) accelerator that everyone believed were critical to the infrastructure. In addition, we depended on a number of database features that we were not supported by the AWS Relational Database Service (RDS), so we couldn't easily migrate to it as a managed service.

I'm convinced that we only found solutions to these problems because of the experience and capabilities we had already established, although the ingenuity of our team in using that experience was quite impressive.

One of our DevOps engineers found that the WAN accelerator and load balancer we used were also available as software via the AWS Marketplace. Inside of a few days, we procured, launched, and configured both components without having to change much of our operational processes.

Next, we migrated the database servers onto Amazon EC2 instances rather than the managed Amazon RDS. It was less than ideal that we still had to manage the database servers ourselves, but it was better than having to lease more datacenter space.

We (mostly) finished the migration in about six weeks. It wasn't perfect, but it worked. We experienced some latency in the continuous database replication from our primary datacenters in New Jersey, largely because I was reluctant to pay for an AWS Direct Connect (AWS Direct Connect lets customers establish a dedicated network connection between their network and one of the AWS Direct Connect locations). We eventually found and made the appropriate database configuration so this was no longer a problem (and eventually installed the AWS Direct Connect), but it was more an operational burden than it was a customer-impacting issue.

And, then, something very interesting happened. The reason we had established the "automate everything" tenet was that we thought it would be more expensive to run in the cloud than on-premises if we didn't optimize for the cloud. But in this case, we didn't fundamentally change the architecture, and we ended up saving 30% by primarily lifting-and-shifting!

Mass migration

At around this same time we were dealing with the shutdown of our Hong Kong datacenter, News Corp, our parent company, had begun to consolidate some of the IT infrastructure and roles from the seven companies in their portfolio (including Dow Jones) into a centralized operating unit. This was an effort to create some efficiencies across the business and cut costs. Paul Cheesbrough, then-CTO at News Corp (now CTO of 21st Century Fox, and still a mentor of mine today) started to socialize these results among the other News Corp companies, and we began to consider what a much larger datacenter migration would mean to all of us.

A business case study across all of the News Corp companies suggested that by consolidating our more than 50 datacenters around the world into six tier-three and tier-four datacenters, and migrating 75 percent of our infrastructure to cloud services in the process (this included our move to Software-as-a-Service products like Salesforce, Workday, and Google Apps), we'd be able to reallocate more than $100,000,000 a year toward revenue-generating activities within about three years.

This was the sort of business case that got the attention of all the executives across News Corp—not just in IT—and pushed us from organically transforming our technology environment to having a fully funded program to migrate our legacy as quickly as possible, leveraging a number of different migration strategies (which are covered in Chapter 6, "6 Strategies for Migrating Your Applications to the Cloud").

By the time I took my role at AWS about a year later, we had migrated roughly 30 percent of our infrastructure to cloud services. It's taken News Corp a bit longer than they planned to get 75 percent of their infrastructure migrated. Today, roughly four years later, they're a little more than 60 percent of the way there. But it only took just over two years to meet the financial goal of reallocating more than $100,000,000 toward revenue-generating activities.

It's all about culture

While I'm proud of these financial results, the thing I'm most proud of is the evolution of our company culture. The Dow Jones Technology department became a driving force in the business, and it was recognized as something that could make a very positive difference in the products we delivered to our customers. During the course of our transition, we went from roughly 400 employees and 1,100 contractors to about 450 employees and 300 contractors. This was a considerable decrease, but a much better mix of motivated people who owned their product areas, and genuinely wanted to move quickly to benefit their customers and the business.

As I prepared to leave Dow Jones for my new position at AWS, the engineering manager from MarketWatch.com, Kevin Dotzenrod, sent me a parting gift: an email with a chart that showed how many software releases they had made in the month before I left. They had gone from Tuesday and Thursday release nights, where if we were lucky we'd have a successful release, to several hundred releases in that month alone – all of which were fully automated and involved only the developer making the change.

I realize that the story outlined here may seem overwhelmingly positive, and a discerning reader might think I'm ignoring the challenges we faced. These changes were hard, and there were times when I questioned our approach, thought I'd be fired, or otherwise just thought it would be easier to give up. We were constantly faced with judgment calls that we had to make with incomplete information and unknown risks. All in all, this was a good learning experience for everyone in the organization, but it wasn't for the faint of heart. Many of the points I make in the chapters that follow were born out of the challenges we (and the hundreds of other companies we work with) faced, and the strategies we used to overcome them.

Bringing this experience to others

Having lived through both the ups and the downs of this experience, I realized that every company in the world is going to have to figure out how to evolve their culture in ways that technology plays a major role. And there is no better enabler for that than the cloud.

Which is ultimately how I ended up at AWS. Today, my job is to help executives transform their people, process, and technology using the cloud by collecting and espousing the best practices from enterprises that are on this journey. I feel very fortunate to have the opportunity to learn from such a diverse set of executives and businesses, and I hope you'll find some of the things that we've learned and outlined throughout this book to be useful in your own organization.

PART I

The Stages of Adoption

◆ ◆ ◆

IF YOU'RE NEW TO CLOUD, you're may be asking yourself questions like, "What does the cloud mean for my organization?" "How am I going to get started?" "What needs to change, and it what order?" "What challenges will I face?" "Who on my team will be involved?" "How will I talk to my peers about it?" This part of the book may have some answers.

Most companies that are doing anything meaningful with the cloud are doing so in pursuit of a broader business driver and/or transformation program. Drivers are often cultural, financial, or innovation-related, but very few executives pursue technology for technology's sake. Most often these efforts are fueled by a desire—or in some cases the necessity—to be more competitive and to have more modern, digital capabilities in one's organization.

A lot of different terms get thrown around for this kind of initiative: IT modernization, cloud-first, mass migration—to name just a few—but the most common term we hear is *digital transformation.*

At some level, it's hard to argue with "digital transformation." Most executives would agree they would benefit from more automation and a team of people who could envision and deliver better customer experiences. Having said that, I think the idea of digital transformation with a beginning, a middle, and an end is *bullshit.*

But, I'm also not naïve. If saying you're going to embark on a digital transformation is what it takes to get your organization to move the needle, or if that's what your management consultants came in and said you need to do, then you might as well embrace it and go. But know that the real goal is not about a transformation that has a finite end state. It's about becoming an organization that is capable of quickly deploying technology to meet business needs, regardless of where the technology comes from.

And, while I don't love the term *digital transformation*, the process of becoming a digital-capable or digital-native company takes time, and is full of hard-fought battles.

Every company's journey will be different, but I have found that there are some recurring patterns and commonalities, and that executives prefer to learn from others who have themselves gone through it. During the course of meeting with hundreds of companies that are at every level of maturity and progress through their own transformation process, I've come up with an imperfect pattern that I call the *Stages of Adoption*. Each of these stages (stage one: project, stage two: foundation, stage three: migration, stage four: reinvention) represents the kind of thing that happens in a large organization during the course of its never-ending journey to becoming a digital company.

Stage 1: Project (Chapter 2)

Not surprisingly, most organizations start with a few ***projects*** where they're experimenting with how to do IT differently and learning what the cloud can do for them. Since most organizations start with few (if any) in-house cloud skills, I always suggest they pick a project that is important enough that people will care, but also not something where there is no appetite for learning (in other words, don't pick something that will get you fired). Once they get a feel for the cloud, they tend to want to do more.

Stage 2: Foundation (Chapter 3)

This is when executives say to themselves, "Okay, there's some real possibility here, now we need to get serious. And to get serious about this at scale, I need to make a couple of ***foundational*** investments so I can scale these new capabilities throughout my organization." This typically includes the creation of a cross-functional team dedicated to their transformation efforts (which we call a Cloud Center of Excellence, or CCoE, Chapter 24-31) and the deployment of an "AWS landing zone" so that they have the right governance and operating model for leveraging the cloud at scale.

Stage 3: Migration (Chapters 4-9)

As this foundational capability gets established, we typically see organizations finding ways that the cloud can help them retire their accumulating technical debt so they can focus more on innovation. Here they develop a business case to quantify the benefits they can achieve by ***migrating*** their legacy systems to the cloud.

Stage 4: Reinvention (Chapter 10)

As the gravity of an organization's IT footprint moves from on-premises to the cloud, the organization typically finds itself in a much better position to optimize both its IT costs and its business capabilities (products and services). Many enterprises, including GE Oil & Gas,[7] find that it's easier to optimize their applications *after* they've migrated them to the cloud, because of the expertise they gained along the way. Many of these organizations begin to feel as though they've ***reinvented*** themselves, and are applying their newfound capabilities across their entire business.

Becoming Cloud-First Along the Way

At some point during these stages, we see a lot of organizations declaring themselves "cloud-first." These organizations have reversed the burden of proof from "Why *should* we use cloud?" to "Why *shouldn't* we use the cloud?" when implementing technology solutions for their business.

Different enterprises arrive at a cloud-first policy at different points in their journey. Some CIOs with confident instincts will declare cloud-first early in their journey; some create elaborate business cases to justify cloud-first

7 https://aws.amazon.com/solutions/case-studies/ge-oil-gas/

before moving anything to the cloud; some have let cloud-first happen to their organization through opportunistic developers or shadow IT; and some have iterated toward a cloud-first posture by opportunistically implementing cloud projects one by one. (I did the latter at Dow Jones).

So, as much as I'd like to articulate the right time for every organization to declare cloud-first, there are too many organization-specific factors to make it that simple.

For one, many enterprises view themselves as a collection of loosely coupled and independently managed business units (BUs). Depending on the enterprise, these BUs will have varying amounts of autonomy in how they make technology decisions. Some enterprises have a highly centralized model—where a central IT function selects and controls which technology should be adopted across the BUs—and some enterprises give the individual BUs autonomy to make their own technology decisions. Most fall somewhere in between.

There is no right or wrong approach for structuring technology decision making across an organization, but there are tradeoffs between centralization (efficiency, standardization) and autonomy (time to market, innovation). Increasingly, most of the executives I talk to favor the latter. Throughout this part of the book, I explore the technology organizational structure of the future, Amazon.com's two-pizza team[8] model, and how a Cloud Center of Excellence fits in.

Although I present these Stages of Adoption as a sequential journey, I've also seen enterprises with many, often unrelated, BUs that are in different stages at the same time. It's very possible that activities from any one stage are happening in parallel across the organization, ideally creating a flywheel effect for the broader organization.

---

8 http://blog.idonethis.com/two-pizza-team/

Hopefully, the Stages of Adoption will give you some idea of what other organizations are going through, and how you might apply this pattern to your own organization. If you'd like to tell your organization's story, please let me know!

CHAPTER 2

Getting Started with the Cloud?

Originally posted on 9/26/16: http://amzn.to/getting-started-with-cloud

◆ ◆ ◆

"The journey of a thousand miles begins with a single step."

—Lao Tzu

In the previous chapter, I introduced a mental model called the Stages of Adoption (SofA), which describes the journey that enterprises travel as they become cloud-first. I've found this journey to be more of a leadership and change management exercise than a technical exercise, and while there is no one-size-fits-all answer, I hope that the SofA will be a useful model for executives to consider as they guide their organizations on their own journey.

This chapter focuses on the first SofA, which I call "Project," and it elaborates on what I've seen within enterprises that are getting started with the cloud.

Not surprisingly, most enterprises start with a handful of projects that help them understand how they can leverage the cloud to meet a business need.

My First Enterprise Cloud Project (as outlined in Chapter 1)

In 2012, while I was the CIO of Dow Jones, my boss (our CEO) had a hypothesis that we all felt was a great business opportunity: If the subscribers of *The Wall Street Journal*—Dow Jones's flagship B2C product—*had* much of the world's wealth, and the subscribers of Factiva and Dow Jones

Newswires—Dow Jones' B2B products—*managed* much of the world's wealth, we could create a valuable platform by giving them a mechanism to connect and communicate with one another.

Dow Jones had never built anything like this before, and we were eager to move quickly. We assembled a very small team of engineers and designers to build out a proof of concept, and we gave them complete freedom to choose whatever tools they thought would get the job done.

Six weeks later, with a little bit of AWS, automation, open source, and a lot of hard work, we had a highly available, disaster-indifferent application up and running. Our newfound ability to deliver technology to the business quickly became our "hero" project, which helped encourage my team (many of whom became anxious until we trained them) and executive stakeholders to come on the journey with us.

What Project Should You Start With?

Generally speaking, I like to see organizations start with a project that they can get results from in a few weeks. The days of multiyear IT projects are numbered, and the majority of executives I talk to are attracted to the cloud because of the agility it brings to their business.

Give your teams a hands-on, time-constrained opportunity to do something meaningful. My experience came in the form of net new development, which is a pattern I've seen many other enterprises follow. Modern web and mobile applications are ideal, particularly because the universe of use cases and reference architectures are well known. I've also seen enterprises start with an Amazon Workspaces[9] deployment, a dev/test environment migration, or a modernization/migration of an existing application.

The complexity of migrating existing applications varies, depending on the architecture and existing licensing arrangements. If I think about the universe of applications to migrate on a spectrum of complexity, I'd put a virtualized, service-oriented architecture on the low-complexity end of the spectrum, and a monolithic mainframe at the high-complexity end of the

9 https://aws.amazon.com/workspaces/

spectrum. I suggest starting with something on the low-complexity end of the spectrum. I will cover these migration scenarios and patterns in much more detail in the "Migration" SofA stage.

What I've found most important is that organizations pick something that will deliver value to the business, but something that isn't so important that there's no appetite for learning. Avoid analysis paralysis, and use your early cloud projects as a way to start experimenting.

Unless there is a strong compelling reason to do so, I'd caution against a complete business transformation program with your first project. There is a rate at which organizations can handle change, and that rate will be unique to every organization. I've found that accelerating past that rate can lead to negative returns. I've often been described as a "cowboy," a term I found endearing until it became counterproductive. Someone once told me that "there's no glory being alone at the finish line." My stomach dropped when I heard this and realized just how cowboy-ish I had been, and I've had to learn to constantly repeat this phrase to myself as I try to strike the right balance.

Who Should Work on Your Early Cloud Projects? (Hint: Attitude Matters)

Regardless of where in your organization you get started, you should expect that your early cloud projects will make some people excited and some people uncomfortable.

Start to nurture the people who get excited, and consider how you can turn them into your own cloud champions/evangelists. I've found that attitude is just as important as aptitude, and your early champions tend to be the curious type who aren't afraid to experiment. Keep an eye on them as your projects evolve, as they may be good candidates to staff your Cloud Center of Excellence (Chapter 25), which we'll explore in the next stage of adoption ("Foundation").

Be empathetic to those that get uncomfortable, and provide them with the tools they need to come on the journey with you. Computer science fundamentals have not changed, but to really take advantage of what the cloud has to offer many traditional functions need to think differently about how they accomplish their goals. Be sensitive to their concerns and check out the chapters on bringing your staff along on your journey: Chapter 15: You Already Have the People You Need to Succeed with the Cloud, and Chapter 16: 11 Things to Consider When Educating Your Staff on the Cloud.

Where Are Early Projects Driven From?

Two or three years ago, it seemed like most cloud projects were driven by individual business units. In many cases, these projects were implemented as *shadow IT*, which is often the case when the business can't get what it needs from a central IT function fast enough. While shadow IT has traditionally been a source of organizational tension, I'm increasingly seeing Cloud Center of Excellence teams (Chapters 24-31) providing IT-approved cloud reference architectures to business units so that they can safely innovate on top of them in a secure, governed, and transparent way. This approach can liberate innovation within different business units while still affording central IT the guardrails it needs to enforce security, compliance, and consistency across a large IT footprint. AWS Service Catalog[10] is aimed at helping enterprises do this at scale.

As cloud has become the new normal, I'm increasingly seeing early cloud projects driven by central IT. Many financial services organizations, for example, are focused on cutting out costs, and look toward the cloud to right size dev/test environments as they go through refresh cycles. In another example, Johnson & Johnson implemented Amazon Workspaces as one of its early cloud projects.[11]

10 https://aws.amazon.com/servicecatalog/

11 https://aws.amazon.com/solutions/case-studies/johnson-and-johnson/

CHAPTER 3

4 Foundational Investments for Your Cloud Journey

Originally posted on 10/11/16: http://amzn.to/cloud-foundation

◆ ◆ ◆

"Good skin is the best foundation for your makeup"

—Holland Rolland

I've found that the journey organizations travel as they become cloud-first is more of a leadership and change management exercise than a technical exercise. And, while there are no one-size-fits-all answers, I hope that the SofA will be a useful model for executives to consider as they guide their organizations on their journey.

It usually takes just a few projects for most organizations to start to realize how much faster they can deliver on the cloud. This chapter covers four areas I typically see organizations invest in so they can scale this benefit across their organization. I call this the "Foundation" stage.

1. Create a Cloud Center of Excellence Team (Chapters 24-31)

I believe the creation of a CCoE is one of the most critical foundational investment an organization can make, particularly if you're looking to evolve your culture. Many organizations I speak to are using their CCoE as a fulcrum to create change across their organization, a trend I captured in Chapter 27: Your Enterprise's Flywheel to the Cloud.

As I described in staffing a CCoE (Chapter 25), I like to see organizations build a cross-functional team of people with a diverse set of perspectives. Traditional roles around system administration, database administration, network engineering, and operations often blend together as they are increasingly automated as code. I strongly believe you already have the people you need to succeed (Chapter 15), and that anyone in these roles today who is eager to learn something new could be an ideal fit for your CCoE. You probably already know who those people are (and aren't).

As you build your CCoE, consider how you want the various business units to engage with it, and how your organization will govern (centralize/decentralize) technology choices.

For example, when we built the CCoE team at Dow Jones, we named it DevOps, deliberately conflating it with a term that describes a run-what-you-build philosophy (Chapter 30). Our goal was to have the DevOps team prescribe an operating model that embodied the best practices, governance, and guardrails we preferred in our enterprise, while still giving each business unit the autonomy to make the decisions it needed to accomplish its goals in a timeframe it controlled. As the DevOps team matured, so did our reference architectures (see below), and we found that more business units wanted to use what the DevOps team offered because it made them faster and more effective, not because we forced them to.

2. Build Reference Architectures to Reuse Across Your Business

Encourage your teams to look for common patterns in the applications they own. If you find a reference architecture that meets the needs of several applications, create scripts that automate the construction of that reference architecture while baking in your security and operational controls. This could be as simple as creating a *golden image* for the various operating systems your teams use, or as complex as a blueprint that describes the architecture and operating model of all the websites you host.

Each reference architecture should consider how it will communicate back to your on-premises assets. As I explain in Chapter 32: Three Myths About Hybrid Architecture Using the Cloud, "I've spoken to many CIOs who want to migrate their infrastructure to the cloud as fast as possible, but realize that meaningful cloud adoption is a journey that takes time. Along that journey, companies need a way to keep their systems running and get the most out of their existing investments." Some organizations create a handful of security groups[12] that are allowed to communicate through their on-premises firewalls in a way that's consistent with their existing controls, and then they reuse these security groups across different reference architectures.

Giving your CCoE visibility across your entire IT portfolio will make it easier for it to find and scale reference architectures. The AWS Service Catalog[13] can help you store, permission, and distribute reference architectures across your organization as you scale.

3. Create a Culture of Experimentation and Evolve Your Operating Model (Chapter 19-20)

The cloud is the single biggest enabler of experimentation I've seen in my career, and many organizations use their cloud journey as a forcing function to revisit their traditional IT operating models.

I'm increasingly seeing organizations revisit how much autonomy they give each business unit to make technology choices. At the same time, they're thinking carefully about how roles and privileges are managed, who's accountable for costs, what tools can/should be used for monitoring and logging, and who can influence changes in the environment.

At Amazon, for example, every service is owned by a *two-pizza team*[14] that is wholly accountable for the service it provides to its customer. This

12 http://docs.aws.amazon.com/AmazonVPC/latest/UserGuide/VPC_SecurityGroups.html

13 https://aws.amazon.com/servicecatalog/

14 http://blog.idonethis.com/two-pizza-team/

includes what technologies are used, the service's roadmap, and the service's operations.

While this run-what-you-build mentality may make some people uncomfortable, I find that more organizations are moving toward it than away from it. Many organizations are pushing their CCoEs to define what an appropriate operating model looks like and bake it into the reference architectures and continuous integration tools they deliver to each business unit. When done with the proper guardrails, this can allow each business unit to release changes much more often.

When I was at Dow Jones, for example, our CCoE built a simple but effective continuous integration pipeline that allowed us to abolish our biweekly release windows in favor of pushing small changes whenever they were ready. And, when I left Dow Jones in September 2014, our CCoE gave me a document describing the 600 releases they made to MarketWatch.com that month alone. It was the most rewarding parting gift I've ever received.

4. Educate Your Staff and Give Your Team a Chance to Learn

Education is the most effective mechanism I've found to get your team to come along with you. I cover this topic in detail under Best Practice Two: Educate Staff, and I can't stress enough how important this is for organizations to remain competitive in today's talent marketplace.

Capital One[15] is, from my perspective, is one of the industry's leading organizations on talent development. Drew Firment, Capital One's former Technology Director of Cloud Engineering, and current Managing Partner at A Cloud Guru, shared his thought leadership on the topic in his post on how Talent Transformation Is Really the Hardest Part of Cloud Adoption.[16]

15 https://aws.amazon.com/solutions/case-studies/capital-one/

16 https://cloudrumblings.io/cloud-adoption-the-talent-transformation-is-really-the-hardest-part-b8f288cee11b

In Closing...

Look at these foundational investments as something that will benefit your organization for many years to come. Don't try to boil the ocean, and remember that you can iterate on and improve your foundation over time. It should be strong, but flexible as you learn.

CHAPTER 4

Considering a Mass Migration to the Cloud?

Originally post on 11/1/2016: http://amzn.to/considering-mass-migration

◆ ◆ ◆

"The story of humanity is essentially the story of human movement. In the near future, people will move even more, particularly if, as some predict, climate change sparks mass migration on an unprecedented scale. The sooner we recognize the inevitability of this movement, the sooner we can try to manage it."

—Patrick Kingsley

My first experience migrating a large number of applications to the cloud in one shot came in 2013 when I was the CIO of Dow Jones. We had implemented a few new projects on the cloud, and established some foundational cloud capabilities through our DevOps team, when we became aware that the data center colocation facility we used to host our Asia-Pacific operations in Hong Kong was about to be torn down. We had two months to find a new home for our dozens of applications running there.

We were pleasantly surprised when we were able to complete this migration in six weeks[17] without having to outlay capital on new hardware or change much of our operational procedures. We found that the AWS Marketplace[18] offered us the opportunity to lease the same load balancer and WAN ac-

17 https://aws.amazon.com/solutions/case-studies/dow-jones/

18 https://aws.amazon.com/marketplace/

celerator we were using in our facility, and that by simply lift-and-shifting our existing databases and applications (this was the first time we didn't rebuild systems from scratch while we migrated), our ongoing operational costs decreased by roughly 30 percent.

This experience led to a business case to save or reallocate more than $100 million in costs across all of News Corp (our parent company) by migrating 75 percent of our applications to the cloud as we consolidated 56 data centers into 6. While News Corp continues its journey toward 75 percent, it was able to realize its savings target in about two years.

I've now been in my current role as the Head of Enterprise Strategy for AWS for more than three years, and I've had the opportunity to talk to hundreds of enterprises that are contemplating migrating large portions of their legacy IT estate to the cloud. As the demand for legacy migrations to the cloud grows, so has the collective industry experience, and my colleagues at AWS have continued to become more deliberate in how they channel this experience to help more enterprises migrate. This chapter is the first of a three-part miniseries outlining some of the things we've learned so far.

What Is a Mass Migration to the Cloud?

mi·gra·tion /mīˈgrāSH(ə)n/: noun: movement of one part of something to another.

People have been taking advantage of advances in technology to migrate systems to more capable platforms since the beginning of time. Handwritten books to the printing press, self-generated electricity to the power grid, human-computed encryption/decryption to the digital computer, mainframes to commodity hardware to virtualization, and so on.

The fundamental process around migration—understand the benefits of the new system, assess gaps in the existing system, plan, and migrate—hasn't changed much over time. I have found, however, that the prospect of migrating a large number of legacy applications to the cloud can sometimes be intimidating to organizations because of the sheer magnitude of change required. Modern enterprises have IT environments that become larger and more complex every day, and organizations rarely have the opportunity to retire technical debt as they continue to build new systems.

For the purposes of this miniseries, we'll consider a mass migration to be the movement of a meaningful portion of your organization's existing IT assets to the cloud, and we'll simply refer to it as a "migration." A migration might consist of a data center, a collection of data centers, a business unit, or some other portfolio of systems that is larger than a single application.

Approaching Migrations

Combining what we know about technology migrations with our experience helping organizations migrate their IT portfolios to AWS, we've developed two mental models that many of our customers have found useful in approaching mass migrations to the cloud.

The first mental model illustrates the pattern we've seen several migrations follow. This five-phased Migration Process might help you approach a migration of tens or hundreds, or even thousands, of applications.

The second mental model, which I sometimes call "The 6 R's," offers six different strategies for migrating individual applications to the cloud.

These mental models—while based on experience—are intended to serve as guiding principles to help you approach your migration. They are not hard-and-fast rules. Every organization has its own unique blend of constraints, budget issues, politics, culture, and market pressures that will guide its decision-making process along the way.

The Migration Process (Chapter 5)

As I mentioned above, the cloud-migration process generally consists of five phases: Opportunity Evaluation, Portfolio Discovery and Planning, Application Design, Migration & Validation, and Operate.

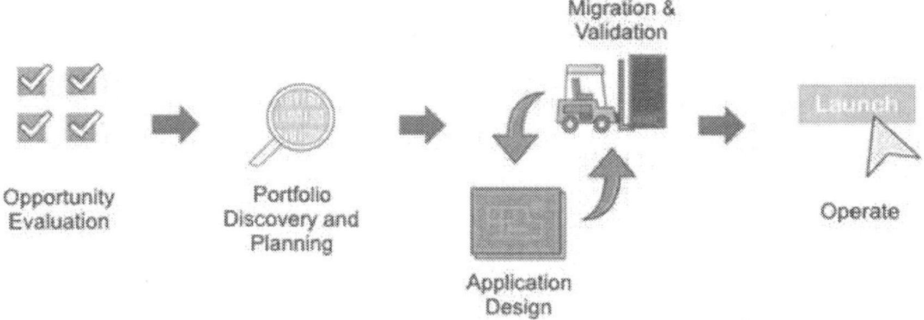

While there's no perfect path or process for every migration, we've found that this mental model helps customers approach their migration, and it has allowed us (AWS) to codify the best practices, tools, and partners that organizations are using to migrate.

For an in-depth view into this "Migration Process," see Chapter 5: A Process for Mass Migrations to the Cloud.

Application Migration Strategies: "The 6 R's" (Chapter 6)

Applications can be migrated to the cloud in a number of different ways, and as with the Migration Process, there can be many shades of gray. However, we find these six approaches to be the most common:

- **Rehosting** (otherwise known as "lift-and-shift")
- **Replatforming** (I sometimes call this "lift-tinker-and-shift")
- **Repurchasing** (migrate to a different product/license, often SaaS)
- **Refactoring** (re-architect or re-imagine leveraging cloud-native capabilities)
- **Retire** (get rid of)
- **Retain** (do nothing, usually "revisit later").

(Note: These strategies build upon the 5 R's that Gartner outlined in 2011)[19]

19 http://www.gartner.com/newsroom/id/1684114

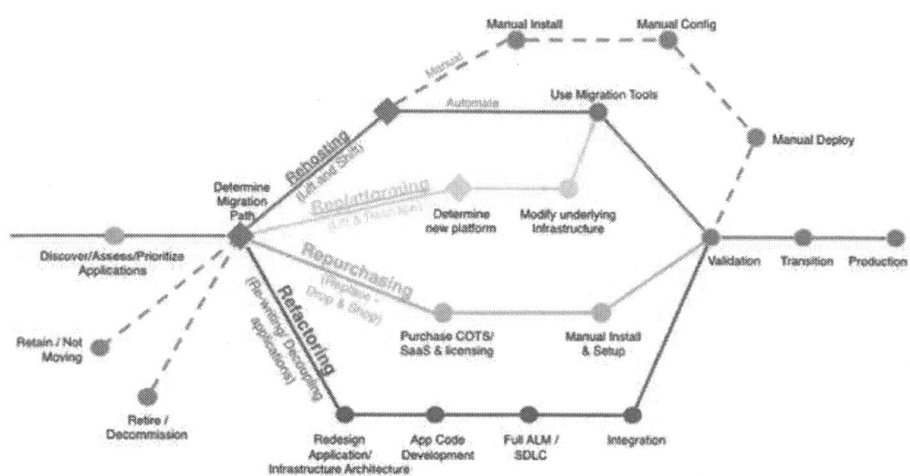

For a more detailed explanation of each of these 6 application migration strategies, see Chapter 6: 6 Strategies for Migrating Applications to the Cloud.

Are You Ready for a Mass Migration?

Mass migrations typically require an organization-wide effort and are most commonly embarked upon by organizations that have some experience with the cloud.

I elaborated on the activities I typically see organizations engage in before they execute mass migrations in Chapters 2 and 3, although I'm finding that, as the cloud market matures and there are more success stories to draw from, more executives are contemplating mass migrations earlier in their journey.

If you have a compelling reason to launch a migration without the benefit of existing experience, you should absolutely start to consider your business case, but I would strongly encourage you to frontload the migration project with some of the activities outlined in these initial stages.

CHAPTER 5

A Process for Mass Migrations to the Cloud

Originally post on 11/1/16: http://amzn.to/migration-process

◆ ◆ ◆

"We cannot and should not stop people from migration. We have to give them a better life at home. Migration is a process not a problem."
—*William Swing*

THIS CHAPTER OUTLINES A FIVE-PHASE "Migration Process" that I hope will help executives who are considering a mass migration to the cloud. You're reading part two of a three-part series. Chapter 4 (the first chapter in this series) introduces the concept of a mass migration, which we'll simply refer to as "migration" throughout the series, and Chapter 6 (the third chapter of the series) describes the six strategies for migrating applications to the cloud. While each of these chapters stands on its own, I believe they go better together.

The Migration Process combines what we (AWS) know about technology migrations and some of our experience helping organizations migrate their IT portfolios to AWS. This process—while based on experience—is intended to provide some guiding principles to help you approach your migration and not meant to prescribe hard-and-fast rules. Every organization has its own unique blend of constraints, budget issues, politics, culture, and market pressures that will guide its decision-making process along the way.

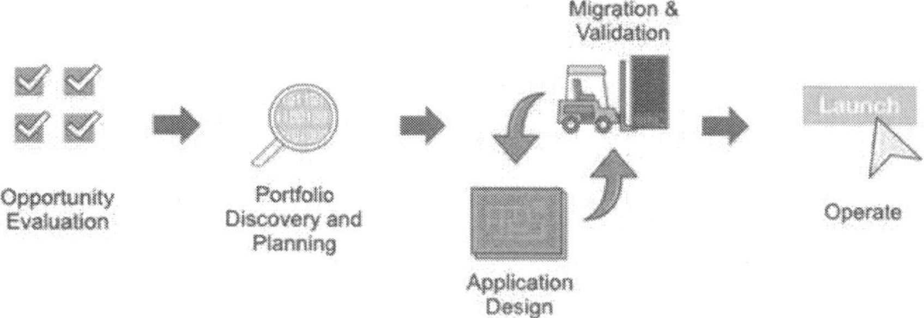

Phase 1: Opportunity Evaluation

What is the business case or compelling event that will drive your migration to the cloud?

Ideally, you'll be building off some experience (see Chapters 2 and 3), and you'll be able to use that experience to inform your business case. In the formative stages of the cloud market, migrations were often driven by instinct—an executive who felt it was the right thing to do. As the market develops and every enterprise is considering what and how to migrate, the need for business cases and/or compelling events to drive organization-wide behavior are becoming more common.

I'm sure that I've yet to see every possible business case or compelling event, but I do see a lot of migrations driven by data center lease expiry, additional developer productivity, global expansion, upcoming M&A activity, and/or the drive for standardized architectures.

One customer we work with, for example, has developed a business case around developer productivity. The customer (rightfully) believes that by migrating its data centers to AWS, and training its developers in the process, each of its 2,000 developers will be 50 percent more productive than they are today. Driven by the elimination of wait time for infrastructure provisioning—and access to more than 80 services they'd otherwise have to build/procure individually—this productivity boost will lead to an additional 1,000 years of developer capacity...each year. The customer intends to use this additional productivity to fund 100 new projects of 10 people each in an effort to find net new growth opportunities. (As a former CIO, this is probably my favorite business case yet. If you have a strong interest in hearing about additional business cases, please send me a note and we'll elaborate on other cases.)

Even if your organization doesn't require a formal business case to migrate to the cloud, I think it's important for leaders to provide clarity of purpose (Chapter 13) and set aggressive—but achievable—goals that their organizations can rally behind. I've seen too many migration efforts stall without this.

As you progress in your migration, you can look to hone in on the value you're creating, how you're communicating that value to your organization, and become more confident in your approach to procuring IT services in a pay-as-you-go, as-a-service model.

Phase 2: Portfolio Discovery and Planning

What's in your environment, what are the interdependencies, what will you migrate first, and how will you migrate it?

This is when organizations typically inspect their configuration management databases (CMDBs), institutional knowledge, and/or deploy tools (like the AWS Discovery Service[20] and/or RISC Networks)[21] to deeply understand what's in their environment. Using this knowledge, organizations can outline a plan (which should be considered subject to change as they progress through their migration and learn) on how they'll approach migrating each of the applications in their portfolio and in what order.

The complexity of migrating existing applications varies, depending on the architecture and existing licensing arrangements. If I think about the universe of applications to migrate on a spectrum of complexity, I'd put a virtualized, service-oriented architecture on the low-complexity end of the spectrum, and a monolithic mainframe at the high-complexity end of the spectrum.

I suggest starting with something on the low-complexity end of the spectrum for the obvious reason that it will be easier to complete—which will give you some immediate positive reinforcement or "quick wins" as you learn.

---

20 https://aws.amazon.com/about-aws/whats-new/2016/04/aws-application-discovery-service/

21 http://www.riscnetworks.com/

The complexity will also influence how you migrate. Because it's easy to lift-and-shift a modern application hosted on a virtualized environment, and there's typically less technical debt associated with something developed 3 years ago versus 20 years ago, we find a strong bias toward rehosting (aka "lift-and-shift"). And, because it's simply not possible to lift-and-shift a mainframe, we also find a strong bias toward feature rationalization and re-architecting. We (AWS and APN Migration Partners)[22] are doing everything we can to make mainframes (and other legacy systems) easier to migrate (contact me for more details), but there's still no silver bullet.

Phases 3 and 4: Designing, Migrating, and Validating Applications

In these two phases, which I often refer to together as the "migration factory," the focus of the migration moves from the portfolio level to the individual application level, and each application is designed, migrated, and validated according to one of the six application migration strategies (Chapter 6).

I recommend taking an approach of continuous improvement. Start with the least-complex application, learn how to migrate while learning more about the target platform, and build toward the more-complex application migrations as your organization becomes more cloud and migration fluent.

To help scale the migration factory quickly, I also recommend creating Agile teams focused on some type of migration theme. You might have a few teams dedicated to one or more of the migration strategies, to common application types (websites, Sharepoint, back-office, etc.), to different business units, or, in all likelihood, some combination thereof. Finding themes for teams to focus on will increase the chances that they learn from common patterns and accelerate the pace at which the factory migrates applications. Ideally, you've established a Cloud Center of Excellence (Chapters 24-31) that can advise and guide teams on their migrations and what to expect as they progress.

22 https://aws.amazon.com/migration/partner-solutions/

Finally, make sure you have a strategy for testing and decommissioning the old systems. The good news is you shouldn't have to purchase or wait for new hardware when you're only going to decommission the old hardware, but you may have to run parallel environments for a period of time while you migrate traffic, users, or content. To minimize this time, make sure that each business owner is involved and ready to validate the migration in real time, and measure the difference in cost and performance as you go.

Phase 5: Modern Operating Model

Finally, as applications are migrated, you iterate on your new foundation, turn off old systems, and constantly iterate toward a modern operating model.

When I was at Dow Jones, we used our migration as a forcing function to adopt a DevOps culture (Chapters 28-31), and many of the executives I speak to today seek a similar path toward Agile, lean, or some other buzzword-friendly approach to application development.

I'd encourage you to think about your operating model as an evergreen set of people, process, and technology that constantly improves as you migrate more applications. You don't need to boil the ocean early on by trying to solve for every scenario you may or may not encounter. Ideally, you're building off the foundational expertise you've developed before you created your business case. If not, use your first few application migrations to develop that foundation, and your operating model will continually improve and become more sophisticated as your migration factory accelerates.

CHAPTER 6

6 Strategies for Migrating Applications to the Cloud

Originally posted on 11/1/2016: http://amzn.to/migration-strategies

◆ ◆ ◆

"How emigration is actually lived—well, this depends on many factors: education, economic station, language, where one lands, and what support network is in place at the site of arrival."

—Daniel Alarcón

This chapter outlines six different migration strategies we see customers implement to migrate applications to the cloud. These strategies build upon the 5 Rs that Gartner outlined in 2011.[23] This is the final installment of a three-part series of chapters on migrations. While each of these chapters stands on its own, I believe they go better together.

Formulating a Migration Strategy

Enterprises typically begin to contemplate how to migrate an application during the second phase of the Migration Process—Portfolio Discovery and Planning. This is when they determine what's in their environment, what are the interdependencies, what's going to be easy or hard to migrate, and how they'll migrate each application.

Using this knowledge, organizations can outline a plan (which should be considered subject to change as they progress through their migration and

23 http://www.gartner.com/newsroom/id/1684114

learn) for how they'll approach migrating each of the applications in their portfolio and in what order.

As outlined in Chapter 2, the complexity of migrating existing applications varies, depending on the architecture and existing licensing arrangements. If I think about the universe of applications to migrate on a spectrum of complexity, I'd put a virtualized, service-oriented architecture on the low-complexity end of the spectrum, and a monolithic mainframe at the high-complexity end of the spectrum.

I suggest starting with something on the low-complexity end of the spectrum for the obvious reason that it will be easier to complete—which will give you some immediate positive reinforcement or quick wins as you learn.

6 Application Migration Strategies: The 6 Rs

The six most common application-migration strategies we see are:

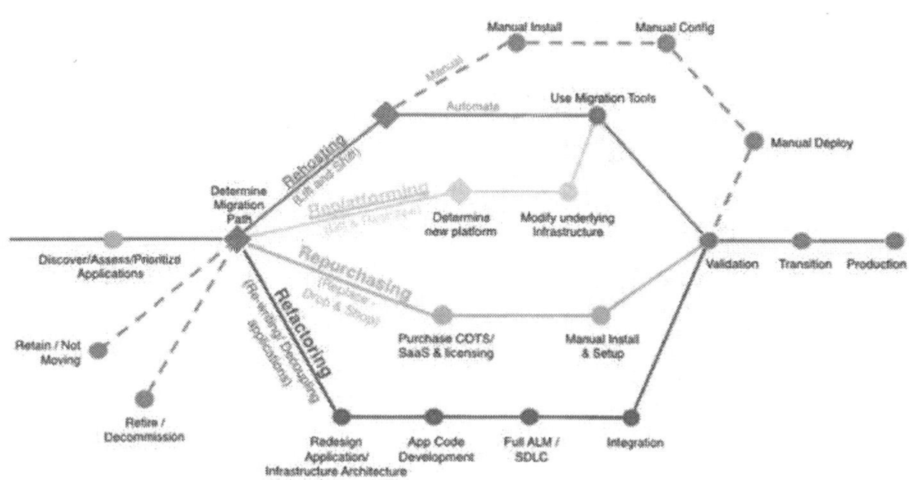

1. **Rehosting—Otherwise known as "lift-and-shift."** We find that many early cloud projects gravitate toward net new development using cloud-native capabilities, but in a large legacy migration scenario where the organization is looking to scale its migration quickly to

meet a business case, we find that the majority of applications are rehosted. GE Oil & Gas,[24] for instance, found that, even without implementing any cloud optimizations, it could save roughly 30 percent of its costs simply by rehosting.

Most rehosting can be automated with tools (e.g. AWS VM Import/Export),[25] although some customers prefer to do this manually as they learn how to apply their legacy systems to the new cloud platform.

We've also found that applications are easier to optimize/re-architect once they're already running in the cloud. Partly because your organization will have developed better skills to do so, and partly because the hard part—migrating the application, data, and traffic—has already been done.

2. **Replatforming—I sometimes call this "lift-tinker-and-shift."** Here you might make a few cloud (or other) optimizations in order to achieve some tangible benefit, but you aren't otherwise changing the core architecture of the application. You may be looking to reduce the amount of time you spend managing database instances by migrating to a database-as-a-service platform like Amazon Relational Database Service (Amazon RDS),[26] or migrating your application to a fully managed platform like Amazon Elastic Beanstalk.[27]

   A large, media company we work with migrated hundreds of web servers it ran on-premises to AWS, and in the process it moved from WebLogic (a Java application container that requires an expensive license) to Apache Tomcat,[28] an open-source equivalent. This media company saved millions in licensing costs on top of the savings and agility it gained by migrating to AWS.

24 https://aws.amazon.com/solutions/case-studies/ge-oil-gas/

25 https://aws.amazon.com/ec2/vm-import/

26 https://aws.amazon.com/rds

27 https://aws.amazon.com/elasticbeanstalk/

28 http://tomcat.apache.org/

3. **Repurchasing—Moving to a different product.** I most commonly see repurchasing as a move to a SaaS platform. Moving a CRM to Salesforce.com, an HR system to Workday, a CMS to Drupal, and so on.

4. **Refactoring/Re-architecting—Re-imagining how the application is architected and developed, typically using cloud-native features.** This is typically driven by a strong business need to add features, scale, or performance that would otherwise be difficult to achieve in the application's existing environment.

   Are you looking to migrate from a monolithic architecture to a service-oriented (or server-less) architecture to boost agility or improve business continuity (I've heard stories of mainframe fan belts being ordered on eBay)? This pattern tends to be the most expensive, but, if you have a good product-market fit, it can also be the most beneficial.

5. **Retire—Get rid of.** Once you've discovered everything in your environment, you might ask each functional area who owns each application. We've found that as much as 10 percent (I've seen 20 percent) of an enterprise IT portfolio is no longer useful, and can simply be turned off. These savings can boost the business case, direct your team's scarce attention to the things that people use, and lessen the surface area you have to secure.

6. **Retain—Usually this means "revisit" or do nothing (for now).** Maybe you're still riding out some depreciation, aren't ready to prioritize an application that was recently upgraded, or are otherwise not inclined to migrate some applications. You should only migrate what makes sense for the business, and, as the gravity of your portfolio changes from on-premises to the cloud, you'll probably have fewer reasons to retain.

CHAPTER 7

Cloud Native or Lift-and-Shift

Originally posted on 1/30/17: http://amzn.to/cloud-native-vs-lift-and-shift

◆ ◆ ◆

"There is always tension between the possibilities we aspire to and our wounded memories and past mistakes."
—Sean Brady

I talk to a lot of executives who are debating different migration approaches for the applications in their IT portfolio. While there's no one-size-fits-all answer to this question, we spend a good deal of time building migration plans with enterprises using a rubric that takes into account their objectives, the age/architecture of their applications, and their constraints. The goal is to help them bucket the applications in their portfolio into one of six migration strategies (Chapter 6).

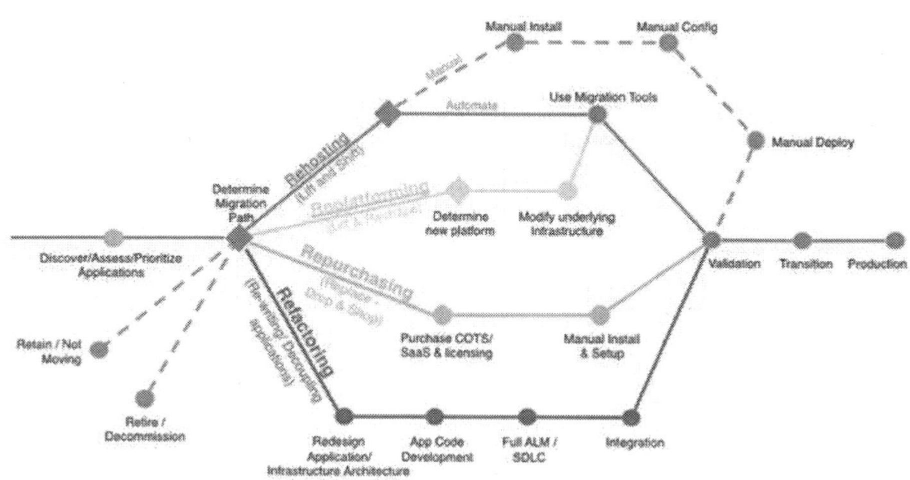

In some cases, the choices are obvious. We see a lot of organizations migrating their back-office technology and end-user computing applications to an as-a-service model ("re-purchasing" toward vendors like Salesforce and Workday); a number of organizations will look for opportunities to retire systems that are no longer in use; and some organizations will choose to later revisit systems that they don't feel they have the appetite or capabilities to migrate yet (i.e. the Mainframe, though You Can Migrate Your Mainframe to the Cloud, Chapter 9).

In other cases, the approach isn't so obvious. In Chapter 7, I touch on the tension between re-architecting and rehosting (a.k.a. "lift-and-shift"). I've heard a lot of executives—including myself, before I learned better—suggest that they're only moving to the cloud if they "do it right," which usually means migrating to a cloud-native architecture. Other executives are biased toward a rehosting strategy because they have a compelling reason to migrate quickly (for example, a data center lease expiry), want to avoid a costly refresh cycle, or simply need a quick budget win, which tends to be in the neighborhood of 30 percent when you're honest about your on-premises TCO.

Somewhere in the middle of rehosting and re-architecting is what we call re-platforming, where you're not spending the time on a complete re-architecture, but, rather, making some adjustments to take advantage of cloud-native features or otherwise optimize the application. This common middle ground includes right-sizing instances using realistic capacity scenarios that can easily be scaled up rather than overbought, or moving from a pay-for product like WebLogic to an open-source alternative like Apache Tomcat.[29]

So, which approach is more often right for your organization?

Without talking to you about your specific opportunities and constraints (which I'm happy to do; just drop me a note), it's hard to give a definitive answer, but I can highlight a few anecdotes that should help shape your perspective.

The first is a quote from Yury Izrailevsky's blog.[30] Yury is the Vice President of Cloud and Platform Engineering at Netflix, and is a well-respected thought leader in our industry.

> *Our journey to the cloud at Netflix began in August of 2008, when we experienced a major database corruption and for three days could not ship DVDs to our members. That is when we realized that we had to move away from vertically scaled single points of failure, like relational databases in our datacenter, towards highly reliable, horizontally scalable, distributed systems in the cloud.*
>
> *We chose Amazon Web Services (AWS) as our cloud provider because it provided us with the greatest scale and the broadest set of services and features. The majority of our systems, including all customer-facing services, had been migrated to the cloud prior to 2015. Since then, we've been taking the time necessary to figure out a secure and durable cloud path for our billing infrastructure as well as all aspects of our customer and employee data management. We are happy to report that in early January 2016, after seven years of diligent effort, we have finally completed our*

29 http://tomcat.apache.org/

30 https://media.netflix.com/en/company-blog/completing-the-netflix-cloud-migration

cloud migration and shut down the last remaining data center bits used by our streaming service!

Given the obvious benefits of the cloud, why did it take us a full seven years to complete the migration? The truth is, moving to the cloud was a lot of hard work, and we had to make a number of difficult choices along the way. Arguably, the easiest way to move to the cloud is to forklift all of the systems, unchanged, out of the data center and drop them in AWS. But in doing so, you end up moving all the problems and limitations of the data center along with it. Instead, we chose the cloud-native approach, rebuilding virtually all of our technology and fundamentally changing the way we operate the company...Many new systems had to be built, and new skills learned. It took time and effort to transform Netflix into a cloud-native company, but it put us in a much better position to continue to grow and become a global TV network.

Yury's experience is both instructive and inspirational, and I'm certain that Netflix's re-architecting approach was right for them.

But most enterprises aren't Netflix, and many will have different drivers for their migration.

When I was the CIO at Dow Jones several years ago, we initially subscribed to the ivory tower attitude that everything we migrated needed to be re-architected, and we had a relentless focus on automation and cloud-native features. That worked fine until we had to vacate one of our data centers in less than two months. We re-hosted most of what was in that data center into AWS, and sprinkled in a little re-platforming where we could to make some small optimizations but still meet our time constraint. One could argue that we would not have been able to do this migration that quickly if we didn't already have the experience leading up to it, but no one could argue with the results. We reduced our costs by roughly 30 percent. This experience led to a business case to save or reallocate more than $100 million in costs across all of News Corp (our parent company) by migrating 75 percent of our applications to the cloud as we consolidated 56 data centers into 6.

GE Oil & Gas[31] rehosted hundreds of applications to the cloud as part of a major digital overhaul.[32] In the process, they reduced their TCO by 52 percent. Ben Cabanas, then one of GE's most forward-thinking technology executives, told me a story that was similar to mine—they initially thought they'd re-architect everything, but soon realized that would take too long, and that they could learn and save a lot by rehosting first.

One of my favorite pun-intended quotes comes from Nike's Global CIO, Jim Scholefield, who told us that "Sometimes, I tell the team to *just move it.*"

Cynics might say that rehosting is simply "your mess for less," but I think there's more to it than that. I'd boil the advantage of rehosting down to two key points. (I'm sure there are others; please send me a note about them and we'll post your story…)

First, rehosting takes a lot less time, particularly when automated, and typically yields a TCO savings in the neighborhood of 30 percent. As you learn from experience, you'll be able to increase that savings through simple replatforming techniques, like instance right-sizing and open source alternatives. Your mileage on the savings may vary, depending on your internal IT costs and how honest you are about them.

Second, it becomes easier to re-architect and constantly reinvent your applications once they're running in the cloud. This is partly because of the obvious toolchain integration, and partly because your people will learn an awful lot about what cloud-native architectures should look like through rehosting. One customer we worked with rehosted one of its primary customer-facing applications in a few months to achieve a 30 percent TCO reduction, then re-architected to a serverless architecture to gain another 80 percent TCO reduction!

Re-architecting takes longer, but it can be a very effective way for an enterprise to re-boot its culture and, if your application is a good product-market fit, can lead to a healthy ROI. Most important, however, re-architecting can set the stage for years and years of continual reinvention that boosts business performance in even the most-competitive markets.

---

31 https://aws.amazon.com/solutions/case-studies/ge-oil-gas/

32 https://aws.amazon.com/blogs/aws/ge-oil-gas-digital-transformation-in-the-cloud/

While I still believe there's no one-size-fits-all answer, I'd summarize by suggesting that you look to re-architect the applications where you know you need to add business capabilities that a cloud-native architecture can help you achieve (performance, scalability, globality, moving to a DevOps or Agile model), and that you look to rehost or re-platform the steady-state applications that you aren't otherwise going to repurchase, retire, or revisit. Either migration path paves the way for constant reinvention.

CHAPTER 8

4 Reasons to Reconsider Lift-and-Shift to the Cloud by Joe Chung, Enterprise Strategist & Evangelist at AWS

Originally posted on 12/6/17: http://amzn.to/4-reasons-lift-and-shift

"...Reform the environment and not man; being absolutely confident that if you give man the right environment, he will behave favorably."
—*Buckminster Fuller*

As an enterprise strategist at AWS, I often talk to customers about strategies that will help them move workloads to the cloud. Occasionally, I'll hear from senior executives who don't want to take any of their legacy workloads to the cloud; instead, they want to focus on developing net new architectures using serverless services like AWS Lambda. Even with the potential cost savings, I'm sympathetic to why an organization wouldn't want to take any of its legacy technical debt to the cloud avoiding the "mess-for-less" approach. Also, given that we live in an era of intense security scrutiny, organizations apply higher standards in the cloud than in their on-premises data centers. This potentially causes refactoring on applications. But, based on my experience and what I've seen from a wide range of customers, lift-and-shift should be one of your core migration paths for taking workloads to the AWS cloud.

Stephen Orban, Global Head of Enterprise Strategy for AWS, has made a very strong case that explains why organizations should look at lift-and-shift as part of their migration strategy. Some of the benefits Stephen cites include reduction of cost and improved performance and resiliency. I'd like to dive a little deeper in this post, because I've found that real-life examples illustrating how lift-and-shift can help organizations frequently lead customers to consider a balanced and holistic migration approach.

Before I get into the reasons why lift-and-shift helps inject new life into applications, I'd like to introduce what may be a new mental model for how to think about software applications. I think of applications as being organic in nature. They are born, evolve, morph, communicate, and interact with other organisms in the environment in which they exist. To extend the analogy further, these applications communicate with other applications and live in an ecosystem or environment that is the data center. I believe the ability of these applications to perform and evolve is just as much dependent on their environment as the code or DNA that governs their behavior. The argument I'd like to make here is that the AWS cloud provides a better environment—in terms of size and diversity of services—that is well beyond what most on-premises data centers can provide.

Reason 1—SSDs Rule

AWS provides 13 families of compute, ranging from memory-optimized computer to optimized storage to optimized server instances. Most organizations aren't able to provide this broad choice, despite the flexibility that virtualization provides. That's unfortunate, because one benefit of this variety is the boost in performance that occurs when solid-state drives (SSDs) are leveraged, particularly for storage I/O-intensive workloads like databases. The price of all storage types continues to go down, but it's still relatively expensive for organizations to upgrade their fleet of physical hosts with SSDs. Having said that, though, SSDs are 2 to 5 times faster than spinning disk, so the performance gains can be substantial for certain classes of workloads. And, with AWS, organizations can be judicious in the application of SSD-backed instances. Or, like my previous organization, they can give everyone a performance bump by just moving all databases to SSD-backed instances.

Reason 2—Covering Application Sins

Most people think about the cloud's elasticity from a scale-out perspective, but scale-up is just as valid. This can be done on-premises, but AWS provides an upper threshold that's greater than most environments. For example, one of AWS' largest instances in memory and CPU comes from our X1 family of virtual servers.[33] The x1e.32xlarge[34] has 128 vCPUs, 4TB of memory, and it's backed by SSD storage with dedicated bandwidth to EBS (14,000 Mbps). This is an instance that is typically used for workloads like SAP HANA.[35]

One customer I know had an application that was in a critical period and realized there were some bad queries causing performance bottlenecks. Changing the code was too risky, so the database server was upped to an X1 instance and then ramped back down to a more reasonable instance size once the critical period was over. Being on the application development side of the IT house, I always appreciated when infrastructure had the ability to cover application sins. I'd rather catch application issues earlier in the development cycle, but it's sure nice to know that AWS can provide help when you're in a bind.

Reason 3—Horses for Courses

The relational database (RDMS) has been the *de facto* back-end for applications over the past 40 years. While the RDMS is great at many kinds of queries there are some workloads that the RDMS is simply not well-suited for. Full-text search is a good example, which explains why Lucene-based technologies such as Apache Solr[36] and ElasticSearch[37] are so popular and much better suited for this use case.

Another story from my professional past—One of the architecture principles I had established in my past is "Horses for Courses" to help our teams

---

33 https://aws.amazon.com/ec2/instance-types/x1/

34 https://aws.amazon.com/about-aws/whats-new/2017/09/general-availability-a-new-addition-to-the-largest-amazon-ec2-memory-optimized-x1-instance-family-x1e32xlarge/

35 https://www.sap.com/products/hana.html

36 http://lucene.apache.org/solr/

37 https://info.elastic.co/branded-ggl-elastic-exact-v3.html

make better technology decisions by choosing the best technology for the given use case versus going with what they know or are comfortable with. An example of this principle is I once worked with an application team that was trying to develop innovative ideas as the business was growing. Users were frustrated with the lack of innovation and development agility and complained greatly when it came to in application search. The idea we had was to stand up an ElasticSearch instance alongside the application, integrate the application data over to ElasticSearch, and then do a minor refactor of the front-end web application. (ElasticSearch provides some great REST-based APIs.) What I love about this story is that the team didn't have to take a big risk refactoring the application and instantiating Amazon ElasticSearch[38] or Amazon CloudSearch.[39] Plus the team did not need to invest in specialized skills provisioning and managing NoSQL clusters. The AWS cloud provides a stable of many service "horses" to help evolve applications.

Reason 4—Evolving Monoliths

A lot has been written about microservices,[40] but, distilled down, it's clear that their primary benefits are independent deployment and scalability. And, if microservices offer the right size of granularity or "bounded context,"[41] then the blast radius of many types of risk can be mitigated (e.g. performance, changes, etc.).

Companies like Netflix and Amazon have implemented microservices architectures to help innovate and scale their applications. But an essential area of microservices that's generally misunderstood is the independence aspect, or how solid the boundaries should actually be between other microservices. One litmus test I deploy with teams that are implementing microservices is pretty simple—if I whack your database, how many other teams or microservices will be impacted? The usual, and sheepish, response I get is that the back-end is shared with a number of other teams. My belief is that, in order to

38 https://aws.amazon.com/elasticsearch-service/

39 https://aws.amazon.com/cloudsearch/

40 https://aws.amazon.com/microservices/

41 https://martinfowler.com/articles/microservices.html

be independently deployable and scalable, the microservice should be isolated from the code repository, presentation layer, business logic, down through the persistence store.

If my definition of microservice isolation resonates for you, then the ramifications can be quite expensive from an infrastructure perspective. In on-premises infrastructure, spinning up a new code repository, web servers, application servers, and database servers can get really expensive (both to provision and operate); this will also likely slow the provisioning process. But spinning up these infrastructure components is fast and cheap in the cloud, especially if you leverage services like Amazon RDS[42] or AWS Lambda.[43]

One of the best examples of how to evolve a monolith is contained in a presentation by gilt.com that has been delivered several times at re:Invent. What's great about the presentation is that the evolution of the gilt.com application can be applied to many enterprise applications. In a nutshell, Gilt needed to evolve its ecommerce platform because of scalability and agility issues. So, it started by standing up microservices alongside its application and kept doing this to the point where it had "a forest of microservices" that grew up around the core application, which was originally written. I could make a strong argument that it would have been really hard to stand up all those microservices in an on-premises environment, especially if there was diversity in the front- and back-end technologies.

If the "mess-for-less" approach has been holding you back, I hope this post has helped evolve your thinking and set the stage for lift-and-shift to become a pillar of your migration strategy.

42 https://aws.amazon.com/rds/

43 https://aws.amazon.com/lambda/

CHAPTER 9

Yes, You Can Migrate Your Mainframe to the Cloud

Originally posted on 1/9/17: http://amzn.to/migrate-mainframe-to-cloud

◆ ◆ ◆

FOR MANY LARGE AND WELL-TENURED enterprises, the mainframe is often cited as a central point of gravity that stalls or elongates a large cloud migration. Many enterprises feel that they have few people who have the domain and technology expertise to execute a mainframe migration, and those who are still working on the mainframe can be harder to motivate for a cloud migration (though I do believe you already have the people you need, Chapter 15). While there is no silver bullet to magically lift-and-shift *and* modernize your mainframe applications as you migrate it to the cloud, there are reasonable approaches leveraging various migration strategies (Chapter 6). To explain, I'll turn it over to AWS' Erik Farr, who has spent much of the last year working with Infosys on an AWS mainframe modernization practice.

◆ ◆ ◆

In the most recent series of blogs that Stephen published on mass migrations (Chapters 4-9), he often talks about a spectrum of complexity for workloads that are being migrated to the cloud. In this spectrum, he puts virtualized, service-oriented architecture workloads at the low end and monolithic mainframes at the high end of complexity, and for good reason. Mainframes have often been with organizations for decades and are usually running mission-critical workloads that have specific performance and security requirements that ensure smooth business operations. When talking with customers about their overall IT landscape and cloud-migration strategy, it's easy to skim past the mainframe workloads and put them into the "revisit" bucket for a future date. However, for companies that have a compelling event to get off their mainframe, or are starting to revisit their landscape, the time is now for a mainframe migration.

I have been fortunate enough to get a deeper understanding of common approaches to mainframe migrations to AWS during my time helping Infosys, an AWS premier partner, create their mainframe to AWS migration solution. They have been a leader in managing, developing on, and modernizing mainframes for decades, and they are extending that experience into migrating mainframe workloads as a core competency. Using their Knowledge Curation Platform (Ki), they are able to analyze the customer mainframe code to understand exactly what's running and what's not.

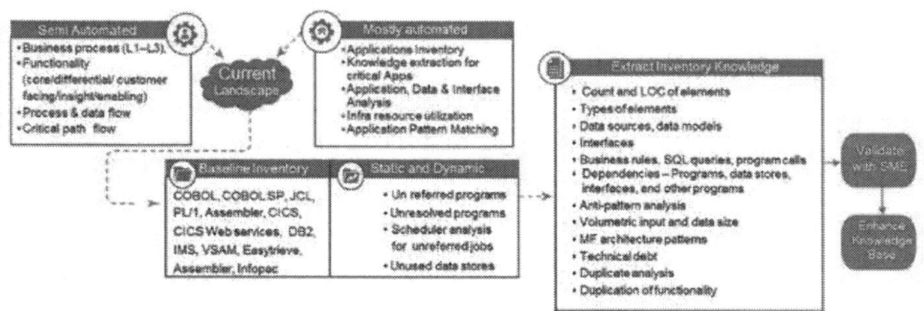

The outputs of this process, which often takes less than six weeks, are then used to help the customer create a business case and ultimately a roadmap for the full mainframe migration project.

There are three main approaches to mainframe migrations that we see customers exploring—re-hosting of workloads, batch-job migration and full re-engineering. Each have their pros and cons and ultimately customers decide based on risk tolerance, business case and following their overall cloud strategy. Here is a quick breakdown of these migration approaches:

Re-Hosting

A re-hosting solution runs existing mainframe applications on an x86–64 based Amazon EC2 instance using a mainframe emulator (i.e. Micro Focus Enterprise Server, TMaxSoft OpenFrame, Oracle Tuxedo ART). This migration is seamless from an end-user perspective and it does not require changes to standard mainframe technologies like 3270 Screens Web Cobol, JCL, and DB2. There is often a bit of re-platforming in this approach as well, like moving older and difficult-to-maintain databases to newer RDMBS engines and hosting on Amazon RDS.

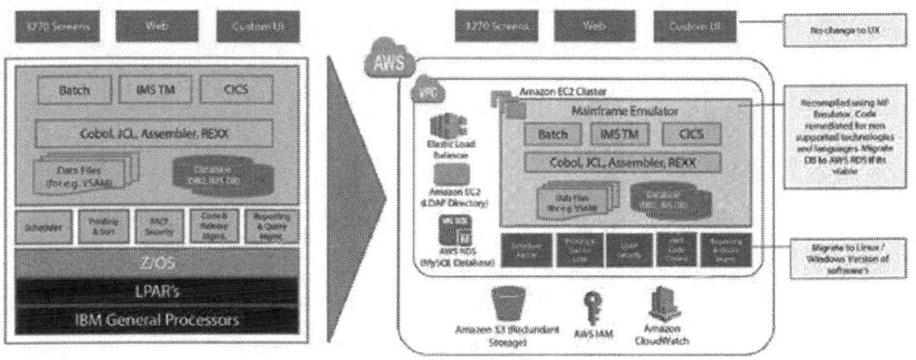

Batch Job Migration

Batch jobs often form a large portion of the mainframe application portfolio, and while some are business-critical, usually a significant number of these jobs are of low business value and consume a large amount of MIPS. Whether they are file based or near-real-time processes, offloading the heavy lifting to the AWS Cloud will enable customers to gain additional insights to their data and reduce MIPS consumption on their existing mainframe.

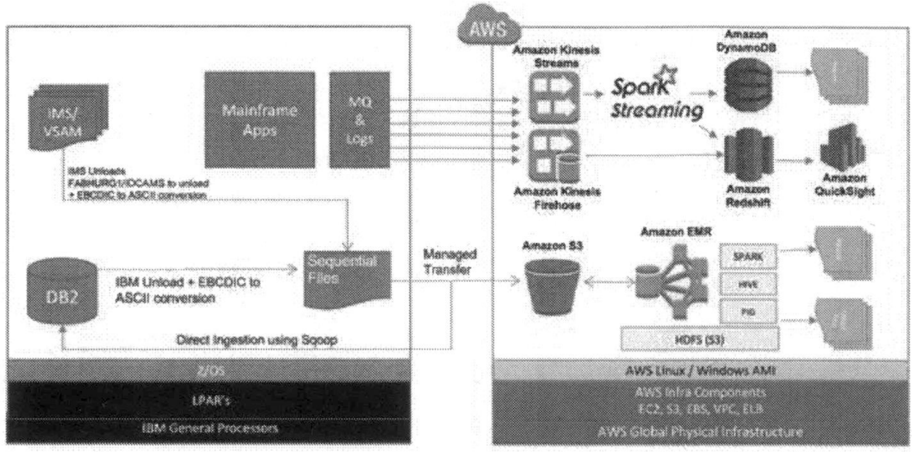

Re-Engineering

The re-engineering approach is recommended when the existing mainframe application is no longer able to meet future-state business requirements or an Agile target architecture. This approach will create a new application with similar performance and equal or enhanced functionality. Typically, this is done using cloud-native techniques, leveraging micro-services (i.e. Amazon API Gateway, AWS Lambda), Containers and Decoupling (i.e. Amazon EC2 Container Service, Docker containers, Amazon Simple Queueing Services) and Data Analytics, Artificial Intelligence and Machine Learning (i.e. Amazon EMR, Infosys Mana for AI, or Amazon Machine Learning).

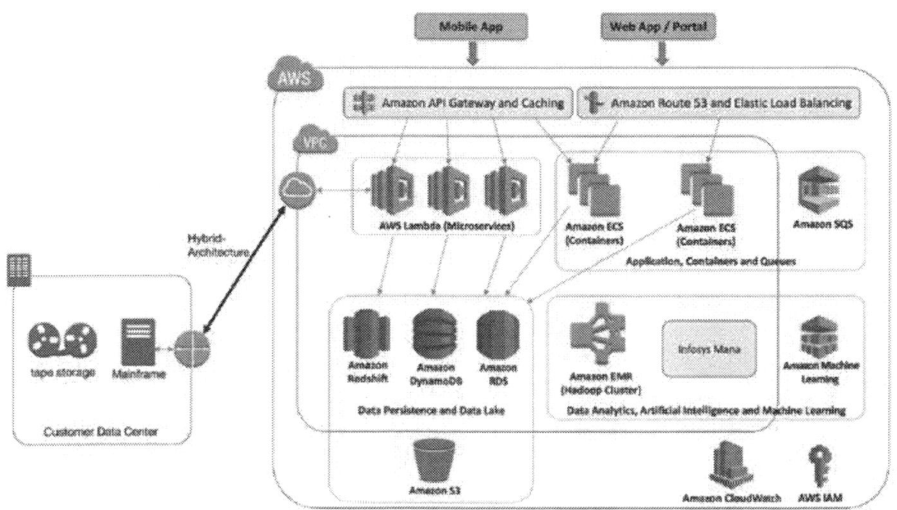

Regardless of the approach taken, it's important for companies to understand that mainframe workloads should be considered in their cloud migration strategy. This will often result in significant cost savings, increased agility and a future-proofed architecture. For more information on the topic of mainframe migration and how AWS and Infosys can help, please review the mainframe migration to AWS whitepaper my colleagues Sanjeet Sahay, Tom Laszewski, and I co-authored with Infosys.[44]

44 http://www.experienceinfosys.com/Mainframe-Modernization-Aug16-13

CHAPTER 10

Always Be Reinventing & The Cloud of Youth

Originally posted on 1/25/17: https://amzn.to/constant-reinvention

◆ ◆ ◆

"The only thing that is constant is change."

—Heraclitus

Most executives I talk with tell me that their journey to the cloud is more about business and cultural transformation than it is about technology adoption. To that end, this part of the book narrows in on a mental model that I call the Stages of Adoption, which highlights the pattern of activities we see inside large organizations that are reinventing their business using the cloud. I think of this pattern as an iterative and transformational journey, and one of my goals is to give executives who are interested in transforming their organization an approach to do so.

When I first published the opener for this series, I called the fourth and final stage of adoption "Optimization." I was trying to suggest that, as the gravity of your IT portfolio shifts from on-premises to the cloud, each application will be easier to constantly optimize once it is migrated from on-premises to the cloud. While this is true—and I'll elaborate on this point in a moment—I've come to believe that the term Optimization undersells the possibilities for organizations that make it to this stage in their journey.

Most large, cloud migration efforts are backed by a business case that quantifies an end state. When I was at News Corp, for example, our business case was to migrate 75 percent of our infrastructure to the cloud over three years to achieve $100M in annual savings. This type of objective seems to have become quite common—dozens of executives have since told me that they are looking to migrate 75-90 percent of their IT portfolio to the cloud in the next three years.

But realizing a business case objective like this is only the beginning. Organizations on this journey also have the opportunity to constantly reinvent their people, process, technology, and, perhaps most important, their culture. I sometimes think of this journey as a perpetual quest for a fountain of youth that will allow enterprises of all ages to continue to compete in a rapidly evolving marketplace. (Since its inception in 1955, for example, the Fortune 500 has seen between 20 and 50 companies fall off the list each year. Advances in technology are largely behind this steady rate of turnover, with the cloud being the most recent cause of large-scale disruption.)

So, to more precisely articulate what we see in organizations that are investing in cloud-first strategies as they constantly evolve their business, I'm rebranding the fourth—and never-ending—stage of adoption to "Reinvention."

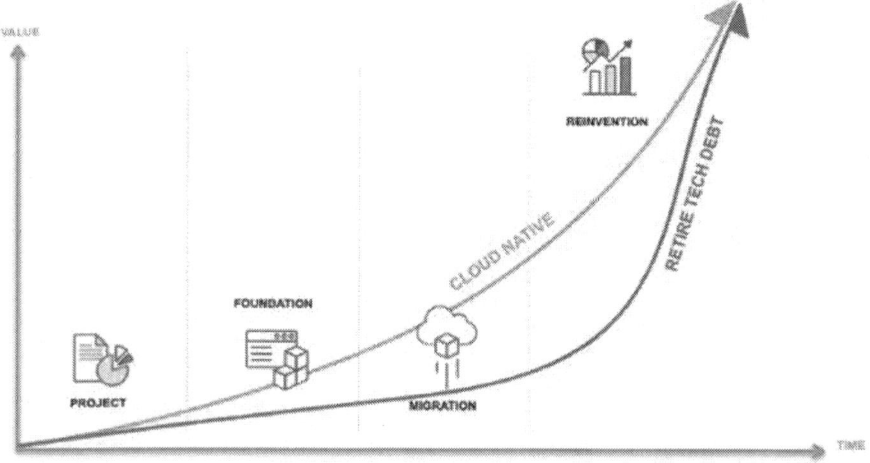

Before I close out this chapter, I'd like to issue a call to arms to anyone who has experience leading their organization through the Stages of Adoption. Other executives are eager to hear about your journey, and I'm eager to host your experience alongside the others who are sharing theirs in Part III of this book.

PART II

7 Best Practices

MEANINGFUL TECHNOLOGY CHANGE IN A very large organization is very rarely just about the technology. It's about people, it's about leadership, and it's about creating a culture that encourages safe-to-fail experiments and smart risk taking instead of creating fear among those who are expected to move the organization forward.

The seven best practices I outline in this part of the book represent an incomplete, non-exhaustive, and opinionated list of what I think are some of the most important things you ought to be thinking about when leading your organization on any kind of change program. While technology is integral to each of these best practices, much of it comes down to leadership's ability to lead, motivate, inspire, reorganize, and influence the people they work with.

These best practices include:

1. **Provide executive support** – projects are much more likely to succeed when the boss supports them, and large-scale change management typically comes from the top. This best practices details some of the things we've seen leaders do to help their organizations transform faster.
2. **Educate staff** – people can sometimes be afraid of what they don't know. I've found that finding the ones who aren't afraid to lead the way (attitude is just as important as aptitude, in many cases) and investing in training and enablement for everyone can be among the most effective ways to get people over their fears.

3. **Create a culture of experimentation** – having access to a seemingly infinite amount of on-demand IT resources can change the game for any organization, provided the culture promotes the use of it. Failure is a lot less expensive when you can just spin down what didn't work.
4. **Pick the right partners** – the ecosystem of system integrators, digital consultancies, managed service providers, and tools around cloud has grown substantially over the years. Your partners of yesterday may or may not be your partners of tomorrow.
5. **Create a Cloud Center of Excellence** – most organizations that are doing anything meaningful with the cloud have a team of people dedicated to deeply understanding how cloud technology can be used across a distributed organization, and can usher in the best practices and governance that can allow you to move fast while maintaining the right amount of centralized control.
6. **Implement a hybrid architecture** – the cloud is not an all-or-nothing value proposition. Any enterprise that has been implementing their own IT infrastructure for any period of time will have a hybrid architecture as part of their journey.
7. **Implement a cloud-first strategy** – once your organization has some experience with implementing cloud at scale, it may be time to make it a strategic imperative to accelerate the results across your organization.

Each of these seven best practices is a mini-series on its own. They're based on the experiences that I—and my many colleagues throughout the industry—have had transforming some of today's most successful organizations. I hope they will give you some perspective on how others have faced the struggles of trying to stay modern and compete in the global marketplace using the cloud, and I welcome your feedback and possible contributions!

BEST PRACTICE ONE

Provide Executive Support

◆ ◆ ◆

CHAPTER 11

Today's IT Executive Is a Chief Change Management Officer

Originally posted on 9/30/15: http://amzn.to/CIO-chief-change-management-officer

◆ ◆ ◆

"Success is about dedication. You may not be where you want to be or do what you want to do when you're on the journey. But you've got to be willing to have vision and foresight that leads you to an incredible end."
—*Usher*

As more and more enterprises consider the cloud, today's IT executive has an opportunity to assume a new role, one that drives both technical excellence and business value across their entire organization.

At the very least, today's IT executive needs to provide executive support throughout their organization's journey to the cloud. Executive support is the first of seven best practices I write about in my Enterprise Cloud Journey series. The remaining six practices are: educate staff, create a culture of experimentation, pick the right partners, create a Cloud Center of Excellence, implement a hybrid architecture, and implement a cloud-first policy.

There are three areas I've seen IT executives focus their energy on when leading their organizations on the journey. In this chapter, I offer a preview into each and go into detail on all of them in the chapters that follow.

Remember—the journey is an iterative process, and one that will take time. It's not just about changing your organization's technology—it's about changing the way your IT department delivers technology and adds business value. The technology shift and new business model that come with the cloud give you an opportunity to look at job functions, finances, product development methodologies, and much more across your entire organization. It sets the stage for a once-in-a-career opportunity to be the IT executive who drives transformation for the betterment of the business, whether your business's motivations are financial, competitive, or both. This means you get to determine what fits and what doesn't, and create the environment that best suits your business.

I'd argue that today's IT executive needs to play the role of the Chief Change Management Officer (which I'll refer to as a CCMO). Technology can no longer be viewed as something that simply supports the business. Today's IT executive is optimally positioned to understand this and subsequently drive the changes required to keep up with an increasingly competitive and increasingly technical landscape. Across all industries, this CCMO will need to lead change throughout the rest of the executive team and their staff, and decisively manage execution.

Here are three responsibilities that I believe are critical to the success of the CCMO:

Merging business and technology. Cloud adoption offers more than technology shift. It also offers a new way to do business. This is something that everyone at the executive level should care about. It's the IT executive's job to consider the executive team and how each respective function is impacted or could be impacted by the journey. There are both clearly positive outcomes (financial, agility, global reach, etc.) and some challenges (hiring, training, fear of the unfamiliar). In order to position a changing IT environment in a way that will help each executive meet his or her goals, you first need to be empathetic to those goals and challenges, then show how goals will become easier and challenges less daunting on the journey.

Providing clarity of purpose. Just as it's important to tie technology to business results together for your executive stakeholders, tying your team's roles back to the business benefit will help them understand how they fit in—especially when it involves changes to their roles. Early in my executive career, I was somewhat naive in thinking that, just because I issued a department-wide directive, everyone's actions would follow. It wasn't until I identified the things that were really important and communicated them over and over and over again that they started to stick. If anything, the cloud creates a lot of new opportunity for your staff, and as long as they're willing to learn, there are a number of new ways they'll be able to contribute to the business.

Breaking (Making) new rules. Most traditional IT operating models won't allow you to take full advantage of what the cloud has to offer. In a world where competitors like Uber, Airbnb, Dropbox, and many others can come out of nowhere with novel technologies and fast-moving operations, you're going to want to consider new rules that allow your organization to keep up. This, even more than the other two, is something that has to come from the top IT executive. Unchecked rule breaking at every level of the organization is probably something worth avoiding.

CHAPTER 12

Today's CIO on Merging Business with Technology

Originally posted on 10/14/15: http://amzn.to/CIO-merge-business-and-technology

◆ ◆ ◆

"Start with the end in mind."

—*Stephen R. Covey*

In the previous chapter, I asserted that today's technology executive needs to play the role of the Chief Change Management Officer (CCMO) in leading his or her organization on the Enterprise Cloud journey. This chapter explores the first of three themes associated with this responsibility: merging business with technology (managing across). The other two, providing clarity of purpose (managing down) and making (breaking, really) new rules (managing execution), will be explored in the chapters that follow.

Today, more than ever, successful technology executives must help their executive counterparts understand how technology fits into—or, even better, powers—their business. Providing the organization with this understanding will illustrate to your executive peers that you have a command over your organization's business objectives and that you're a critical member of the executive team.

The current business landscape is being disrupted by companies that are built and run by executives and entrepreneurs who not only understand how technology fits into their business, but who are also defining the role technology plays across entire industries: Airbnb for hotels, Uber for car services, Nest Labs for home automation, and Dropbox for storage are just a few examples. While this creates pressure for traditional enterprises to keep pace, it also creates an opportunity for IT executives everywhere. No one is in a better position to translate how technology can meet the increasing demands of the marketplace than those who have spent their careers working in technology. This is especially true for those of us who have been working in large companies for most of our careers. We speak the enterprise lingo, understand what constraints are hard and which are soft, and what levers you have to pull for each of your C-level peers. Companies can no longer expect to be successful with their technology executive(s) working behind the scenes.

And, because the cloud takes away much of the undifferentiated heavy lifting traditionally associated with enterprise IT, today's IT executive can leverage it to devote more time and resources towards the activities that drive the business and keep the organization competitive. The cloud is a key ingredient being used by these new disruptive forces. Using the same ingredient won't necessarily give you the ideas you need to grow your business, but it will even the playing field while opening up additional possibilities.

Here are a few ideas for those of you looking to lead your organization on your journey:

Empathize with Your Peers

The cloud is more than a technology shift. It's a business shift, and one that everyone at the executive level should care about. It's your job to consider your executive team and how its functions are impacted, or could be impacted, by the journey.

There are too many types of executives for me to cover in this chapter, but:

CFOs are typically attracted to lower up-front costs and the ability to pay only for what you use. I've seen some friction around the variability of costs from month to month, but I almost always find that the total cost of ownership is lower, especially when you're freed from the burden of capacity planning and maintenance activities. Work closely with your controllers every month as you learn more about your environment to forecast spend, govern resource utilization, stagger the purchase of Reserved Instances (RIs), and consider how you capitalize labor costs as more of your resources become focused on product development (creating assets) over time.

CMOs are typically looking to keep the company's brand fresh and respond to changing market conditions. What would the implications be of being able to update your brand website several times a day instead of once a month? How would an infinitely scalable data warehouse help CMOs better understand their customers? What experiments might they try with a small fraction of their users if it cost little to nothing to try?

VPs of HR will want to see that you're looking after your staff properly and how you're hiring for new skills. Take advantage of AWS Training and Certification, and feel free to make our training expertise a part of your own training curriculums. I explore how to educate your staff under Best Practice Two, and—spoiler alert—everyone on your team can help you make the journey if they're willing to learn. Also, network with other companies who are on the journey to find out about how they're hiring for new roles and managing the transition with existing staff. For example, how does DevOps fit into your organization, and what would it mean to run-what-you-build?

CEOs care about all of these things, and how the company will stay competitive. Use what you learn from the other executives to help shape a complete vision, and show how, by leveraging modern technology, you'll be able to do things that would not have been possible given the same constraints.

At Dow Jones, I set a goal to take a few executives out for a meal each month. During the time we spent together, I did nothing but listen to their frustrations. I used what I learned to adjust our strategy, and made sure that I communicated back to them how their influence altered our direction. This is a simple (and enjoyable, if you like people and food) way to show empathy toward their needs, build trust, and earn their support. The key here is not just to listen, but to also take action based on what you learn.

Enlist Help

You don't have to do this alone. Think of your account managers as shepherds for your journey. They're happy to work with you and your executive team to help shape the message around and benefits of moving to the cloud so that it aligns with your business. If the influence you need is beyond the scope of the account manager's expertise, they'll find the appropriate people, whether they're inside or outside of AWS. We're happy to create opportunities for you to network with like-minded peers—not just at our events, but at any juncture in your journey. I had several reference calls with other companies in my last role, and learning from other executives is both educational and validating.

The AWS Partner Network and AWS Training and Certification are also great resources to help you accelerate your journey. I'll touch more on these when I address them as best practices in their own right, but I find a lot of companies that partner with their HR departments to institutionalize AWS training on top of our programs. At Dow Jones, our DevOps team partnered with HR to develop DevOps days that they regularly held to evangelize our evolving tools and best practices. This is a great way to scale skills across a large and geographically distributed team. Again, your account managers can help make the right connections across both of these areas.

Evolve the IT Brand

I talk to a lot of IT executives that aspire to improve their department's brand. I spent more than a decade of my career developing software that drove the business at Bloomberg. One of the reasons I moved to Dow Jones was to help them shift the mindset away from IT being a cost center and toward a discipline that drove and empowered the business. I felt that I owed it to every person in my department for their hard work and dedication, and it was very helpful in getting them on board with the changes we were making.

AWS was part of the foundation for making this shift, but most of the hard work at the executive level revolved around understanding each executive's pain points, what they wanted to get out of IT, and aligning technology to help them meet their goals. After a few months of using the cloud to deliver better results faster, we spent several months retraining the executive team and their departments to refer to us as technology instead of IT. It may seem subtle, but it made a meaningful difference in the tone and productivity of our conversations, and signaled a changing contribution by the department to the overall company.

CHAPTER 13

What Makes Good Leaders Great?

Originally posted on 10/22/15: http://amzn.to/what-makes-good-leaders-great

◆ ◆ ◆

"It's a lack of clarity that creates chaos and frustration. Those emotions are poison to any living goal."

—Steve Maraboli

Leaders lead in many different ways. Some lead by fear, some by example, some with charisma, and some lead through others. And while every leader's style is slightly different, experience has taught me one thing that stays the same: people are most likely to follow those they understand.

People believe in what they are able to understand. When it comes to change management, they'll typically revert to what they're comfortable with—the status quo—when they don't understand the direction in which they're being led. Leaders can resolve this dilemma by providing clear and concise direction. The ability to provide clarity of purpose separates the great leaders from the good ones.

Today's technology executives should consider themselves Chief Change Management Officers (CCMO) when leading their organization's journey to the cloud. In addition to handling the merging of business and technology, the CCMO is also responsible for providing clarity of purpose. That means being able to articulate your strategy, how your team fits into that strategy, where there is and isn't flexibility, staying determined, and staying patient.

Organizations move to the cloud for different reasons—some to save money, some to expand globally, some to improve their security posture, and some to improve agility. Through my experiences, I've found that companies begin to embrace cloud as a platform across the entire organization once they realize how it helps them devote more of their resources to what matters to the business. Those are the activities that matter most to your customers and your stakeholders. And unless you're an infrastructure provider, these activities are not related to managing infrastructure.

Whatever your short- or long-term motivations may be, I'd encourage you to make them known and make them measurable. Clearly articulate your motivations and goals to your team and your stakeholders, and hold everyone accountable for moving the needle in the right direction.

Early in my leadership tenure, I thought—naively—that just because I was the boss everyone would do what I said. I learned the hard way that this is, of course, not how leadership works. It wasn't until I started to clearly articulate what was important about our strategy that the behavior of my team started to change. Before presenting a new idea or goal to my team, I had to consider how everyone fit into this strategy and how it tied back to the business and everyone's careers. Then, I had to capitalize on every opportunity to reinforce these points.

This meant talking strategy at quarterly town halls, on internal blogs, during sprint planning sessions, and using every meeting as an opportunity to relate the work being discussed back to our strategy. Sometimes it felt redundant, but the bigger your team is, the less likely each individual regularly hears from you. Remaining determined and being consistent with your communication is key.

Fear of the unknown is one of the most common points of friction in any change management program. I'll address this point in several upcoming chapters when I cover the Educate Staff best practice of the cloud journey. It's worth mentioning in this context that a great way for leaders to address this friction is to give everyone on the team clarity around what will happen with their roles.

Making it clear what everyone's options are in light of the changing direction will give them a clear path to understanding how they can participate, and likely some peace of mind. When I was the CIO at Dow Jones, we gave everyone in the department training *and* gave them the opportunity to move to new roles within the company. We made it clear that we wanted everyone to be a part of the journey, and sometimes that meant they had the opportunity to take on something new. It was in everyone's best interest to take advantage of the wealth of institutional knowledge they held, and in many cases, it became even more valuable when directed toward a different area or discipline. That knowledge is hard to replace, and I'd argue you should make every effort to keep it.

In almost any strategy that involves change, there will be some elements you need to stick firmly to, and some that may be more suggestive. Making it clear to your team which is which gives everyone the opportunity to continue pushing boundaries in the appropriate areas, and shows that the organization is still willing to learn.

At Dow Jones, we made automation a hard requirement for everything we did at the beginning of our journey. Once we became skilled enough with our cloud operations, we were able to make financially appealing business cases to migrate dozens of data centers to AWS. At this point, a "lift-*tinker*-and-shift" strategy was better suited to move us toward these goals. This required some clarity of purpose—we had to communicate this several times—to get right, but once we relaxed our automation constraint and applied a spectrum of migration techniques our progress accelerated substantially.

Every enterprise's cloud journey will hit some bumps in the road. I wish I could say that everything is going to be perfect and that the industry has figured out how to prescribe what every company should do every step of the way. At AWS, we are committed to becoming more prescriptive based on what we see working for our customers, but it's unlikely the whole process will be completely turnkey. I've found that it's best to treat the bumps you hit as learning opportunities, not to chastise your team for making mistakes (although you shouldn't accept the same mistake twice), and swiftly address skepticism that goes against your purpose. Don't let those who would be more comfortable reverting to the status quo influence the potential of your vision. This isn't always easy, but your patience and perseverance will pay off.

Remember, practice makes permanent.

CHAPTER 14

Great Leaders Make New Rules

Originally posted on 11/2/15: http://amzn.to/great-leaders-make-new-rules

◆ ◆ ◆

"I am free, no matter what rules surround me.
If I find them tolerable, I tolerate them; if I find
them too obnoxious, I break them.
I am free because I know that I alone
am morally responsible for everything I do."
—*Robert A. Heinlein*

GOOD LEADERS ENFORCE THE RULES. Great leaders know when the old rules no longer apply and that it's time to make new ones. As Heinlein suggests in the quote above, sometimes this means actually breaking the rules. But before they do either, great leaders wanting to influence behavioral change across the organization must first know the existing rules and then decide the ifs, whens, and hows of altering them.

Leading an organization on its journey to the cloud is one of the best opportunities technology leaders will have to make new rules. I would even argue that a technology executive-turned-Chief Change Management Officer (CCMO) has an *obligation* to inspect his or her processes and determine which rules are still appropriate for governing a cloud-enabled enterprise.

New Rules for New Missions

Many of us are familiar with process-based frameworks such as ITIL, ITSM, and plan-build-run. These were developed over the last few decades in order to standardize the way IT was delivered and operated in large organizations. The creators of these various frameworks prided themselves on being able to improve some combination of efficiency, effectiveness, quality, and costs by clearly defining roles, responsibilities, and processes in the organization.

These methodologies made sense when everyone used them to govern similar activities, like managing infrastructure. But, today, companies are increasingly looking to focus on the activities that delight their customers and make their organization different: Talen Energy wants to focus on generating power from a fleet of power plants that use diverse fuel sources. Nike wants to bring inspiration and innovation to every athlete in the world. GE wants to build, move, power, and cure the world. Before, managing infrastructure would be the table stakes for such missions. Now, the cloud provides the table stakes, and so it follows that today's CCMO should keep what makes sense from their existing process-based frameworks, but not be afraid to make new rules to govern their new, more modern, and increasingly digital operating models.

Look for Organization-Wide Opportunities

Regardless of where you are on your journey (or any change-management program), I urge you to consider what your roles, responsibilities, and processes will look like in the cloud-first world of tomorrow. This will take some exploring, and will be different for every organization. Operations, IT audit, and financial management are among the topics I frequently discuss with enterprise executives when it comes to changing the rules.

I should note that this list is by no means exhaustive—it would be impossible cover every angle and nuance here. I'd love to hear about some of the others you're finding, and welcome your responses!

Operations. I have written numerous pieces for enterprises considering switching to DevOps. These pieces include a number of rule changes to consider:

Focus on creating a customer-service-centric IT department that strives to understand what customers (internal or external) need, and remains open-minded about what and how solutions are delivered.

The run-what-you-build concept, meanwhile, focuses on exactly what it sounds like. In my experience, this practice tends to be one of the most difficult changes for enterprises to make, perhaps because it is so far from the traditional IT process-based frameworks. There are many, many good reasons to adopt run-what-you-build and the inherent rule changing that goes with it, and I've yet to come across an organization that didn't reap plenty of benefits from the shift.

Finally, it helps to know what you can expect as you make these and other operational changes. Remember to remain patient—making changes to rules that have been around for decades or longer won't happen overnight.

Auditing process. Auditors are an essential part of any enterprise's journey. Right now, many executives still associate the phrase "audit function" with negative thoughts and headaches because they believe an audit could delay their progress. But that isn't a productive or progressive way of looking at the situation, *especially* when you're trying to establish new rules. Audits are your friend, not your enemy. Use them to educate everyone that you're better off with the new rules that you're making and get feedback. Collaborate with your auditors early and often, and explain what you're trying to accomplish. Get their input and I'm sure they'll improve your thinking and your results.

When I was with Dow Jones, I was very anxious about explaining our plan to adopt DevOps and run-what-you-build to our auditors. This anxiety made us prepared, though the stress was somewhat misplaced. Once we illustrated that our controls were greatly improved *because* of the new rules we were employing around automation, our auditors became *more* comfortable with our future direction. By showing them early that we no longer had ownership spread across siloed teams sitting next to one another but communicating through tickets, and that the opportunity for human mistakes was much less, we were able to gain the necessary confidence and trust of our auditors.

These same tactics apply when dealing with your security and legal teams. Involve them early and often, and partner with them to ensure that everyone's needs are met. Make sure to be empathetic to your executive stakeholders, and find ways to address their needs with your rules.

Financial Management. In nearly every case, moving from large, up-front capital investments—where capacity is uncertain and often overbought—to a pay-as-you-go (and only for what you use) model leads to better cash flow. Having said that, managing variable expense may change the way you're used to governing your finances. Typically, it's best to work closely with your finance department to make new rules that allow you to capitalize on the levers cloud offers and get the most out of your budget.

At Dow Jones, our cloud expenses grew slower than our infrastructure investments declined. We may have been getting a lot done, but eventually our growing bill caught the interest of our finance team, and they became our partners in optimizing our budget.

As our resources became increasingly focused on product development, we reached a productive monthly cadence with our controllers around forecasting, Reserved Instances (RI) purchases, and capitalizing an increasing percentage of our labor costs. We learned that it's best to stagger RI purchases over the course of several months as your compute needs evolve, and that there are a number of partners who can help with financial management. Cloudability is one of them, and they recently posted a great article on staggering RI purchases. This piece does a much better job of explaining this than I could here.

As I noted, these are just some of the rules worth scrutinizing on your journey. I'd love to hear about some of the others you encounter. Whatever they are, don't be afraid to make new ones.

BEST PRACTICE TWO

Educate Staff

◆ ◆ ◆

CHAPTER 15

You Already Have the People You Need to Succeed with the Cloud

Originally posted on 11/18/15: http://amzn.to/you-already-have-the-people-you-need-to-succeed-with-the-cloud

◆ ◆ ◆

"Education is the most powerful weapon which you can use to change the world."
—Nelson Mandela

I FEEL FORTUNATE TO HAVE the opportunity to talk to a number of executives from a wide range of companies about their business and IT strategies. Every executive and company has their own unique set of challenges, but they all share the need to equip their staff with the skills that will help them move toward their future aspirations. This is no different when it comes to the cloud. While this may seem obvious, several executives have told me that the perceived lack of cloud skills in their organization is the primary reason they haven't made as much progress as they'd like on their journey to the cloud.

Educating your staff is the second of seven best practices I've observed enterprises with successful cloud strategies follow. Providing executive leadership is the first, and I'll explore the others in subsequent chapters. Educating your staff can turn skeptical employees into true believers, and will make a huge difference in how quickly you're able to leverage the cloud to deliver results to your business.

You Already Have What You Need

People fear the unknown, and change makes some uncomfortable. One the most powerful things you can do to alleviate that fear is to educate. You may also look to acquire new talent that already has the skills you're looking for, but this typically only works in small doses and can be difficult to scale.

Most organizations already have a wealth of institutional knowledge and cultural practices that are well established in tenured staff members. This can be used to the organization's advantage if the existing staff is given an opportunity to learn how to marry institutional knowledge and culture with cloud technologies. In other words, everyone you need to move forward with the cloud is already there, you just have to enable them.

The following points illustrate some of the areas I suggest executives consider when educating their staff on cloud technologies. I typically try to focus my writing on strategic and leadership guidance devoid of any AWS-specific services or solutions, but I couldn't avoid pointing to some of the AWS programs that suit this topic so well. I'm sure you can think of others, and I'd love to hear about them!

AWS Training and Certification

AWS's self-directed and instructor-led training courses can help your team get started quickly and keep skills current over time. I won't repeat the details that are very eloquently provided on the website, but I will say that every company I've talked to that's using our training programs now benefits from better cloud operations. Most report the reduction of friction between teams within their organizations, too.

When I was at Dow Jones, we trained nearly every technical person on our team with what became the AWS Technical Fundamentals course. Over time, many of the individuals interested in meaningful adoption took more advanced courses too.

We eventually institutionalized training of our own. Our DevOps team started to host "DevOps Days" where others in the organization learned about the best practices, frameworks, and governance models we developed on top of the cloud.

This type of grassroots education made a meaningful impact on how people worked, and helped us reinforce elements of the culture we were trying to build in the context of a cloud-first tomorrow. The training grew to be one of the most effective mechanisms we had for knocking down internal roadblocks. It became very difficult, for example, to attend a DevOps Day and not become enamored with what we were doing with the cloud. I've since talked to several other large companies taking a similar path. They're working with the AWS training and certification team to create and scale large training programs that suit their own specific organization's needs.

If you still feel like your staff is resisting, it may be worth sharing this chart from 2015 that illustrates job trends from indeed.com:

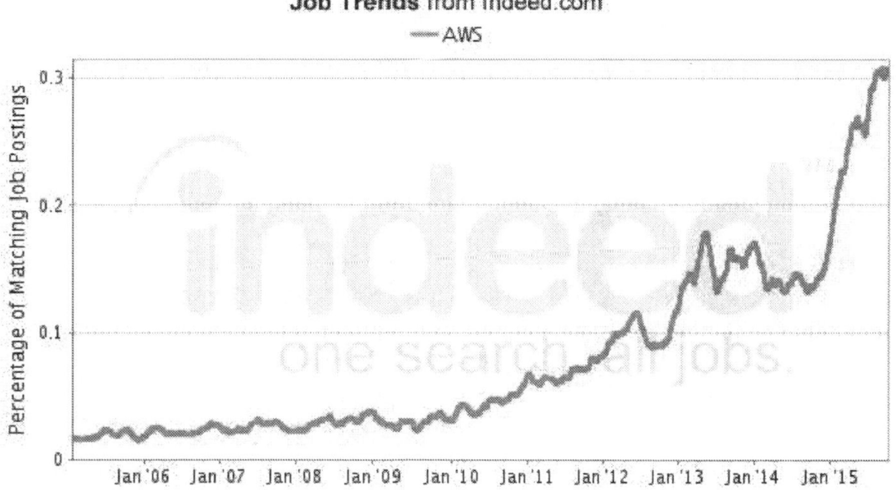

There is a clear and steep rise in demand for cloud skills, and I don't see this trend changing anytime soon. I think it's pretty safe to say that cloud training is something that will pay dividends for you and for your employees for many years to come.

Leverage the Ecosystem

You may be leading your organization's cloud journey, but you don't have to do it alone, especially when it comes to education. Talk to your peers, attend cloud-related events, and read about what other companies are doing. It's amazing how fast the cloud ecosystem has grown, and how many born-in-the-cloud businesses have found success in such a short amount of time. There's a wealth of information online illustrating what many companies have accomplished, and how you can leverage what they've learned.

The AWS Partner Network is one way to browse the ecosystem, and is full of resources that you can learn from. Whether you're looking for a tool to help you with a specific need, or an implementation partner to help you with a large migration, there are a wide variety of partners to choose from. You can always look to your AWS account manager to help you find the right one. I'll dive deeper into the partner community in Best Practice Four: Pick the Right Partners.

Last but not least, AWS Professional Services has helped hundreds of executives identify the roles and skills needed to execute a cloud strategy. The AWS Professional Services team does this by assessing an organization's current readiness and helping the organization obtain the skills they need based on AWS Professional Services's experience helping hundreds of similar companies. Through these engagements, AWS Professional Services has developed the AWS Cloud Adoption Framework, which they've made freely available for any organization that would like to use it as a resource as they transform their organization toward a cloud operating model.

There's No Substitute for Experience

I've yet to come across a use case where someone with the appropriate skills and a can-do attitude couldn't find a place for themselves in the cloud. While I think most people can imagine that anything's possible, it can be harder for those who don't have the experience to prove it.

Training is a great way to expose everyone to new concepts and illustrate examples, but I've always felt the best education comes in the form of experience. Give your teams a hands-on, time-constrained opportunity to do something meaningful to your business with the cloud, and see what happens. Ask them to build a website, create an API for some of your data, host a wiki, or build something else tangible that fits into what your teams already do. I'm always surprised by how quickly the right motivation mixed with a bit of time pressure can lead to results. Scarcity breeds invention, and I've seen some pretty innovative things happen in a short amount of time when the goals are clear and the tools are predetermined.

These hands-on experiences might become game-changing innovations, or they may simply provide some education that you parlay into your next project. Either way, they'll help you move your agenda forward, and give your team a great opportunity to learn.

CHAPTER 16

11 Things to Consider When Educating Your Staff on Cloud

Originally posted on 12/3/15: http://amzn.to/educate-staff-on-cloud

◆ ◆ ◆

"Tell me and I forget. Teach me and I remember.
Involve me and I learn."
—*Benjamin Franklin*

My last post discussed how you already have the necessary resources to leverage cloud technologies, provided you enable your staff with the appropriate education.

So how do you, the Chief Change Management Officer, educate your staff so that they can accelerate your journey? Every organization's journey will be unique, but there are some commonalities that I've seen in organizations that do this well. Here are 11 considerations that speak to these commonalities:

1. **Start with something meaningful, but basic.** Your teams will quickly see the practical benefits of cloud technologies when they accomplish something important to the business. I've seen a few companies progress slower than they'd like by focusing on projects that don't move the needle. Of course, you don't want to bet the farm with your first few projects, but you will want to start with projects that are meaningful enough to illustrate business benefit.

There are a number of good ones to start with—a simple website, a mobile application, an API to easily access data, or a file backup/disaster recovery improvement. Your teams will be able to apply what it learns to more projects faster if their education is rooted in a practical application.

2. **Leverage AWS training.** AWS offers a wide variety of great training programs. These programs have helped hundreds of companies hone their cloud skills. AWS uses every training engagement as an opportunity to improve, and has developed a diverse curriculum and a variety of delivery mechanisms that allow organizations to customize training that meets their specific needs. When I was at Dow Jones, we trained nearly every technical person on our team with what became the AWS Technical Fundamentals course. In addition to equipping our staff with new skills, the training also removed some of the fear of the unknown commonly found when the journey is just beginning.
3. **Give your teams time to experiment.** Creating a culture of experimentation is the next best practice on the journey, and it is particularly relevant when motivating your staff to learn. Innovation comes from experimentation, and because the cloud takes away the need for large up-front investments to try new things, there is nothing holding your team back from creating the next disruptive product in your industry. Give your team some freedom to implement existing projects in new ways.
4. **Set goals that encourage learning and experimentation.** Most companies set goals and/or KPIs for their staff and tie these goals to performance. Using these existing mechanisms is a great way to reinforce your strategy and produce the behavior you're after. You can create goals around the completion of relevant training courses, how much budget is freed up, or how your operational excellence has improved by leveraging the appropriate cloud architectures. Doing this shows that leadership is serious about giving everyone the opportunity to experiment and learn.

5. **Set time constraints, and pace yourselves.** This is especially important as you move toward a culture of experimentation. At the end of the day, results are what matter. You can help your team members balance experimentation with using what they already know by setting deadlines on each project. Sometimes your teams will make compromises as a result of these constraints, and as you progress, you'll need to define a mechanism for how to deal with these compromises. But your team will always be learning and improving its skills for the next project.
6. **Spot and deal with change resistance.** All of these considerations are aimed at curbing your staff's resistance to change by giving people the tools they need to succeed. But even with all of these opportunities, there will likely be individuals in your organization who will continue to resist. My post about providing clarity of purpose speaks to this challenge. Look to understand the apprehension that comes from your team, be open-minded about what's working and what's not, and swiftly deal with unnecessary friction. Which leads me to my next point…
7. **Don't be afraid to give people new roles.** Moving to the cloud in a meaningful way is as much a cultural shift as it is a technology shift. I've found that giving people an opportunity to take on new roles can help them overcome their resistance to change. My preference has always been to look inside the company first, as institutional knowledge is an expensive and typically unnecessary loss. I held six very different roles during my 11-year tenure at Bloomberg. This abundance of opportunity is one of the key reasons I stayed as long as I did. Finding ways to give your staff new opportunities will keep them engaged and can help with employee retention.
8. **Show your staff how they fit into the bigger picture.** It's much easier to get excited about your job when you know how it fits into the organization's big picture. Make sure you consider each role and communicate how and why it matters to your team. Again, I'd look

to how your organization aligns its objectives with departmental and/ or individual goals, and find a way to tailor that to each role.

9. **Go to industry events and see what others are doing.** Most people learn a lot from the successes and failures of others. I've been developing cloud-enabled technology strategies for large companies for more than five years now, and I'm still amazed at what I learn from attending AWS re:Invent, AWS summits, and other technology events. Give your staff time to network and bring new ideas back home. Considering many ideas, even some that you're confident you won't pursue, is a great way to create teachable moments and reinforce your strategy.
10. **Learn from your partners.** There are tens of thousands of organizations in the AWS Partner Network. Many of them are probably already in your existing stable of partners, but there are likely some new ones you can learn from, too. I've been amazed by how many large enterprises are turning to the smaller, younger, "born-in-the-cloud," system integrators likeCloudreach, 2nd Watch, and Minjar to accelerate their cloud strategies and change their IT culture.

    And this one goes to 11….
11. **Institutionalize your own flavor of training in your organization.** As you progress on your journey, you will hopefully find that a few teams or individuals in your organization will want to share what they learn with others. This will ideally come from your Cloud Center of Excellence, which I'll later cover as another best practice in your journey. While I was with Dow Jones, our DevOps team periodically hosted DevOps Days, where they shared the cloud best practices, frameworks, and governance models they developed with others in the organization. I've spoken to several other Fortune 500 companies that have built similar programs that are specific to their organizations.

CHAPTER 17

A Must-Have Secret Weapon To Modernize Your Business: Training Your Team On Cloud

Originally posted on 5/8/17: http://amzn.to/cloud-secret-weapon-training

◆ ◆ ◆

"The task of the modern educator is not to cut down jungles, but to irrigate deserts."

—*C.S. Lewis*

I FEEL VERY FORTUNATE THAT I've been able to learn how hundreds of executives from the world's largest companies are transforming their businesses using modern technologies and the cloud. Transformational change is not easy—few things in business worth doing are—and, from what I can tell, the biggest resistance to change usually comes from within. People can (naturally) be afraid of what they don't know. The best way I've found to get team members over their fear of the unknown—both as a CIO of Dow Jones and as the Head of Enterprise Strategy for AWS—is to teach them.

This is why I think Maureen Lonergan—my personal friend and AWS's Head of Training and Certification[45]—has one of the most important jobs on the planet. Maureen and her team are committed to training and educating as many people as possible on all things cloud.

45 https://aws.amazon.com/training/

And today, I'm delighted to host a chapter from Maureen that outlines how you might approach training your teams.

Many large and small enterprises are considering a transition to cloud technology, but wonder how their teams can best leverage the technology for their business. As the Director of Training and Certification at AWS, I believe the best way to get the most out of your cloud investment is to invest in training to help build cloud skills within your organization. Doing so will enable you to leverage the skills of your existing staff, reach your business goals sooner, and feel confident that your organization is getting the most out of the cloud.

In this chapter, I look at why training is such an important and valuable step of the cloud journey, and how, specifically, AWS can help you navigate the transition to the cloud and turn your employees into true experts.

You already have the people you need

In Chapter 15, Stephen writes about the importance of educating existing staff about the cloud. He noted that "everyone you need to move forward with the cloud is already there, you just have to enable them."

Training can help your staff leverage the fundamental IT skills and institutional knowledge they already have to transition to cloud roles. Training current employees saves you time and money since you won't have to hire new staff to fill cloud-based roles.

Essentially, regardless of your cloud platform, the sooner you evaluate the roles you currently have and the ones you need, then invest in the training to develop your employees, the easier your job becomes.

Training helps you reach your business goals sooner

Training your staff will allow them to better use the cloud so you can accomplish your objectives more efficiently. Cloud training gives your employees the skills they need to innovate faster.

Training is particularly important for organizations undergoing complex migrations. Here are a few key ways training can help accelerate a transition:

- Training will help your employees understand how to use the cloud. For example, they can learn to efficiently manage, operate, and deploy applications using AWS.
- Alleviating your team's anxiety by teaching them the unknown can build internal buy-in.
- Training will give your staff a common language, and allow them to work together more effectively.
- A trained staff, whether with AWS or another platform, will be able to spot the services and solutions they need much faster, which means you can quickly develop better solutions for your customers.

Validate knowledge with certifications

Encourage staff to get certified so everyone feels confident in the team's skills. A core group of AWS Certified staff can help lead your organization through the change and implement best practices. Certification can help you identify individuals who are ready to be promoted within your organization.

If you do need more cloud experience within your organization, look for certified candidates so you can fill any remaining holes with confidence.

A tour through AWS Training and Certification

AWS Training and Certification helps build cloud skills to make your transition to the AWS Cloud easier so you can get the most out of your investment, faster.

There are several training options with AWS:

Awareness Days. Before or during training, you can ask AWS to come to your company and hold an Awareness Day. This is an especially useful resource if you're having a hard time selling the cloud in your organization, or just simply need someone to come in and present a clearer picture of the cloud's benefits. Awareness Day sessions cover elements like general AWS advantages, how to become an Agile organization, and the many ways the cloud will help you innovate. You can contact the AWS Training team to schedule an Awareness Day.[46]

Role-based training. AWS offers role-based learning paths for employees in Architecting,[47] Developing,[48] or Operations[49] roles. Each path includes training, labs, and certifications that are most relevant for how they will work with AWS. Each path leads to associate and professional certification exams so employees can validate their new skills.

Customized training. You can work with AWS on building a customized training strategy, including a step-by-step guide and timeline that lays out who should take what training. This way, your staff will have a clear roadmap to follow. Here is an example of how training can be broken into phases for your organization:

Phase 1: Cloud awareness and essentials training for a very broad range of employees

Phase 2: Role-based foundational training for technical employees and key lines of business

Phase 3: Associate certification for select technical staff with relevant experience

Phase 4: Advanced and specialty training for select technical staff as required

Phase 5: Professional certification for select technical staff with relevant experience

46 https://aws.amazon.com/contact-us/aws-training/

47 https://aws.amazon.com/training/path-architecting/

48 https://aws.amazon.com/training/path-developing/

49 https://aws.amazon.com/training/path-operations/

Online Training. Once your staff knows the basics, they can use free or low-cost labs to get practice using AWS. They can also explore free online course offerings on topics like big data and security. This is a simple, cost-effective way to go about getting your staff the skills they need for your organization's cloud.

Accessibility. Whether you prefer in-person or online, self-guided or instructor-led, AWS has an option to suit your organization. Training is available across the globe and in eight languages through AWS and the APN Partner Training network. That means training can be delivered in your location using local language and customs.

Beyond knowledge

AWS Training and Certification can help you prepare your staff for your move to the cloud. In the end, training is about more than just building knowledge and awareness. It's about helping your business accomplish your goals sooner for less. With the right training, you'll have a cloud-knowledgeable staff to help you leverage the cloud so you can innovate more and get to market faster. AWS works with a network of authorized AWS Training Partners and delivers training across the globe. You can get started building your training strategy by contacting AWS Training and Certification today.

CHAPTER 18

A 12-Step Program to Get from Zero to Hundreds of AWS-Certified Engineers

Originally posted on 7/15/17: http://amzn.to/12-steps-to-1000s-of-cloud-certifications

◆ ◆ ◆

"Don't wish for what you haven't got; it blinds you to the possibilities of the present"

IN THIS CHAPTER, JOHNATHAN ALLEN—EMEA Enterprise Strategist and Evangelist for AWS—explains how to build a vibrant team of AWS-Certified Engineers, efficiently and effectively.

◆ ◆ ◆

As an AWS Enterprise Strategist, I have the privilege of meeting executives from around the globe who are faced with a wide range of business and technology challenges. Each customer is unique. Many of the challenges, however, like history, tend to rhyme.

One of those rhymes is the skills challenge in the market, and the belief that not having the right people on staff stops you from moving faster, saving money, and expanding your business on the cloud. It's certainly true that the number of job postings with the words "AWS" and "cloud" have materially increased as people realize the power of letting AWS do the undifferentiated heavy lifting in the infrastructure space. But I don't think that this escalating demand, or the perception that you don't have the talent that you need, should get in the way of your enterprise cloud success.

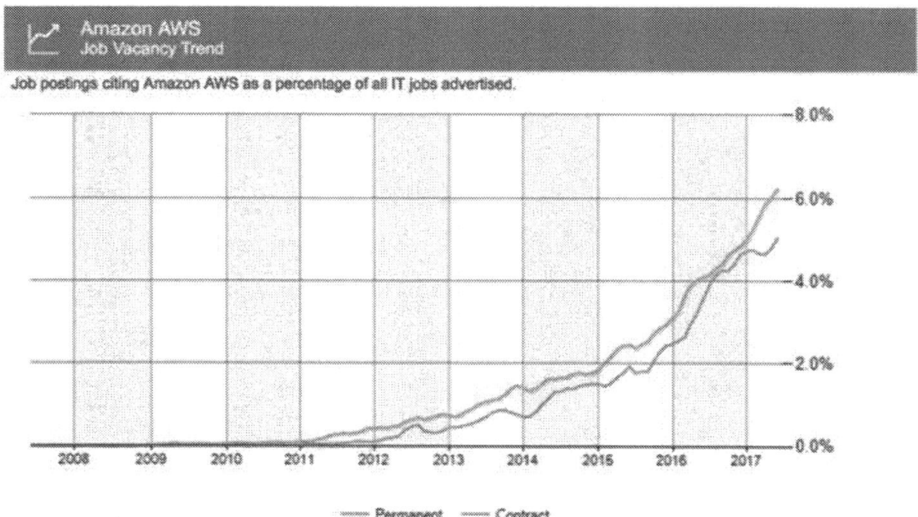

Stephen Orban, Head of Enterprise Strategy at AWS, has written convincingly about this in Chapter 15: "You Already Have the People You Need to Succeed with the Cloud." And, to reinforce this point, I'd like to share the story of when I faced a major skills challenge. That was back in 2014, at the start of my cloud journey.

I was Capital One's CTO in the UK then, and I found myself thinking deeply about the perceived skills gap in my engineers. These engineers were really talented, but they were predominantly skilled in legacy on-premises technology; as a result, they offered largely siloed infrastructure skill sets.

Seeking change, I then proceeded to make the oft-repeated mistake of creating a unicorn job specification and placing it joyfully in the external job market. I was surprised and disappointed when my job posting was met by a profound echo of silence in my inbox.

I was clearly missing a crucial fact.

The highly skilled, proactive, and dedicated team I had was the team I needed. The team members just needed a path, an incentive, and someone with empathy to listen and address their totally human fears of the technology unknown.

This realization about talent transformation and the enterprise cloud journey led to a significant amount of best practice and human learning for me. I have to be honest, though; mistakes were made and time was lost along the way. But we established a path that eventually worked and ultimately contributed to Capital One's UK success. This contributed to helping Capital One scale its technical talent to a profoundly high level globally. In fact, a full 2 percent of all AWS-certified developers now work at Capital One.[50]

With the benefit of hindsight, here are the 12 steps that worked for us.

50 https://www.cloudtp.com/doppler/capital-one-pushing-frontiers-banking-focus-technology-talent/

Step 1—Acceptance

Mental health specialists say that acceptance is the first step toward recovery; and that's totally applicable here, too. Your engineers must accept the fact that they have the ability to learn AWS cloud skills and become experts. It's also incredibly important for technology leaders within your organization to accept this. As Stephen Orban explains, and as my tenure at Capital One shows, the talent you already have is the talent you need. These are the people who have many years of critical experience developing and running your existing systems.

Step 2—Training

After this acceptance, you should then swiftly start with the AWS Technical Essentials course.[51] This classroom course is an eye-opener, and a delightful peek into the art of the possible. It's also excellently facilitated by AWS's own training team, or one of our Approved Training Partners.[52]

Step 3—Hands-on time

There is no compression algorithm for experience. So, hands-on time is now required. Even if it's a little clunky, engineers need to play away and configure stuff in a safe space. Also, at this point, it feels like there are a million ways to the possible, and it's all a bit overwhelming. Your engineers can get either very excited or slightly disillusioned. Recognition of the normal change curves everyone goes through (some are short, some are long—it's personal) is absolutely critical. Continual encouragement is key, too.

51 https://aws.amazon.com/training/course-descriptions/essentials/

52 https://aws.amazon.com/partners/training-partner/

How People Respond to Change

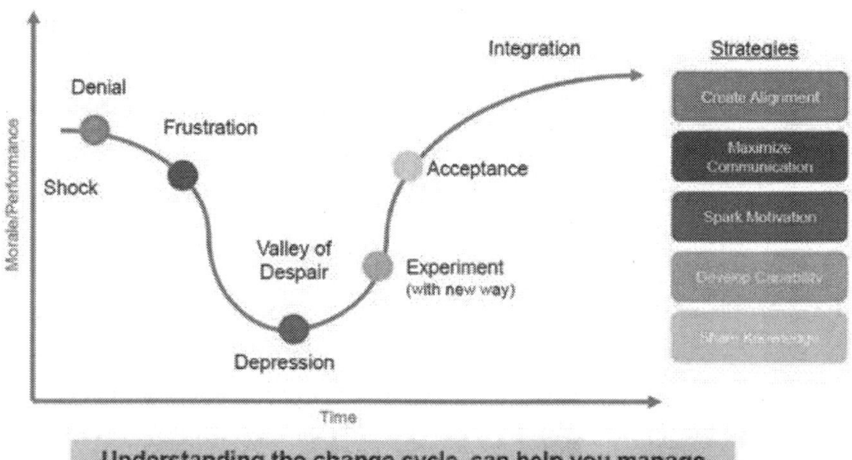

Understanding the change cycle, can help you manage change in your unit

Step 4—Create your two-pizza team53

The first engineering team you put together should consist of a thorough mix of core skills—Network, Database, Linux Server, Application, Automation, Storage, and Security. The team will make some progress. It will probably look at tools like Terraform[54] and others. It will also write some AWS CloudFormation[55] code. The team will make mistakes. All of this is perfectly natural.

Step 5—Bring in some experts

There is no compression algorithm for experience (continued). So, now you should bring in some real experts. Indeed, adding some expert-level engineers who have the right attitude when it comes to sharing their learnings and best

53 http://blog.idonethis.com/two-pizza-team/

54 https://www.terraform.io/

55 https://aws.amazon.com/cloudformation

practices is essential at this point. At Capital One in the UK, I worked closely with CloudReach[56] to bring in a number of its professionally certified-level, field-proven AWS engineers to do just this. And I integrated these expert engineers into different teams to propagate specialties where they were needed. This had a transformative effect. Humans learn from other humans by watching, asking questions, and repeating. Even better, engineers like to learn from fellow engineers. And, working in small teams, they get the chance to ask questions and try things they won't do in a classroom setting. We even got the process down to one day. During that short timeframe, a new engineer joined the team, buddied up with an expert, and was then shown through the CloudFormation and associated Continual Integration/Continual Development (CI/CD)[57] best practice that had emerged.

Step 6—Make it real

At this juncture, the goal of the Agile two-pizza team should be to build something real and in production. This can be your foundational Amazon Machine Image (AMI)[58] to host a small app, and associated network setup. The objective is to find something important but not critical to start with. Set the goal of getting it done in weeks, not months. Track progress. Show an interest. Set a demo deadline. And be there to see progress as well as the end results. A word of advice—don't let the team boil the ocean here. Only work with the AWS building blocks you need. (You don't need to master all 90+ building blocks from the get-go.) There will be plenty of time later to expand into the others as you need them for your solutions. The advantage of experimentation is key and the ability to discard and start again as many times as required to learn becomes as natural as walking with AWS.

56 https://www.cloudreach.com/

57 https://aws.amazon.com/getting-started/projects/set-up-ci-cd-pipeline/

58 http://docs.aws.amazon.com/AWSEC2/latest/UserGuide/AMIs.html

Step 7—Scale the learning with cellular mitosis

As this first team achieves a level of AWS proficiency and delivers a product, you now need to oversee a cellular mitosis[59] of this first team. And you need to gently but consciously split this first team who have gained the experience and best practice, into two new four-person teams, and then introduce four more engineers into each team. This will be difficult and should be handled with care. Being honest with the team members and positively acknowledging their collective achievement will be crucial. As well as asking for their help to pass on the learnings and best practice to their new teammates. Keep splitting and reform teams in this Mitosis-driven approach until all engineers rotate into a team.

Step 8—Certification

Working with either AWS Technical Training[60] or one of our excellent partners,[61] you can now start down the path to certification. Encouraging the use of services like A Cloud Guru[62] can also provide engineers with a process that enables them to pass the certification in their own time and at their own pace. I advocate starting with the Associate-level certification[63] and building up to the Professional-level certification.[64] I am going to pause here, to stress this point. I really cannot over-emphasize the importance of this often-overlooked step. At Capital One, we saw a direct correlation between engineer certification, the movement of apps, and the building of new systems on AWS. Capital One even patented[65] a process for measuring transfor

---

59 https://www.khanacademy.org/science/biology/cellular-molecular-biology/mitosis/a/phases-of-mitosis

60 https://aws.amazon.com/training/course-descriptions/

61 https://aws.amazon.com/partners/training-partner/

62 https://acloud.guru/

63 https://aws.amazon.com/certification/certified-solutions-architect-associate/

64 https://aws.amazon.com/certification/certified-solutions-architect-professional/

65 http://pdfpiw.uspto.gov/.piw?PageNum=0&docid=09680696&IDKey=B687549475AA&HomeUrl=http%3A%2F%2Fpatft.uspto.gov%2Fnetacgi%2Fnph-Parser%3FSect1%3DPTO2%2526Sect2%3DHITOFF%2526p%3D1%2526u%3D%25252Fnetahtml%25252FPTO%25252Fsearch-bool.html%2526r%3D1%252

mation. The process of certification of engineers shows demonstrable expert progression and allows the common AWS language to propagate and become the *de facto* method that underpins solutions.

Step 9—Scaling the certification and associated leadership

Experience at Capital One and with many of our customers—plus scientific study—has shown that you need to reach a critical mass of 10 percent of engineers[66] advocating a platform before the network effect[67] takes hold. So, scaling this learning and certification to 10 percent of your engineers is a major milestone in your journey. From here onward you get a compelling Halo Effect[68] which starts to influence how your company is seen externally and not just internally. Those engineers externally to your organization who only want to work with Cloud Native companies, will start seriously considering working for you. And, so thus in turn, the pace increases exponentially of your transformation as you attract or convert more talent to be Cloud literate.

Step 10—Recognize and reward expertise (in a very loud and proud way!)

Your goal as an IT executive is to shout from the rooftops the names of every engineer that passes every certification exam. Reward and recognize technical progress in any way that you can. That means—meals, vouchers, drinks, special team chair, novelty awards, you name it. At Capital One, we had a global roster of every person and every AWS certification he or she obtained. Certification was viewed as a tangible and visceral achievement. Nearly every engineer I've ever met craves peer respect, and certification—combined with what you build—contributes to community kudos.

---

66 https://www.sciencedaily.com/releases/2011/07/110725190044.htm

67 https://en.wikipedia.org/wiki/Network_effect#Types_of_network_effects

68 https://en.wikipedia.org/wiki/Halo_effect

Step 11—Take the challenge yourself

When I was standing at a town hall meeting, recognizing and rewarding the engineers who had progressed, thanks to certification, one of the sharper sparks in the audience spoke up loudly. "If you believe so passionately in certification, when will *you* take the exam?" That stopped me pretty squarely. I hadn't taken an industry exam for a long while. But, as somebody who likes to practice what I preach, I stepped up to the plate. And I passed my AWS Associate Architect certification exam. Now, I could proudly stand on that stage, too! Taking the exam acted as an excellent forcing mechanism, ensuring that I gained a broad, yet sufficiently detailed, overview of the key AWS building blocks.

Step 12—Create a unifying job family portfolio

Finally, and at the right time, you will need to offer a concrete job family track for your technical employees. At Capital One UK, these are some of the job family tracks we created in IT—

Technical Program Manager (TPM)—Typically responsible for the Agile execution, release train congruence, and team interdependencies.

AWS Infrastructure Engineer (IE)—Previously data center systems engineers, who were typically Linux/Wintel/Network, etc. Now creating CloudFormation code for different AWS building blocks as required for the product teams. AWS experts.

Software Development Engineer (SDE)—Writing logic and working with data constructs in a variety of software languages.

Software Quality Engineer (SQE)—Using test-driven design principles. Ensuring that testing is considered and executed throughout the lifecycle.

Security Engineer—Ensuring that security is holistic.

Engineering Manager—The manager responsible for both intent and supervising a group of engineers comprised from the above skill groups.

As you follow this path, it's important that some glass ceilings get broken. In particular, it's essential that engineers who don't manage people now have the ability to get to very senior levels—including that of Director and above—and still not be managing people. These promotions should respect technical depth and associated competency development, as well as technical leadership maturity as it broadens. As a leader seeing your employees scale new heights and attain hard earned promotions is always the most rewarding part of the role. Many members of my team who took the great opportunities available proudly achieved promotion. We also broke the glass ceiling ourselves, and as I was leaving Capital One UK, one of my proudest moments was promoting a founding member of our Cloud Center of Excellence to the Infrastructure Engineering Director level. This person remains an individual contributor, hands-on AWS expert, and a good friend.

Following these 12 steps as a path to talent transformation, can unleash your teams so they achieve greatness things for your customers.

Remember—"All of your assumed constraints are debatable."

BEST PRACTICE THREE

Create A Culture Of Experimentation

◆ ◆ ◆

CHAPTER 19

Create a Culture of Experimentation Enabled by the Cloud

Originally posted on 1/4/16: http://amzn.to/cloud-culture-of-experimentation

◆ ◆ ◆

"Speed matters in business"
—Jeff Bezos

Keeping your business competitive in today's market is hard, though in many markets that's always been the case. *Wired* points out that, since its inception in 1955, the Fortune 500 has seen between 20 and 50 companies fall off the list each year.[69] Technology has a lot to do with this steady rate of turnover. More specifically, the cloud has been one of the key, if not *the key*, enabler of this trend over the past few years. The cloud allows companies with a small amount of capital come out of nowhere and disrupt entire industries. Airbnb, Pinterest, Uber, and Spotify, for example, didn't even exist 10 years ago. Now they're redefining entire industries with businesses powered by the cloud.

What do these disruptive companies (and most startups) have in common? They started as experiments. No one was sure whether or not they'd work.

Experiments Are No Longer Just for Startups

The good news is that the cloud can help every company experiment and remain competitive, regardless of that company's size or tenure. Having said

69 http://www.wired.com/2012/06/fortune-500-turnover-and-its-meaning/

that, the bigger the company and the more established its IT operations are, the more things may have to change to get the most out of the cloud.

For companies that are successful at maximizing the benefit of the cloud, change is seen as opportunity. These companies' executives aren't afraid to challenge the status quo, and creating a culture of experimentation is one of the most common changes these executives look to make. I was certainly trying to cultivate that type of culture when I was the CIO of Dow Jones. I've come to admire many other companies doing the same—Capital One, GE, Johnson & Johnson, and News Corp, to name just a few. All of these companies are relentless about challenging the status quo in an effort to keep up with their customers and stay ahead of their competitors.

This trend is the reason that creating a culture of experimentation has landed its spot as the third best practice on the enterprise journey to the cloud. For those looking to create a culture of experimentation, this chapter serves as an introduction to what will be a miniseries on the topic. The remainder of the chapter focuses on how the cloud makes experimentation easier, and I'll dive deeper into how today's technology executive can create a culture of experimentation in subsequent ones.

How Does the Cloud Make Experimentation Easier?

A market leadership position and access to capital aren't enough to keep even the most well-established enterprises competitive today. Here are a few ways that the cloud makes experimentation easier, particularly for big companies.

You don't need access to capital to experiment. Throughout my career, I've spent countless hours trying to justify the ROI on a capital investment for resources I *thought* were needed for a potential product. I was rarely, if ever, able to get capacity planning right, and almost always overbuilt my infrastructure. In a few cases, it took my team longer to justify an investment than it took to build the first version of the product. Because the cloud is pay-as-you-go and only-for-what-you-use, you no longer need months to justify what you can experiment with in days. Those just getting started have access to even simpler options. For example, some AWS services have free tiers and cost nothing to try.

There are no costs to absorb for projects that don't work out. Sometimes even the most compelling vision doesn't end up a product/market fit. I've built my fair share of products that didn't pan out. I'm not ashamed of this, because each time I learned something, but it sure does hurt to keep those assets on your balance sheet. It sometimes hurts worse to feel like you have to use those assets for something they weren't intended for. Wasting a 16-core machine to run your company's wiki page is, to state the obvious, less than ideal. Today, if your product doesn't work out, you can spin down the resources and stop paying for them altogether.

The cloud is optimized for automation. Leveraging automation to take care of tasks that can be repeated in software allows you to spend more time developing products that impact the company's bottom line.

You can focus on the things that matter most. The cloud gets rid of much of the heavy lifting associated with enterprise IT. "We don't do load balancers anymore, we just do load balancing," Talen Energy's Bruce Kantor told me recently. At the end of the day, this is what compels executives to adopt cloud as a platform across their entire business. It frees them of the burden of that heavy lifting and allows them to repurpose those precious resources toward the activities that drive revenue.

CHAPTER 20

4 Dos and Don'ts When Using the Cloud to Experiment

Originally posted on 1/25/16: http://amzn.to/dos-donts-cloud-experimentation

◆ ◆ ◆

"The best way to show that a stick is crooked is not to argue about it or to spend time denouncing it, but to lay a straight stick alongside it"
—D.L. Moody

In the previous chapter, I described how the cloud is making experimentation easier, cheaper, and less risky for companies of all shapes and sizes. The more that companies realize this, the more having a culture of experimentation becomes table stakes to stay competitive in today's market. Experimentation breeds innovation, and there's never been a better time to execute on new ideas.

So where do you start? Here are four things to consider and four things to avoid when building a culture of experimentation in your organization.

1(A). DO manage expectations. Not every experiment will deliver the results you envision, but every experiment is an opportunity to learn and improve your operations. If your organization is not used to the concept of *failing to learn*, start small and make sure everyone knows which projects you consider experiments. Manage your stakeholder's expectations by being clear about the purpose of the experiment, what you hope the outcome will be, how you're going to measure and test the result, and what you hope to learn from it. I've found that most executives appreciate experimentation with uncertain outcomes if they know how the organization will be better off for having tried it and learned something.

1(B). DON'T start with a project where everyone is set on a specific outcome. If you're acting as a change agent trying to create a culture of experimentation, don't experiment too early in your journey with a project where your stakeholders demand a specific outcome. I wouldn't advise that you start experimenting with your end-of-year billing run, for instance. A CEO I once worked for told me that it's okay to fail, except when it isn't. Be satisfied with incremental progress and slowly increase the number of experiments you run, but don't outpace the organization.

2(A). DO encourage your teams to propose experiments. Every organization has its own way of determining which projects get technology resources. Unfortunately, some organizations now treat the technology or IT department as a cost center and have pushed ideation too far away from those implementing it. Good ideas can come from anywhere, of course, and most technology professionals have a unique perspective that will surface when it comes to outside projects. This is especially true in organizations that are just getting started with the cloud—the individuals using the cloud for their projects are in the best position to propose experiments that leverage capabilities that are unique to the cloud to benefit the business. Help champion your team's proposals and position your staff to have an influence on which projects get invested in with the executive team.

2(B). DON'T pursue an experiment until you know how to measure it. You want to spend time on the right experiments and ensure the lessons learned from them will improve your operations and your products. Before you let your team to move forward with an experiment, you should agree on what they will measure during the experiment, and how. If you're testing a new feature on your website, what are the metrics that will make it successful? Page views? Number of clicks? Abandonment? This small, but important act of due diligence will force your teams to think through why they're proposing an experiment in the first place. It will also force your team to prioritize the right experiments.

3(A). DO consider DevOps to institutionalize experimentation. A DevOps culture can be a powerful way to codify experimentation into your organization. Marrying run-what-you-build with automation can drastically reduce the time it takes to release changes, allowing you to release more often and quickly rollback changes that don't work. Mature DevOps organizations also develop A/B testing frameworks that allow them to experiment on slightly different user experiences with different user cohorts in parallel to see what works best.

3(B). DON'T doubt your team. Doubt is one of the most powerful ways to discourage your team and open the door for failure. As you learn to properly scope experiments, measure them, and iterate on them quickly, you should find that you're able to adapt your approach before you need to doubt it. Making sure your teams are thinking about the right way to measure experiments and asking hard questions is healthy, but you should be looking to help the team work through issues rather than doubt their ability to deliver. People tend to follow leaders who believe they will succeed.

4(A). DO encourage the whole organization to participate. As you start to deliver results faster through experimentation, other areas of the organization will become attracted to your methods. Involve those people. Try a hackathon that includes different business areas, have your stakeholders help define how you'll measure experiments, and ask the organization for areas they've always wanted to experiment with. While not every company chooses to give its employees time to experiment, those that do typically tout it as a competitive advantage. At the very least, these kinds of inclusive activities will improve employee morale and retention. In my brief tenure so far at Amazon, I've found that anyone able to think through and articulate an experiment in writing typically gets the opportunity to try it. This is a special part of our culture and a great tool for attracting and retaining innovators and builders.

4(B). DON'T let experiments slow or halt delivery. Don't let your teams off the hook to deliver just because something is an experiment. While it's okay to fail and learn, it's not okay to under deliver on the experiment.

Software still needs to ship to be tested; it often needs to be measured with real traffic in production. Just because it's an experiment doesn't mean you should start measuring it late or let its quality suffer. You're still running a business, after all.

What is your organization doing to enable a culture of experimentation?

BEST PRACTICE FOUR

Pick The Right Partners

◆ ◆ ◆

CHAPTER 21

Accelerate Your Cloud Strategy with Partners

Originally posted on 2/8/16: http://amzn.to/accelerate-cloud-with-partners

◆ ◆ ◆

"You can do what I cannot do. I can do what you cannot do. Together we can do great things."
—Mother Teresa

Different organizations take different approaches to partnering with third parties for technology expertise. Some are biased toward building their own technology; others outsource some or all of the development, maintenance, and ongoing operations of their technology to one or more partners. Regardless of where your organization sits on the spectrum, you're almost certainly partnering with a handful of hardware, tools, and/or cloud providers to develop products and services for your internal and external customers.

I've spoken with hundreds of executives who are in the process of evolving their organization's technology strategy over the past few years, and many are re-examining their approach to partnering as they begin to understand how the cloud can help them transform their business. This chapter explores some of my observations on how the technology ecosystem is changing in the wake of the cloud, and kicks off a miniseries on the topic of engaging partners, which is the fourth best practice in my Enterprise Cloud Journey series.

Making Sense of the Fast-Growing Ecosystem

I'm continually amazed at how fast the ecosystem around the cloud grows. I've attended AWS re:Invent for the last four years, and each time I've marveled at how much larger the partner expo was than the year before. To put this into perspective, the number of partner booths more than doubled between 2012 and 2015, and walking the floor to learn about the latest tools and services went from an hour-long stroll to a day-long expedition. I can't think of a better place to discover where the market is headed and spot trends around where VCs are placing their bets.

This growing ecosystem may make finding the right partner for your needs seem difficult, but having multiple vendors competing for your business can also work to your advantage. Your AWS account manager and our AWS Partner Directory can help you narrow down your selection, and the AWS Marketplace can help you discover and deploy solutions from a wide range of providers and categories in seconds. If you can't find what you're looking for in the AWS Marketplace today, let us know.

Transforming Your Culture

It's encouraging to see how open minded large organizations have become to partnering with the smaller, leaner, and less "proven" organizations that are building tools, professional services, and managed services that cater to enterprises. When I started buying technology on behalf of my organization more than 15 years ago, I was taught to only partner with the large and established companies with long track records and large scale. Now I see many large Fortune 500 companies partnering with providers younger than my 4-year-old daughter to help them with their hairiest problems. In some cases, doing so helps them transform their entire business.

Many technology executives leading their organization toward a digital and customer-first tomorrow realize that they'll be able to move faster if they adopt some of the cultural aspects that are native to the younger, born-in-the-cloud providers. While I was the CIO at Dow Jones, one of my primary motivations for partnering with AWS was to assimilate some of Amazon's culture with our own. I wanted the same tools that enabled Amazon to be laser focused on the customer and move quickly. I was also eager to develop a DevOps culture that encouraged experimentation. Many of these younger providers—2nd Watch, Cloudreach, Cloud Technology Partners, Minjar, New Relic, App Dynamics, Chef, Puppet, CloudEndure, to name just a few—are finding new business for the very same reason.

This is definitely not to say that the stable of large, existing service providers and tools aren't also quickly evolving to take advantage of this shift. In many cases, it's more appropriate to leverage an existing relationship to transform your business and/or culture. AWS recently announced a new joint business group with Accenture, and we are working together to help several large enterprises transform their business with offerings around cloud strategy and migrations, big data, analytics, and IoT. Expect more of these announcements in the years ahead.

Finding Proven Partners in Your Focus Areas

You should always aim to partner with organizations that align with your business objectives. If you're looking to establish a DevOps competency and want your team to learn how to run-what-they-build, for example, make sure your partner can demonstrate the ability to help you do just that. This is one of the reasons AWS developed the AWS Competency Program. We want to make sure that you're successful on our platform, and this program will help you find partners that are capable of facilitating your success in the areas on which your organization is specifically focused. We are currently helping the ecosystem develop competencies in the areas of DevOps, mobile, security, digital media, marketing and commerce, big data, storage, healthcare, life sciences, Microsoft workloads, SAP, Oracle, and migrations.

Whatever your organization's stance is on partnering, we'd be happy to help you find the right partners to achieve your goals.

CHAPTER 22

Don't Let Traditional Managed Services Providers Hold Your Cloud Strategy Back

Originally posted on 2/13/17: http://amzn.to/dont-let-msp-hold-you-back

"You cannot discover new oceans unless you have the courage to lose sight of the shore."
—Andre Gide

It's hard for large organizations to keep up with the pace of technology evolution, and I've come to admire those who have repeatedly proven that they're strong enough to survive. Companies like GE, Capital One, News Corp, and Netflix are committed to constantly reinventing themselves, and they're increasingly turning to the cloud as a means to do so. More specifically, these companies—and the thousands of enterprises that share this common resolve—are using the cloud to offload much of the undifferentiated heavy lifting traditionally associated with enterprise IT so they can focus more resources on delivering value to their customers.

Constant reinvention isn't easy, and most executives I speak to agree that it's a journey that takes time and deliberate effort. This is true, regardless of what type of business you're in, and I spend a lot of time trying to help both customers and managed services providers (MSPs) through this journey.

As I explain in the next chapter, many MSPs are well out in front of this curve. 2nd Watch, Cloudreach, Accenture, Infosys, Wipro, REAN Cloud,

8K Miles, Bulletproof, Cloud Technology Partners, Logicworks, Minjar, and Rackspace are just a few of the MSPs that have committed to helping their customers reinvent their business using the cloud (for a complete list of AWS MSP Partners, look here: https://aws.amazon.com/partners/msp/).

Unfortunately, however, many traditional MSPs continue to hold their customers back. Like many companies featured in Clayton Christensen's book, *The Innovator's Dilemma*, these traditional MSPs are spending more time protecting their existing revenue streams than helping their customers remain competitive.

I wasn't terribly surprised to read a recent report from CompTIA that 44 percent of the MSPs surveyed said they only support cloud services when asked to do so by their customer.[70] I was, however, pretty surprised to receive a candid email from an executive at a large and well-known MSP that articulated his company's position on cloud. As the executive concedes, some MSPs are spreading FUD (Fear, Uncertainty, and Doubt) about the cloud to buy themselves time at the expense of their customers. Says the MSP executive,

> *The only way we can salvage our market share for now is to fuel [fear] because the hard truth is that we simply do not have the arsenal to counter AWS's dominance. More importantly, we constantly bombard these messages (vendor lock-in, security, et al) with the operational executives that are still (a vast majority in large enterprises) stuck in the traditional IT thinking and their existence threatened by the cloud wave."*

The full (anonymized) version of the e-mail follows below—

> *Dear Mr. Orban,*
>
> *I recently started following you on Medium after I stumbled upon your article on mass migrations. Earlier yesterday, I read your article on the*

70 https://www.comptia.org/about-us/newsroom/blog-home/comptia-blog/2016/07/21/why-cloud-is-the-stuff-of-msp-nightmares

myths about hybrid architecture. Thought would share my 2 cents on your "fear" of architecting applications to work on multi-cloud environments.

In my humble opinion, the fear is instilled by the major IT Managed Services Players (MSP) in a vain attempt to salvage their business. I must admit, one of those that's drilling the need for architecting solutions to work on multi-cloud environment. As you aware, most MSPs have been quite late into the cloud game and still playing catch-up with AWS. The only way we can salvage our market share for now is to fuel these fears because the hard truth is that we simply do not have the arsenal to counter AWS's dominance. More importantly, we constantly bombard these messages (vendor lock-in, security et al) with the operational executives that are still (a vast majority in large enterprises) stuck in the traditional IT thinking and their existence threatened by the cloud wave. Everybody knows that if you do not embrace cloud you simply die. So, to come around it, you simply introduce more complexities in the guise of simplifying IT!

The last decade has been about managed services and AWS is simply taking it away from the MSPs especially that's been slow on uptake. Though I strongly believe that architecting applications for multi-cloud is an overkill and limits to the lowest common denominator, our only strategy for now (though slowly getting ineffective) is to continue to fuel these fears

Initially thought of posting this as a comment on Medium, but honesty on a public forum means shooting myself on the foot and hence the note to your email.

Looking forward to reading more of your wonderful insights

To be fair, I empathize with this executive's perspective. Change is hard, and MSPs have to help hundreds of enterprises change while they change themselves. Change at this scale can be harder than it is for an enterprise that has fewer P&Ls to manage.

But it's not impossible...

Logicworks started helping enterprises manage their IT environments long before cloud became mainstream, and it's successfully transitioning its business at breakneck speed. In fact, it recently received a $135 million investment led by Pamplona Capital to accelerate this transition.[71]

Kenneth Ziegler, CEO of Logicworks, says,

> *We disrupted our own business starting in 2012 because of two key reasons: 1) customers were increasingly asking for us to help them make sense of IaaS offerings and 2) by that point, AWS had become a superior technology platform, which meant we could build repeatable, scalable solutions around it to not only achieve the compliant and secure solutions our customers were looking for, but through our automation platform we could now exceed previous standards by reducing human error and providing programmatic enforcement of desired configurations.*
>
> *The heavy lifting that we used to do manually as a traditional MSP has been replaced by managed services bots, which our clients subscribe to, and the DevOps expertise they have access to enables our customers to transform their business faster, regardless of where they are on their journey. The courage to stop defending our traditional IT install base has led to growth well beyond our initial expectations.*

Cloudreach, one of AWS's premier born-in-the-cloud partners, prides itself on intelligent cloud adoption, and has 350 enterprise customers in 7 countries. Launched in 2009, the company brings deep expertise in enabling enterprises' use of the cloud through best-practice guidance and cloud tooling.

Tom Ray, head of Cloudreach in the US, says that in order to deliver the best cloud solutions to enterprises, his team tries to

71 http://www.logicworks.net/news/2016/following-three-years-high-growth-its-amazon-web-services-cloud-automation-software

> *Recruit the right people, expose them to the technology, our mindset, and our methodologies. This takes time, effort and experience…You cannot rush the process.*

Meanwhile, 2nd Watch—also born in the cloud and now one of AWS's leading hyper-scale MSPs—is helping the largest enterprises not only adopt the public cloud, but evolve how it will be managed today and in the future. Says Jeff Aden, the company's co-founder and Executive Vice President of Marketing & Business Development,

> *Large enterprises partner with 2nd Watch so we can walk alongside them to deliver tailored and integrated management solutions that holistically and proactively encompass the operating, financial, and technical requirements for public cloud adoption. In the end, customers gain more leverage from the cloud with a lot less risk.*

That's also part of the value proposition at REAN Cloud, a born-in-the-cloud MSP with core expertise in building and managing DevOps-based managed services that support enterprise cloud transformation. REAN Cloud manages what Gartner calls "Bi-Modal IT,"[72] which allows enterprises to manage their traditional ITIL-led managed services while adapting to cloud-led transformation.

Minjar is another innovative MSP, and it's leading the born-in-the-cloud charge in India. The company's smart Managed Cloud services are powered by an intelligent man + machine model on top of its Botmetric Cloud Management Platform,[73] which blends AWS competencies, technology, and automation to deliver 24x7 AWS cloud operations.

At the same time, Cloud Technology Partners (CTP), a premier cloud professional services company for enterprises moving to AWS, specializes in helping companies accelerate their cloud adoption and digital innovation

---

72 https://c.ymcdn.com/sites/misaontario.site-ym.com/resource/resmgr/MCIO_2015/Presentations/Bimodal_IT_-_Gartner.pdf

73 https://www.botmetric.com/

initiatives. Bruce Coughlin, Executive Vice President at CTP, says that clients often refer to his company's delivery teams as "cloud therapists" because they help organizations think differently about the cloud.

Explains Coughlin,

> *The public cloud is not just another datacenter, so it shouldn't be treated like one. We help shift our client's thinking from "How do I replicate what I do in the datacenter?" to "How do I configure the appropriate infrastructure to enable my developers?" In the end, empowering developers with the tools they need—with the right overarching security and governance controls—helps our clients achieve even their loftiest cloud goals.*

Like CTP, Rackspace recognized the importance of helping businesses move and operate in the cloud. As a result, it fully embraced a strategic shift that enables it to provide top-tier cloud management and support. Says Prashanth Chandrasekar, Vice President & General Manager of the AWS Business Unit at Rackspace,

> *For over 15 years, Rackspace has been focused on helping customers leverage technology to move their businesses forward. We saw a huge demand for AWS from our customers, and made the decision to develop the technology and expertise necessary to enable them to take full advantage of the AWS Cloud. With just over a year in the market, Fanatical Support for AWS is the fastest growing business in Rackspace history, and we look forward to continuing to adapt our capabilities to help our customers build cloud-enabled businesses.*

Regardless of which MSP an enterprise chooses—or whether it chooses one—I've said that each organization has its own unique set of opportunities and challenges that guide and constrain its decisions on the cloud journey.

Chris Wegmann, who leads the Accenture AWS Business Group at Accenture, enriched this thinking in his post[74] —

> *Despite how obvious it may sound, our advice is to start from the finish line and work back. Look at your business goals, your targets—your most important outcomes, and then decide on what migration approach you want to take. Each business has unique objectives, and determining what they are represents the epitome of a more assured cloud journey.*
>
> *For example, is your organization dealing with a physical challenge, such as exiting a data center that needs to be refreshed or a data center lease expiring? A technical debt issue, such as end of life on your OS or hardware? Or do you want to re-architect your applications completely, so that they gain greater elasticity and agility within and outside your organization? It's clear that public cloud can be the catalyst that drives true business transformation. How you get there, however, will vary and evolve based on your business needs.*

In addition to the best practices outlined in this book, which are just as relevant to traditional MSPs as they are to modern-day enterprises, I'd close with one final piece of advice for the MSPs who are struggling with their journey…

Stop fighting gravity. The cloud is here, the benefits to your customers are transformational, and these companies need your help to take full advantage of what the cloud offers them. Eventually, if you don't help them, they'll find someone who will. Train and certify your teams on cloud, adjust your go-to-market so you can help your customers constantly reinvent themselves, and you'll reinvent yourself in the process.

---

74 https://medium.com/aws-enterprise-collection/cloud-migrations-some-tips-from-the-accenture-aws-business-group-5d6742e58aaf

CHAPTER 23

The Future of Managed Services in the Cloud

Originally posted on 3/4/16: http://amzn.to/future-of-managed-services-in-cloud

"You can't do today's job with yesterday's methods and be in business tomorrow"

—George W Bush

The ecosystem around the cloud is growing and changing rapidly, and most of the executives I speak to are (re)considering who they partner with and what they partner for to accelerate the value technology brings to their organizations.

IT Managed Services is an area that has seen substantial changes in the last few years, thanks to the growing popularity of cloud services. This area is served by what the industry calls MSPs (Managed Service Providers), and this group's role and business model is rapidly evolving. This chapter explores a few things your enterprise may want to consider in light of this shift.

"Your Mess for Less" Isn't Enough

Traditionally, MSPs are attractive alternatives for enterprises wanting to outsource steady-state IT operations to someone who can do it cheaper. "Your mess for less" can still be valuable for organizations looking to cut costs, but you should look to your MSPs to do this in a way that is consistent with both your enterprise-IT strategy and where the market is headed.

MSPs are attracted to the cloud for the same reason your enterprise is: the cloud gives MSPs the ability to devote more of their resources to their customers (you), rather than on the undifferentiated heavy lifting typically associated with managing data centers and ubiquitous IT services. MSPs who realize this—Logicworks, Cloudreach, Accenture, 2nd Watch, REAN Cloud, Cascadeo, Mobiquity, to name a few—are able to streamline their operations, focus more on value-added services, and optimize their own cost structure. This results in a combination of better margins for the next-generation MSP and lower costs for you.

I'm also seeing a new trend of MSPs combining their cloud migration expertise with the *as-a-service* model which enterprises that benefit from the cloud have become accustomed to.

In this new type of arrangement, the MSP agrees to migrate an enterprise's existing system(s) to the cloud, takes full ownership of the systems management, and sells the business function back to you (the customer) as-a-service. Imagine being able to keep the business processes around your ERP system without having to manage the infrastructure and have a predictable cost model for business process changes. This new model eliminates the need to establish elaborate ITSM (IT Service Management) processes for change management and the (sometimes astonishing) rate cards that go with these processes. I've certainly felt nickel-and-dimed by MSPs in the past, and I recently spoke to an executive who told me that their MSP tried to charge them $10,000 to create a VPC in their AWS environment—a process which takes minutes and costs almost nothing. I've spent some time determining how to deliver this new value proposition through the AWS and Accenture partnership team, and you can expect to hear more about this.

The Role of DevOps for an MSP

In Chapter 21, I make the point that many enterprises are looking for partners to help them evolve their culture. I also wrote a DevOps series that elaborates on why enterprises are becoming increasingly drawn to DevOps and how to navigate organizational change to embrace it. Several MSPs have combined all of this thinking together and are helping enterprises manage their steady state operations while also helping them leverage DevOps and develop a culture of experimentation.

AWS has established an AWS Managed Services Program that gives MSPs a set of best practices for large-scale cloud operations and periodically uses an independent third-party audit firm to audit MSPs who claim to implement them. Looking for partners who've passed the AWS Managed Services Program audit can give you the confidence that you're engaging with partners that have appropriate cloud expertise and can help you develop your own cloud operating model.

Just as with the AWS Managed Services Program, working with partners who have achieved the AWS DevOps Competency can give you the confidence that you're working with a partner who understands how to implement continuous integration, automation, and other DevOps-centric tools offered by AWS.

If the combination of these competencies is attractive to your organization, here's the list of organizations that have achieved both: 2nd Watch, Cascadeo, Cloudreach, REAN Cloud, Smartronix, Rackspace, and Logicworks.

If you're working with partners who don't have both of these competencies but you think that they should, urge them to consider these programs, then tell me about it. I'd also love to hear your expectations and thoughts for how the MSP landscape has and will continue to evolve in the coming years.

BEST PRACTICE FIVE

Create A Cloud Center Of Excellence

◆ ◆ ◆

CHAPTER 24

How to Create a Cloud Center of Excellence in Your Enterprise

Originally posted on 3/17/16: http://amzn.to/create-cloud-center-of-excellence

"Give me a lever long enough and a fulcrum on which to place it, and I shall move the world."

—ARCHIMEDES

IN 2012, I WAS FORTUNATE enough to be named the CIO of Dow Jones, which at the time was a storied, 123-year-old organization with a strong brand, prolific content, and loyal customer base. My job was to shift the technology group's focus toward product development in order for the company to stay relevant in an increasingly competitive environment, improve operational excellence, and drive down costs.

There were many levers we pulled over the course of our ever-evolving strategy to achieve these goals, including in-sourcing talent, leveraging open-source, and bringing in cloud services so we could focus on the business. But possibly the best decision we made was to create our CCoE, which we called DevOps, to codify *how* we built and executed our cloud strategy across the organization. I knew from seeing change-management programs succeed and fail throughout my career, that having a dedicated team with single-threaded ownership over an organization's most important initiatives is one of the most effective way to get results fast and influence change. My Enterprise DevOps series covers some of these experiences in more detail.

Since then, every enterprise I've met with that has made meaningful progress on their journey has a team of people dedicated to creating, evangelizing, and institutionalizing best practices, frameworks, and governance for their evolving technology operations, which are increasingly implemented using the cloud. These CCoE teams start small, develop a point of view for how cloud technology can be responsibly implemented at scale for your organization, and, if implemented properly, can become the fulcrum by which your organization transforms the way technology serves the business.

Over the course of the next few chapters, I'll explore how enterprises are doing this through the following dimensions:

Build the Team

I recommend putting together a team of three to five people from a diverse set of professional backgrounds. Try to find developers, system administrators, network engineers, IT operations, and database administrators. These people should ideally be open-minded and eager about how they can leverage modern technology and cloud services to do their jobs differently and take your organization into the future. Don't be afraid to enlist those with little to no experience—attitude can be just as important as aptitude, and chances are you already have the people you need in your organization.

Scope (and Grow) the Team's Responsibilities

Your CCoE should be responsible for building the best practices, governance, and frameworks that the rest of the organization leverages when implementing systems on (or migrating systems to) the cloud. Start with the basics: roles and permissions, cost governance, monitoring, incident management, a hybrid architecture, and a security model.

Over time, these responsibilities will evolve to include things like multi-account management, managing "golden" images, asset management, business unit chargebacks, and reusable reference architectures. Make sure you don't get stuck in analysis paralysis, and you will naturally evolve your capabilities with practical experience.

Weave the Team into the Other Best Practices

All of the best practices I've been writing about are dependent on one another. To be successful, your CCoE needs to: find a tremendous amount of support from the executive team, consider how to train the organization on CCoE methods, embrace experimentation to stay relevant, stay abreast of the best tools and partners for your environment, own the organization's hybrid architecture, and become a key player in any cloud-first strategy.

CHAPTER 25

Staffing Your Enterprise's Cloud Center of Excellence

Originally posted on 3/17/16: http://amzn.to/cloud-center-of-excellence-staffing

◆ ◆ ◆

"The future depends on attitude, aptitude, and gratitude—not on knowledge."
—Debasish Mridha M.D.

Starting small, iterating, and growing based on what you learn is a recurring theme in any successful Enterprise Cloud journey. I encourage you to apply that same iterative thinking as you create the team of people who will lead your organization's Cloud Center of Excellence.

You'll start by enlisting a small number of forward-thinking individuals who are willing to learn and excited about how the cloud can impact their organization. Three to five people are enough to make a noticeable difference right away. Then, each month, evaluate the impact the CCoE is having on the organization, make adjustments, and grow the team as the number and size of projects they influence grows.

How do you know when you're choosing the right staff for the job?

Executives often ask me about the types of people to look for and where/how they can hire those people. Typically, I've found that *attitude* is just as important as *aptitude*, which means any large organization already has the people it needs to leverage the cloud. Look for people with a genuine enthusiasm and interest for learning something new. Chances are, you have plenty of people in your organization eager to use the cloud for their projects, and they shouldn't be hard to find. It's fine to augment the team with talent hired from the market, but don't wait to get started until you do so. If every organization waited, we'd be needlessly stuck in a deadlock for talent when it's easy enough to manufacture our own.

Ideally, the people on your CCoE team will come from a diverse set of roles and backgrounds. These can include (but shouldn't be limited to) application developers, system administrators, network engineers, security practitioners, IT operations, and database administrators. Bringing a diverse group of expertise together will give you a team with a broad range of perspectives and likely lead to a more-complete platform. This team's institutional knowledge of your existing products and processes will help guide their decision on how to create and govern the most fitting cloud best practices for your organization.

The *as-a-service* model that most cloud services provide also lends itself well to a cross-functional point of view. Many server and database-administration tasks, for example, are now automated and can be controlled by software. It's still necessary to have those who understand how to optimize applications on servers and databases, but the tasks themselves will benefit from someone who knows how to write code to automate them.

This blending of disciplines is one of the factors behind the rise of DevOps, as well as one of the reasons the CCoE is commonly named DevOps and staffed by roles that sound like DevOps engineers. While "DevOps" and "DevOps engineer" are fairly new terms in the technology vocabulary, I believe the concepts have actually been around for decades. Most individuals playing these roles today come from a variety of disciplines and/or specialties, and they want to expand their horizons and deliver a more diverse value to their organizations.

Of course, every enterprise will have its share of change-averse individuals existing alongside its cloud champions. Sometimes all it takes to convince more-hesitant employees is a nudge in the right direction. I've talked to a few enterprises that did this by staffing their CCoE with one or two skeptics.

If you have leaders in your organization who carry a lot of influence and are wary of your cloud direction, you might consider tying their success to how quickly you're able to gain value from the cloud by putting them in or around your CCoE. This method needs to be managed carefully, but I've seen it work as a force-multiplier for cultural shifts. As these skeptics learn more about how the cloud can benefit your business and their careers, they are more likely to start championing the direction and encourage others in the organization to follow suit.

Finally, where the CCoE reports is less important than the executive support it receives. Your CCoE should be high enough in your organization's power structure that it can create impactful change.

What's your experience been staffing your CCoE? Are there other strategies you've found for making the team gel and be successful? I'd love to hear about it!

CHAPTER 26

Common Responsibilities for Your Cloud Center of Excellence

Originally posted on 4/12/16: http://amzn.to/cloud-center-of-excellence-responsibilities

"The right thing to do and the hard thing to do are usually the same."
—Steve Maraboli

A Cloud Center of Excellence is the team of people responsible for developing the cloud best practices, governance, and frameworks that the rest of the organization can leverage to transform your business using the cloud. Its creation is the fifth of seven best practices that I'm writing about in the Enterprise Cloud journey.

Your organization's CCoE should start small and grow as it adds value to the business. Organizations that do this well set metrics or KPIs for the CCoE and measure progress against them. I've seen metrics range from IT resource utilization, to the number of releases each day/week/month as a sign of increasing agility, to the number of projects the CCoE is influencing. Couple these with a customer-service centric approach, and other business units will *want* to work with your CCoE because they find value *and* because the CCoE is a pleasure to work with.

Chapter 25 dove into how to staff your CCoE. Here, I'll go over some of the common considerations that I've found among the organizations that are successful at growing their CCoE. This chapter should function as a way to get you thinking about the right things to task your CCoE with, rather than an exhaustive list, and it concludes with some additional resources you can leverage for more details.

Remember to start small: you only need to solve for the issues you face in your current projects rather than needing to boil the ocean. You can experiment, measure, and learn as you go.

Identity management. How do you want to map roles and permissions in your cloud environment to the roles and responsibilities that you already have in your organization? What services and features are you comfortable leveraging in what environments? How do you want to integrate with your Active Directory and/or single-sign-on (SSO) platform? AWS's IAM platform, for example, provides fine-grained access across all of the different AWS services. This level of granularity is new for a lot of enterprises, and gives you the opportunity to think through what roles in your organization should have access to what resources/services in what environments.

Account and cost management. Do you want to map accounts to business units and cost centers so you can logically separate your IT services and/or understand business-unit-specific costs? While the business units may be accountable for costs associated with their consumption, it's much easier to centralize cost optimization across a larger portfolio of resources. Your CCoE should think about how to stagger RI purchases, so they can remain flexible with the business, and look at some of the tools (e.g., CloudHealth, Cloudability) that are available to help you with this.

Asset management/tagging. What kind of information do you want to track for each of the resources that you provision? Some examples I've seen include budget code/cost center, business units, environments (e.g., test, staging, production), and owners. When I was at Dow Jones, one of the first growing pains we hit was having our bill escalate as more developers started to experiment. In the course of a few hours, we addressed this by tagging each instance launched in our development VPC as such and writing a script to stop those instances on nights and weekends. This was the first piece of what became a fairly sophisticated tagging and automation library that allowed us to manage our environment as we scaled. I've seen many other customers do the same thing, increasingly taking action based on tags in their production environment as they mature toward highly available architectures and "disaster indifference." (Credit to Wilf Russell from Nike on coining this phrase.)

Reference architectures. How can you build security and governance into your environment from the very beginning, and rely on automation to keep it up to date? If you can find and define commonalities in the tools and approaches you use across your applications you can begin to automate the installation, patching, and governance of them. You may want one reference architecture across the whole enterprise that still gives business units flexibility to add in what they need in an automated way. Alternatively, you might want multiple reference architectures for different classes or tiers of applications. Most likely you'll end up with something in between, but regardless, consider how to automate more of this over time so business units can think less about the underlying infrastructure and more about their applications.

Over time, as the CCoE learns, it can become increasingly prescriptive to more business units and work the right balance of giving them freedom to innovate while still providing guardrails for consistency. Some other considerations that I don't cover here include defining an automation strategy, exploring a hybrid architecture, providing continuous delivery capabilities to enable business units to move more quickly and run-what-they-build, defining data governance practices, and implementing dashboards that give transparency to the metrics/KPIs that are important to your business.

The AWS Cloud Adoption Framework contains a number of perspectives that give prescriptive guidance to help you think through these best practices (and more). You can also leverage AWS Trusted Advisor to proactively identify cost, performance, security, and fault-tolerance optimizations. Last but not least, you can leverage the AWS Well-Architected Framework to benchmark the work your CCoE does against the best practices we've seen across our entire AWS customer base.

CHAPTER 27

Your Enterprise's Flywheel to the Cloud

Originally posted on 4/25/16: http://amzn.to/enterprise-cloud-flywheel

◆ ◆ ◆

"In theory there is no difference between theory and practice. In practice there is."
—Yogi Berra

When I introduced the Cloud Center of Excellence, I noted that your CCoE should become the fabric through which all the other best practices on your journey are woven. In this chapter, which concludes the CCoE series, I offer some thoughts on how the CCoE benefits from or drives the other best practices on the journey.

Executive Support

It's hard for a CCoE to succeed if it's not driven by strong leadership. Whenever I talk with executives about creating their CCoE, I encourage them to make bold moves. That means identifying the people best suited for the team, transferring them from their current roles without backfilling them, and shifting responsibility toward the CCoE so the vacant roles don't matter.

Reporting lines, on the other hand, do matter. It's fine to put the CCoE in an infrastructure-focused organization, but make sure the leaders of that organization aren't afraid of what the cloud might mean for them. There's a good chance that as you grow your cloud capabilities and tip the balance to cloud-based solutions, your CCoE will be the dominant part of your infrastructure team. This requires strong leadership, air cover, and a willingness to continue to move resources into the team as you learn.

Educating Your Staff

The CCoE should be leading the charge to educate the rest of your organization on cloud, how your organization uses it, and evangelizing the best practices, governance, and frameworks that you use to support your business. You already have the people you need to succeed using the cloud, and your CCoE should be their key enabler. Consider how your CCoE can leverage as much AWS Training and Certification as possible, have them layer in your organization-specific content, and scale the delivery of that training to the rest of the organization. When I was at Dow Jones our DevOps team delivered DevOps Days several times per year to anyone who wanted to learn more. Others in the industry are doing this, too: Drew Firment, former Technology Director of Cloud Engineering at Capital One, drove an amazing CCoE education program to spread cloud expertise throughout Capital One. Check out his blog to learn more.

Experimentation

The CCoE provides the guardrails that allow the rest of the organization to experiment quickly, while enhancing the organization's security posture. By implementing reference architectures for common application patterns and developing one or more continuous integration platforms, the CCoE can enable dependent business units to experiment in a consistent and compliant way, allowing the organization to run-what-they-build, fail fast, learn, and deliver value to the business faster than before.

Partners

Partners are, as I've mentioned, there to accelerate your cloud strategy, and your CCoE can help accelerate your partner strategy. You can use your CCoE to stay on top of the evolving partner ecosystem, evaluate new tools, and steward the best practices of how the new wave of cloud tools and consultants are integrated into the complex enterprise environment. Your CCoE should drive discussions with your legal, procurement, security, and other business stakeholders and help them understand your approach to cloud, and what you're comfortable allowing your partners do for your business. Many organizations templatize their approach to bringing in tools so each business unit has the flexibility to choose from a variety of tools, while others look to drive a single standard. Whatever your preference, lean on your CCoE to drive the approach and template.

Hybrid

Cloud is not an all-or-nothing value proposition, and any enterprise that has been running IT for a significant period of time will run some form of a hybrid architecture. Your CCoE should be driving your hybrid strategy, and develop the standards and reference architectures for how your cloud and on-premises applications can call each other and migrate to the cloud over time. When I was at Dow Jones, our earliest hybrid ah-ha moment came the first time we had a native cloud application we had developed call our identity management system that was running on-premises. Our DevOps team studied how Amazon Virtual Private Cloud (VPC) worked for a few hours, mapped how we wanted security groups to work with our internal firewalls, and implemented a secure hybrid architecture that allowed our cloud applications to talk to our on-premises assets. This whole process took a few hours. We immediately turned this into an automated reference architecture that we used over and over for similar scenarios.

Cloud-First

At some point, your CCoE will prove to some (and eventually all) of your business units that they're better off asking themselves why they *shouldn't* use cloud for their projects than asking why they *should.* Using automation and having reference architectures for your legacy and/or compliant applications will lead to faster time-to-marke,t and you should find that your business units *want* to work with your CCoE rather than have to be coerced to. This is a departure from the typical infrastructure and application team dynamic in most organizations, and can be embraced and celebrated in a deliberate cloud-first strategy communicated from the top down.

CHAPTER 28

Considering DevOps in Your Enterprise?

Originally posted on 7/31/15: http://amzn.to/enterprise-devops

◆ ◆ ◆

"Development is an endurance exercise with incremental improvements"
—Sri Mulyani Indrawati

Before I wrote the CCoE series (Chapters 24-27), I wrote a series on DevOps in your enterprise, which has quite a few relevant points to the CCoE model.

DevOps is a relatively new term for a concept I believe has been around a long time. At this point, it's widely accepted as a cultural way of being in some organizations, a confluence of formerly siloed teams that together can produce faster, more frequent, and more reliable results.

I was fortunate enough to start my career in a DevOps culture before the term hit mainstream. When I became a developer at Bloomberg in 2001, the company was already well known for its relentless pursuit of time-to-market, iterative development cycles, and developers owning the ongoing operations of the systems they delivered. It didn't take long for new developers to learn what it was like to troubleshoot a system at 4 a.m. (when London trading opened). I found that these late-night experiences served as great motivation to make our systems more robust.

DevOps may be intuitively obvious to startups because smaller businesses can gravitate toward it with relative ease. But for larger organizations with significant amounts of technical debt, monolithic architectures, and risk-averse business practices, the undertaking can seem intimidating.

The good news is that it doesn't have to be. I encourage companies wanting to shift to a DevOps culture to do so in a DevOps fashion—start with small projects, iterate, learn, and improve. I encourage them to consider implementing strategies that produce commonly accepted practices across the organization, and to begin embracing the idea that, when automated, ongoing operations can be decentralized and trusted in the hands of many teams that will run what they build.

When I was the CIO at Dow Jones, we built our DevOps practice around a small team of people—four or five individuals were enough to get going on several projects. The goal, however, was not just to create a new team but to influence a change in the company's culture. By implementing and inventing frameworks, best practices, and governance, and by automating everything, DevOps became one of our key levers for driving innovation and accelerating product development. We started with small projects, and used the results to showcase how we could successfully execute an increasing number of projects using the same model. Slowly but surely, we began to deliver more features, and improve our time-to-market in the process. What used to be Tuesday and Thursday release nights, where things often went wrong, eventually turned into developers releasing dozens of changes throughout the course of each week.

For those considering DevOps but also juggling technical debt, consider these three tenets to start:

1. **Be customer service-oriented throughout your organization.** Businesses today should think of their internal stakeholders as customers. These customers could be anyone from a marketing department, a product manager, or a developer. Each individual or group needs technology to do their jobs. Teams that puts those needs in the forefront will keep their customers from wandering off to other solutions (Shadow IT), will likely deliver better results (faster, better, cheaper), and

have happier stakeholders. Lack of superior service could leave your customers wanting to work around you, not with you.

2. **Automate everything.** It's widely understood that to get the most out of the cloud, you'll need to be able to reliably reproduce your systems using code. This is particularly true for autoscaling (elasticity). Automation also allows organizations to be much more aggressive with implementing changes: If you make a mistake, you can very quickly go back and reliably reproduce the previous state. Other benefits include better efficiency, security, and auditability. (See my post on automation for more detail.)
3. **Run what you build.** This is often where I see traditional IT become anxious. In a traditional IT model, the operations of an application or service are sometimes managed by those who weren't involved in creating the asset. There were a number of reasons for doing this (e.g., lower-cost resourcing, centralized expertise), but I would argue these reasons are going away. Cloud technologies now handle much of the heavy lifting associated with IT operations, and much of the operations can be automated with software. Developers are familiar with software, which means there's less motivation to separate the operations responsibility of any given task. This is where the term *DevOps* comes from, after all. Since developers will be the ones most intimately familiar with the nuances of the system, they will likely be able to address issues the fastest. And by using automation, it is easy to methodically propagate changes and roll back or address issues before they impact customers. I encourage centralized DevOps teams to do what they can to make development teams increasingly independent, and not be in the critical path for ongoing operations/releases.

For those that are interested in dipping their toe in the water, there's no time like the present. Start small and be satisfied with incremental improvements. Cultural changes don't happen overnight. Slowly begin applying these concepts across your portfolio, and both new and old ways of working can improve. As you gain experience, you can parlay each learning to the next, leverage your growing inventory of automation, and hopefully see better results.

In the next chapter, I explore a bit more about what it means to be a customer service-centric IT organization.

CHAPTER 29

Two Reasons Customer Service is Key to Enterprise DevOps

Originally posted on 8/11/15: http://amzn.to/customer-service-devops

◆ ◆ ◆

"Your customer doesn't care how much you know until they know how much you care."

—Damon Richards

Customer service is, as I outlined in my introduction to this DevOps series (Chapter 28), one of three tenets I encourage organizations to consider when implementing a DevOps culture.

Today's world is full of technology solutions. There are a myriad of options available to all of us to meet just about any need. For those of us delivering technology solutions, doing good business means not just delivering a great product, but also delivering great customer service. The better the customer service, the less likely your customers will seek solutions from your competitors.

In the most traditional sense, customers are the people who buy your products and services, like the shoppers on Amazon.com, or the enterprises using AWS.

Inside of enterprise IT, your customer is often someone you work with. An internal stakeholder could be anyone in the organization relying on various technologies to get their jobs done. Sometimes they are in another department (marketing, sales, etc.) and sometimes they are other technologists.

Who consumes the products and services of an internal DevOps organization? Of course, the answer will depend, but often they will be the application developers and other technology teams in the company, since faster product development is often a key motivator for implementing centralized DevOps in the first place. A centralized team that collaborates and listens across departments will be able to better anticipate needs and deliver better customer service than one that is solely concerned about the challenges they face in isolation.

There are at least two reasons to keep customer service at the forefront of your organization:

1. Customer-service-centricity improves the IT brand

Twenty years ago, enterprise technology needs were served exclusively by IT. Technology was thought of as complicated. It was something that required a great deal of expertise to do well. Unlike a DevOps culture where teams run what they build, organizations were biased toward centralizing IT into the hands of the few that understood how to procure and deploy it. This left IT's customers—the rest of the organization—little choice on where to go to get their IT needs met.

Today, however, there are so many more products and solutions that solve your customers' problems. Technology continues to become more consumerized. More people are using computers, smartphones, websites, apps, than ever before, and they have more choices at home and at work. This trend is changing the way technology leaders need to think about customer service—particularly within their own organizations.

My experience has taught me that when someone finds an easier way to execute a task, they'll likely take it. If they aren't getting the service they need from IT, they'll try to find that service elsewhere. The newsroom might download editing software because IT can't or won't deliver its own version fast enough. HR may look for a scheduling tool outside the internal calendaring environment. Marketing may go to a third party to have the brand's website redone. The industry knows this as "Shadow IT," which can make it much more difficult to effectively manage and secure a large IT environment. The reality, however, is that Shadow IT exists because internal stakeholders are simply not satisfied or don't know how to get what they want from IT.

A centralized DevOps organization that remains customer-service-centric has a much better chance of avoiding these scenarios. When you're thinking about your customer from the very beginning, you will be able to empathize with their needs and concerns from the start, and determining how solutions to those needs fit into the overall company. Instead of saying, "You can't use that to do your job," ask "What are you trying to accomplish and how can I help you be more effective?" Every time an app team implements a workaround for something the DevOps team can't deliver, there's an opportunity for the organization to learn how and why that happened, and decide if they should do things differently moving forward. Is there something they can do to alleviate the need for a workaround in the future? The answer may very well be "no," and in many cases, it will be okay to accept a workaround, but I encourage organizations to be deliberate about it. This is one of the ways IT can become an enabler rather than a point of friction. It is the kind of collaboration that incentivizes customers to work with you and not around you.

2. Customer-service-centricity is good for your career

In a DevOps model, where application teams run what they build, ownership and customer service go hand in hand. I've been fortunate enough to have ownership as a key performance indicator at every company I've worked for. It was one of Bloomberg's core values, we made it one for IT at Dow Jones, and it's one of Amazon's leadership principles.

Ownership simply means that any individual responsible for a product or service should treat that product or service as his or her own business. Products and services can take any number of forms: a website, a mobile application, the company's e-mail service, desktop support, a security tool, a CMS, or anything that you deliver to your customer.

Ownership creates better customer service because it places responsibility and reputation directly on the shoulders of the person overseeing the product. This person, in turn, will be motivated to listen to others, be aware of the customer's alternatives, and constantly keep insights into how the product is performing. Someone in charge of the product can't simply "pass the buck" when a problem occurs. They are accountable to see issues through to their resolution, and get help when they need it.

Individual careers will benefit here: Anyone willing to own a product and cultivate a healthy customer relationship will gain a reputation around the company for being reliable, trustworthy, and dependable.

These are just two reasons that customer service is so important inside of a large and complicated organizations, and especially important when considering DevOps. There's a good chance that you have encountered some of your own, and I'd love to hear about them.

CHAPTER 30

Enterprise DevOps: Why You Should Run What You Build

Originally posted on 8/31/15: http://amzn.to/run-what-you-build

◆ ◆ ◆

"You build it, you run it"

—Werner Vogels

It's an all-too-common scenario: You're spending time with your family and your phone suddenly steals away your attention. The dreaded air horn alerts you to a SEV1 failure. Your application—one that periodically suffers from a memory leak that operations "fixed" by restarting it—is now exhausting server resources within minutes of coming online. The application is effectively unusable. The operations team isn't equipped to do much other than restart or rollback, but the last good copy is months old. Who knows what else changed since then? It's up to you to fix the leak, but you're miles away from the office and your computer.

Incidents like this are far too common in a traditional enterprise IT model, where development and operations sit on opposite sides of a wall. But it doesn't have to be this way. DevOps is not just for startups. It can be used in the enterprise too. Like automation and customer service, "run what you build" can be an effective tenet for improving enterprise IT delivery using a DevOps model.

In the traditional setting, developers architect and engineer a solution, then hand it over to operations. Sometimes they're kind enough to give some guidance on how to deal with production issues, and sometimes they have little-to-no knowledge of the production environment to begin with. When these teams remain separate entities, each has little information on how the other works and what they need. The operations team often has runbooks, SOP (Standard Operating Procedures), or some other mechanism to address issues as they arise in production. These can be quite effective when you need a fix fast, but when the root causes aren't identified and addressed, it's like using chewing gum to patch a leaky boat. Eventually, you're going to sink.

DevOps Can Provide a Better Way...

The cloud has helped tear down this wall because with it, your infrastructure starts to look a lot like software. The API-driven nature allows you to treat your infrastructure as code, which is something developers understand. Now that everyone is much closer to the infrastructure, operations naturally becomes more of a key requirement.

Meanwhile, software is increasingly sold as a service, and your customers are rightfully demanding constant improvements. They may tolerate a mistake here and there, but only if those mistakes are addressed right away and don't keep happening. In order to keep up with these changes, you need to listen for clues and insights that your customers may not clearly communicate directly to you. Like you, they're busy with other things, and when they call to give you feedback it's likely they're unsatisfied. While any customer interaction is a learning opportunity, you may be better off having them on your terms. These insights are much harder to find with a wall between development and operations—operations may be sweeping problems under the rug with quick fixes, and developers will have a lower bar for operational excellence if they have too much of a safety net.

All of these things are good reasons for moving away from the traditional IT model and towards a DevOps culture, where development and operations come together into a singular focus. I try to encourage executives to make *run what you build* a crucial tenet in their DevOps-driven organizations. Here are just a few benefits and behaviors that I've seen organizations reap:

- **Design for production.** Run what you build forces development teams to think about how their software is going to run in production as they design it. This can help your teams avoid the last-minute scrambling that often occurs when teams try to force fit what they've built to a production environment to meet a deadline. I can't remember how many times I've seen this materially hurt quality. You change something at deployment time to address something that's different between production and development, run what you think are the relevant tests, and later discover that this change caused a bug somewhere else in the system.
- **Greater employee autonomy.** The run-what-you-build mentality encourages ownership and accountability, which, in my experience, leads to more independent, responsible employees and even career growth in the organization.
- **Greater transparency.** No one wants their personal time interrupted. Whoever is taking the calls will do everything they can to avoid getting them in the first place. Your teams will naturally want greater transparency in the environment and will implement proactive monitoring so they can identify issues or concerning patterns before they become widespread problems. In addition to finding problems before they happen, this sort of transparency should make it much easier to find root causes for issues that still make it through.
- **More automation.** Developers hate repeating manual tasks, so if they find they have to do something over and over in production to address an issue, they're more likely get to the root cause, and automate things along the way.
- **Better operational quality.** Things like transparency and automation will make your teams more efficient, and will continue to raise the bar for operational excellence.
- **More-satisfied customers.** Run what you build forces the entire IT team to understand more about the customer. That knowledge will

no longer be limited to a product or sales team, and these insights can be incredibly useful when used as a feedback loop for constant product improvement.

I'm sure you can think of other benefits. What have you found to be the case for your organization?

CHAPTER 31

Enterprise DevOps: What to Expect When You're DevOps'ing

Originally posted on 9/11/15: http://amzn.to/what-to-expect-when-youre-devops-ing

"You cannot create experience, you must undergo it"
—Albert Camus

I'm wrapping up my DevOps in the Enterprise series with a piece on what to expect once your organization has some DevOps experience. These are just a few of the things I've experienced or seen in organizations that embrace automation, customer-service-oriented IT, and a run-what-you-build mentality.

Expect to Grow Your DevOps Practice Slowly

Like most things worth doing, implementing a culture of DevOps takes time. I encourage anyone going down this path to start small and deliberately. Measure the impact of each organizational change you make, embrace what works, and celebrate the things you learn from what doesn't work. This helps the organization grow toward a culture of continuous improvement. The most challenging part of the whole process is getting started. As you become more and more comfortable with a DevOps culture, the unique challenges your organization may face should become obvious, and the solutions for those challenges won't be far behind.

When we implemented DevOps at Dow Jones, we started with just four people and grew the team slowly by adding one or two more members to the team from other areas of IT each month. This allowed us to build up some experience and best practices, and grow in line with the number of projects to which we were applying DevOps. I wouldn't recommend trying to grow much faster than this. Slow and deliberate growth allows you to set realistic expectations with your stakeholders, which includes your team, for how quickly things will change. It also allows you to consume resources in proportion to the overall business benefit, which may help you navigate around unnecessary politics surrounding resource allocation.

Roughly 18 months into our journey, after we felt we had built a large enough inventory of best practices, automation, and governance models, we became comfortable moving the majority of our infrastructure resources into our DevOps team. Our goal with this change was to have these individuals adapt their traditional roles to the DevOps mentality using the experiences the DevOps team built up over time. People didn't drastically alter how they did their jobs overnight. They did, however, start to change, little by little, the way they managed all of our systems.

Be Open Minded About Where and How You Apply DevOps

There is no one-size-fits-all way to implement and gain experience with DevOps. Every organization is unique. Not everything needs to—or should—change. Be prepared to measure what works and what doesn't. Find a way to tie your DevOps mentality and/or team to a business benefit—which can come from any part of IT. The industry often emphasizes how DevOps and a culture of innovation applies to product development, but I have seen these practices be just as applicable to back-office, end-user computing, and other parts of IT. Being open-minded about the types of projects you take on will allow you to stay focused on nurturing your DevOps team and understanding how it can work best for you.

Here are some of the benefits I've seen organizations celebrate as they mature a culture of DevOps:

Constant releases. A DevOps culture should be conducive to smaller changes being made more frequently. I talk about this in the previous chapter, where I list several benefits that can be summarized as greater efficiency, more resources aligned to business needs, and better operational excellence. All these things lead to a better experience for your customers (internal or external). Be prepared to manage the expectations of your business stakeholders as this happens, and don't get too far ahead of them. Be sensitive to the fact that your stakeholders may view a constantly changing product or environment as a risk. It will take time and maturity to build and prove the mechanisms that you need to do this responsibly. Building trust is essential, and building trust to do something new takes time. There's no glory in being the only one at the finish line.

Globally distributed apps. Watching an application scale up and down across different regions of the world as each time zone conducts its business is one of the most rewarding experiences I've had as an IT executive. As your DevOps team understands how to automate and manage a fleet of resources across different regions, it will become straightforward to distribute your applications globally. Pushing your services closer to customers will lower latency, making your system more efficient, cost effective, and, of course, delight your customer. As your mastery of DevOps improves, it will become increasingly easy to distribute your applications globally.

The data center migration. Everything IT does should be driven by the business. And when an IT exec can take something considered a traditional IT initiative and turn it into a real business case, they start to cement their place as a business executive overseeing IT, rather than simply an IT exec. Using your inventory of automation and globally distributed applications, you can develop compelling business cases to migrate some or all of your data centers to the cloud. I've seen this happen with increasing frequency over the course of the past year.

I experienced this after about several months of running a DevOps team at Dow Jones. We were leasing a data center in Hong Kong that was going to be closed in just a few months' time. We had to quickly find somewhere else to host our infrastructure. I felt that we had a strong enough momentum with our DevOps practice and cloud expertise that it would have been a shame to take a step backwards and lock ourselves into another data center commitment.

After some initial resistance, the team found a way to engineer around all the perceived roadblocks, and we completed a full data center migration to AWS in six weeks. While this particular deployment looks much different today than it did when we completed the migration, I think it remains a great testament to what happens as you build expertise and manage expectations over time. There's no way we would have been able to achieve that migration without the experience we gained leading up to it.

BEST PRACTICE SIX

Implement A Hybrid Architecture

◆ ◆ ◆

CHAPTER 32

Three Myths About Hybrid Architectures Using the Cloud

Originally posted on 3/9/15: http://amzn.to/3-myths-hybrid-cloud

◆ ◆ ◆

"The hardest thing in life to learn is which bridge to cross and which to burn."
—David Russell

I began to develop my point of view on hybrid architectures as a CIO leading the delivery of several business solutions on top of cloud services. Over the years, I have been fortunate enough to engage in several dozen conversations with CIOs and CTOs from large companies that have further shaped my thinking on this topic. At the same time, I've read many articles and blogs that discuss hybrid architectures, and it's not clear to me that the industry has a common understanding of what hybrid architectures using the cloud look like.

Companies embrace cloud technologies for many different reasons. Cloud adopters have benefited from increased agility, lower costs, and a global reach. For many of the CIOs I speak with, it really boils down to their ability to funnel precious resources from the things that don't bring in business to the things that do. In other words, the undifferentiated heavy lifting associated with managing infrastructure to the activities associated with building the products and services that their brand is known for.

That said, most enterprise IT organizations have established infrastructure and governance that they operate today. I've spoken with many CIOs who want to migrate this infrastructure to the cloud as fast as possible, but realize that meaningful cloud adoption is a journey that takes time. Along that journey, companies need a way to keep their systems running and get the most out of their existing investments. In my post on the enterprise cloud journey, I talk about how companies use AWS Virtual Private Cloud (VPC) and Direct Connect to extend their on-premises infrastructure with AWS to create a hybrid architecture. This is the hybrid architecture that has always made the most sense to me, and the step that many companies are taking on their way to maximizing their benefits from the cloud.

Beyond this, the conversation around hybrid becomes a bit convoluted. I am seeing three trends in market commentary that I believe sound good at first, but don't hold up once you start to peel back the onion. These three myths are:

Myth One: Hybrid is a permanent destination. Permanent is too strong a word to describe this point of view. Large companies with significant legacy systems will run hybrid cloud architectures for some time, likely measured in years. Each organization's cloud journey will be a bit different, and everyone will move at a pace that they're comfortable with. Still, I find it hard to imagine a future where many companies will be running their own data centers. It's probably more than 3 years out, but I'm confident it's less than 15. There are at least four factors that are working toward accelerating this transition:

1. **The economies of scale that cloud providers achieve are continuing to grow with adoption.** These benefits, one way or another, will benefit cloud consumers.
2. **The pace of innovation coming from cloud technologies is unprecedented.** AWS released 516 new services and features in 2014, 722 in 2015, and 1,017 in 2016.

3. **The technologies that companies depend on to run their business (e-mail, productivity, HR, CRM, etc.) are increasingly being built on the cloud.**
4. **The technologies and businesses that exist to help companies migrate to the cloud are growing rapidly in number.** To get an idea, check out the AWS Marketplace and the AWS Partner Network.

Myth Two: Hybrid allows you to seamlessly move applications between on-premises infrastructure and the cloud. On the surface this may seem attractive, but there is a fundamental flaw with this premise. It assumes that the cloud and on-premises infrastructure are equally capable. I appreciate how many companies have become well equipped to manage their infrastructure. At the same time, companies are moving to the cloud for the features and capabilities that their data centers don't have: true elasticity, security posturing, pay-as-you-go and only-for-what-you-use, and the constant stream of innovation. Architecting your applications to seamlessly work across your data centers and the cloud will limit you to the functionality of the lowest common denominator.

Myth Three: Hybrid allows you to seamlessly broker your applications across several cloud providers. There is a nuance to this argument that I believe is worth exploring. Companies are using a variety of different cloud solutions to meet the needs of their business. This generally includes a mix of infrastructure services as well as packaged solutions that run somewhere other than the company's data center (and very often on AWS). This makes perfect sense. IT executives should look at the problem they're trying to solve and select the best tool to solve it given their constraints.

What scares me is when companies fall into the trap of trying to architect a single application to work across multiple different cloud providers. I understand why engineers are attracted to this—it is quite an accomplishment to engineer the glue that is required to make different clouds work together. Unfortunately, this effort eats into the productivity gains that compelled the organization to the cloud in the first place. I always thought of this as taking me back to square one. Instead of managing your own infrastructure, you're now managing the nuances between several others. Like Myth Two, this also limits the functionality to the lowest common denominator.

I also understand that companies may go down this road to keep their vendors honest, and to avoid being locked into a single provider. On one hand, I would debate the risk of one of the big cloud providers going away, and it seems unlikely that the direction of the cloud computing industry is headed toward punitive business tactics. On the other hand, I feel there is a better way to mitigate this concern. Companies that architect their applications using known automation techniques will be able to reliably reproduce their environments. This best practice is what enables them to take advantage of the elastic properties of the cloud, and will decouple the application from the infrastructure. If done well, it becomes less of a burden to move to a different cloud provider if there is a compelling reason to do so.

Technology choices are not always easy, and often imperfect. Creating a hybrid architecture doesn't have to be.

CHAPTER 33

A Hybrid Cloud Architecture Ah-Ha! Moment

Originally posted on 6/2/16: http://amzn.to/hybrid-cloud-moment

◆ ◆ ◆

Each week I meet a few more executives who are transforming the way technology delivers value to their business using the cloud. Motivation for getting started with the cloud varies, but a consistent theme in my conversations is that the cloud allows organizations to devote more resources to their core business, move faster, and be more secure.

This transformation won't happen overnight, and I often refer to the process as a journey. During this time, your enterprise still needs to operate its existing IT assets in order to keep the business running. While most enterprises I speak with are in the process of migrating some or the entirety of their IT portfolio to the cloud, they've also realized the cloud is not an all-or-nothing value proposition. As each enterprise realizes this, they're able to bridge their on-premises IT assets with the cloud and use that bridge to migrate the gravity of their IT portfolio to the cloud over time.

In the previous chapter, I wrote about three myths around hybrid architectures in the cloud, which I still encounter when discussing hybrid cloud architectures with executives today. If you're still shaping your organization's hybrid cloud architecture perspective, I encourage you to consider the points I made about these myths.

The rest of this chapter details the ah-ha! moment my team and I had when I was the CIO at Dow Jones and we first implemented a hybrid cloud architecture.

A Hybrid Ah-Ha! Moment

In 2012, my boss (and then CEO of Dow Jones) had a hypothesis that we all felt was a great business opportunity: If all subscribers of the *Wall Street Journal*, one of Dow Jones' flagship B2C products, *had* much of the world's wealth, and all subscribers of Factiva and Dow Jones Newswires, Dow Jones' B2B products, *managed* much of the world's wealth, we could create a valuable platform by giving them a mechanism to connect and communicate with one another.

We were starting from scratch and wanted to move quickly. We assembled a very small team of engineers and designers to build out this concept, giving them the freedom to choose whatever tools they thought would get the job done. Six weeks later, with a little bit of open source, automation, AWS services, and a lot of hard work, we had a highly-available and disaster-indifferent application up and running. Our newfound ability to deliver technology to the business quickly became our *hero* project, and it helped us encourage my team and executive stakeholders to come on the journey with us.

As we integrated this application into more of our products, we found that we also needed to integrate it with some of our internal-only identity management systems. Some of these systems were not (and should not be) exposed to the internet, and were therefore unreachable from our application running on AWS in the public internet.

Engineers across our networking, infrastructure, and development teams began to look for a solution to this problem. After a little bit of research, we found we could leverage Amazon VPC to create a virtual network within our internal IP address space and put our application inside of the VPC.

After reading the AWS documentation and deciding how we would manage the integration of AWS Security Groups with our internal firewall rules, the team went to work. Inside of 45 minutes, they created the VPC, took a snapshot of the instances we were running on the public internet, brought the instances up in the VPC where they were assigned IP addresses from our internal subnet, routed inbound traffic to the new instances, enabled connectivity from the instances to our internal identity systems, and completed the migration.

We were amazed at how simple this was to set up, and even more amazed by the opportunity we realized we had for enhancing and extending our existing legacy systems with systems we built in the cloud.

Over the next several years, our DevOps team (otherwise known as our Cloud Center of Excellence) codified what we learned during this exercise by automating VPC creation and governance into a handful of reference architectures for different areas of our business. With this simple, but powerful strategy, we used this hybrid architecture model to build and enhance all of our existing systems in the cloud without having to migrate everything at once.

Since then, I've spoken to many executives who have had similar ah-ha! moment experiences. Once they realize they don't have to scrap all of their existing infrastructure investments and can still take advantage of the cloud, a number of possibilities open up. This gives their teams time to learn, ride out existing investments/depreciation schedules, and still benefit from the elasticity, agility, security, and cost characteristics of the cloud.

Have you had an ah-ha! moment setting up your hybrid architecture? I'd love to hear about it!

BEST PRACTICE SEVEN

Implement A Cloud-First Strategy

◆ ◆ ◆

CHAPTER 34

What Cloud-First Looks Like

Originally posted on 7/5/16: http://amzn.to/what-does-cloud-first-look-like

"Surround yourself with the best people you can find, delegate authority, and don't interfere as long as the policy you've decided upon is being carried out."

—Ronald Reagan

Change is hard. The larger and more complex an organization grows, and the more it gets used to doing things a certain way, the harder change becomes. Still, change always arrives, and I believe this tension of change being hard but inevitable is one of the reasons 20 to 50 companies fall out of the Fortune 500 every year.

In this part, I write about seven best practices I've seen employed by organizations that aren't afraid to reinvent themselves using the cloud. These practices help organizations of all shapes and sizes transform the way technology is used to support the business and remain competitive. I've also seen these practices turn countless technology executives into heroes capable of devoting their company's resources to the things that matter most to the business—the products and services that make their organizations unique—and do so faster and more securely.

Many of the executives looking to accelerate this change within their organizations are instituting a cloud-first policy to reverse the burden of proof from "Why should we use the cloud?" to "Why shouldn't we use the cloud?" for all of the organization's technology projects.

Declaring a cloud-first policy is the last best practice I'll cover in this series, and I'll use this chapter to cover some of the common questions I get around what cloud-first looks like.

Where Are Organizations Declaring Cloud-First Policies?

Some executives apply this policy to individual business units, others across their entire organization. The scope often depends on the experience of each business unit, their goals, and their constraints. GE, for example, is a highly distributed organization with many different businesses that operate largely independent of one another, with some business units much further along their cloud journey than others. GE Oil & Gas is well along their journey and is living in a cloud-first operating model; other business units are close behind. Capital One, on the other hand, is cloud-first across their entire business.

Who Administers a Cloud-First Policy?

When applied across the entire organization, the cloud-first policy tends to impact many departments outside of central IT/technology. Procurement, legal, finance, business development, and product functions can all contribute to making cloud-first a reality. The more these departments know how to make cloud technology vendors work for them, and know why the organization is looking to leverage the cloud—to focus more on what matters to their business—the more active a role they can play in driving the organization to make cloud-first decisions.

My team and I implemented a cloud-first policy whilst I was the CIO of Dow Jones, and one of the first things we did was to create an escalation path with our finance department to highlight any request for a hardware-related capital expense. Any department that felt it needed to procure hardware instead of leverage our cloud capabilities had to explain why they couldn't accomplish what they were trying to do in the cloud before their purchase order would be approved. It didn't take many escalations for everyone to understand how serious our intentions were. Over time, our legal, procurement, and product teams started asking similar questions.

When Should You Declare a Cloud-First Organization?

When I first started this series on best practices, in September 2015, I planned on the series culminating with the point that a cloud-first policy comes after an organization has a lot of experience using the cloud in their business. This was my experience at Dow Jones. But, since then, I've met with hundreds of additional executives, all at different stages of the journey, and learned that many organizations institute a cloud-first policy much earlier in their journey—in some cases before they have any experience at all.

Some organizations have business cases so compelling they don't feel they need years of experience to be confident cloud-first is for them. A Fortune 100 enterprise I work with believes their developers will be at least 50 percent more productive when fully trained on and working in an AWS environment. This organization has more than 2,000 developers, and, as a result, will benefit from 1,000-plus man-days of additional development time per year as a result of their migration and cloud-first efforts. The idea of this is so attractive they *started* their journey with a cloud-first mentality.

Administer Sensibly

Anyone who's worked with me (hopefully) knows that I'm not a big fan of top-down policy unless it's absolutely necessary. When used sparingly, however, I've found it can be an effective way for leaders to create a change in behavior, accelerate that change, and help everyone understand what the organization's priorities are. Well-implemented policies come with a thorough communications plan that helps the organization understand the policy, the rationale behind it, and how it will impact their role. Communication, in my view, is one of a few characteristics that makes good leaders great.

PART III

Other Voices/Other Views

As I previously mentioned, I have talked with hundreds of tech executives and AWS partners about how cloud has impacted their world. In this part, I've included a collection of real-life stories about the critical importance of culture during large-scale cloud transformation. These authoritative, first-person accounts come from some of the most forward-thinking executives in business and technology—people like Bryan Landerman, CTO, Cox Automotive, Terren Peterson, vice president, Platform Engineering – Retail & Direct Bank at Capital One; Paul Hannan, CTO, SGN; Natty Gur, vice president and CIO of the Friedkin Group; and Jay Haque of The New York Public Library, and others.

In addition, I have invited key members of my AWS team—including Jonathan Allen, Phil Potloff, Ilya Epshteyn, Joe Chung, Thomas Blood, Miriam McLemore, and Mark Schwartz—to add their own perspectives and experience into the mix. I'm super fortunate to be able to work with these folks, all of whom have led transformations at some of the world's largest and well-known organizations.

For those of you who have been regular readers of the AWS Enterprise Collection,[75] there may be some thematic and strategic echoes in the pages that follow. But, there's still plenty of fresh and—hopefully—thought-provoking content in this collection.

75 https://medium.com/aws-enterprise-collection

Finally, bringing these thought leaders together means allowing their diverse viewpoints to stand on their own—not melding, muddying or mashing up their opinions in one monolithic chapter. This modular approach allows you to fully appreciate each individual contributor's insight and intelligence, and to apply the imparted knowledge within your own organization as you transform.

Moving forward, I would love to hear from those of you with additional experiences. If you've got a strong story to tell—good or bad—please let me know, and let's talk about posting it in future updates to this book. Everyone benefits from hearing the experiences of others!

CHAPTER 35

Capital One's Cloud Journey Through the Stages of Adoption by Terren Peterson, Vice President, Platform Engineering – Retail & Direct Bank at Capital One

Originally posted on 4/5/17: http://amzn.to/capital-one-cloud-journey

"He that will not apply new remedies must expect new evils; for time is the greatest innovator."

—Francis Bacon

Over the last few years, I've had the pleasure of working with hundreds of thought-leading executives who are leading large-scale cultural shifts[76] in their organizations. Few have done this better than Capital One, which has built a culture that seems to attract a number of executives that are not just great leaders…they're also builders and innovators that will shape the future of digital banking. Today I'm lucky to be able to host a guest chapter from Capital One's Terren Peterson, who has taught me quite a bit about what it takes to be successful leading a large-scale cloud migration.

76 http://amzn.to/culture-eats-strategy-for-breakfast

This contribution by: Terren Peterson

When Stephen asked me to write about our Cloud journey, I saw it as a privilege given that the move forward with AWS has been a broad team effort where thousands of engineers at Capital One have played different roles.

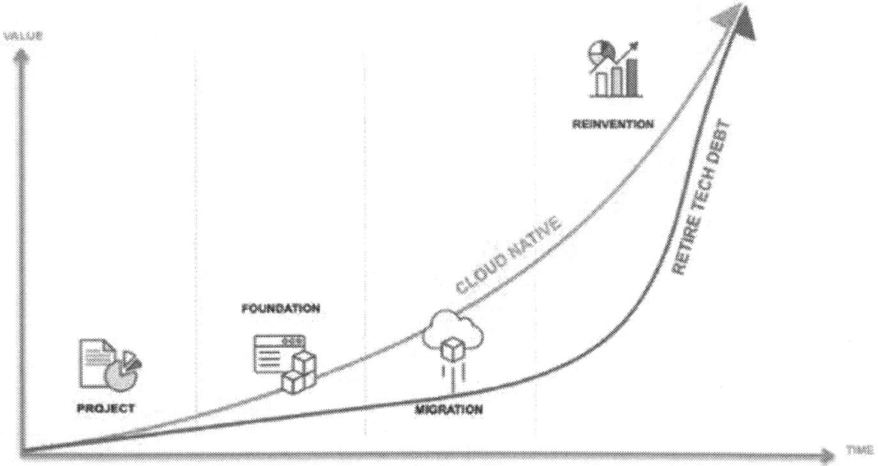

Stages of Adoption

In reviewing our journey over the past few years, I'm using the Stages of Adoption methodology that Stephen has outlined in earlier blog posts. It's a great structure to organize a multi-year effort, providing milestones to track progress along the way.

For context, Capital One is one of the nation's largest banks and offers credit cards, checking and savings accounts, auto loans, rewards, and online banking services for consumers and businesses. In 2016, we were ranked #1 on the *InformationWeek* Elite 100 list of the country's most innovative users of business technology.[77]

We are using or experimenting with nearly every AWS service, and are actively sharing our learnings through AWS Re:Invent as well as sharing some of our tooling through open source projects like Cloud Custodian.[78]

---

77 http://www.informationweek.com/2016-informationweek-elite-100-winners/d/d-id/1325060

78 https://github.com/capitalone/cloud-custodian

Stage 1—Project

Back in 2013-14, we started out our Public Cloud journey with what we called our "Experimentation Phase," leveraging AWS in our innovation labs[79] to test out the technology and operating model. In this initial stage, we had a limited number of individuals that touched the technology, and minimized the need for education to the broader organization. Those that did participate were highly motivated software engineers, some of which had familiarity with AWS before joining our company.

The Lab was a great place to start given the focus on new application development, and creating small-scale learning environments to prove out new products and servicing tools. Having a small footprint enabled us to test out different security tools, and how different processes and methods from our Private cloud environment externally.

After a successful trial in the Lab, the recommendation was made to continue to use Public Cloud based on the security model, the ability to provision infrastructure on the fly, the elasticity to handle purchasing demands at peak times, its high availability, and the pace of innovation.

Stage 2—Foundation

Moving into 2015, we added development & test environments to our AWS footprint, and enabled our first production deployments. This was a big step forward in the number of technology associates that needed expertise in the services, which influenced our thinking on how to scale our expertise.

79 http://www.capitalonelabs.com/

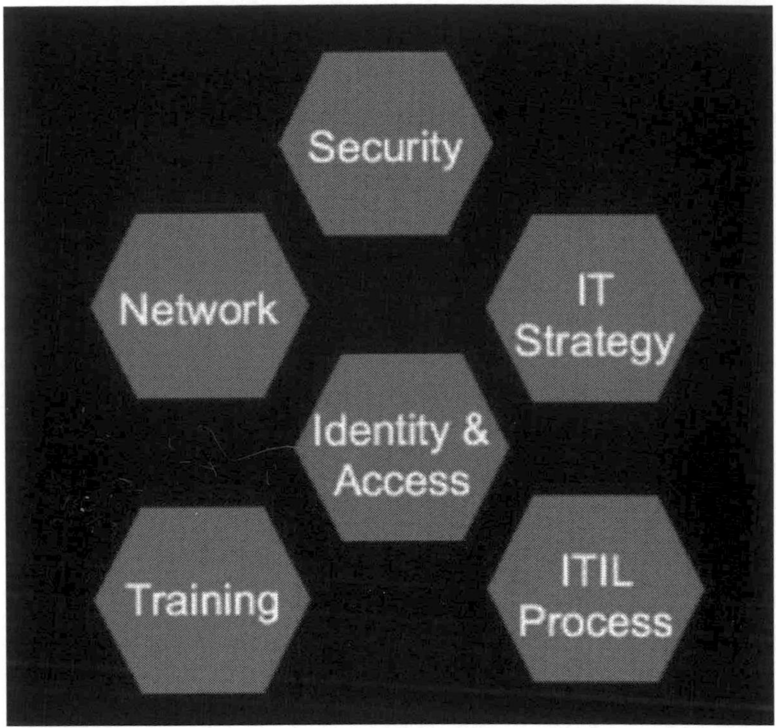

Foundational Elements of Capital One's Cloud Journey

It also initiated a period of investment as we began to use services like Direct Connect to extend our virtual network into AWS datacenters. Effort was required to integrate access management tools to make the environment seamless between our on-premises environment and the AWS US Regions. This reduced friction in our application delivery processes, and assisted in the transition to a Cloud-First infrastructure approach for all new applications.

During this time, we worked closely with multiple groups inside of AWS to establish Cloud engineering patterns. This included Professional Services, Technical Account Managers, Solutions Architects, and AWS Product Teams.

As the demand for the number of Cloud experienced associates expanded, we saw the clear need to build a Cloud Center of Excellence. This team was given the task to capture best practices and learnings from projects within internal teams, as well as build an education curriculum. This included establishing metrics and goals to quantify how many of our associates had been trained, and how many had achieved a level of expertise using the formal AWS certification program.

Stage 3—Migration

At ReInvent in 2015, we shared publicly our target to leverage our AWS competency to reduce our number of datacenters from eight in 2014, down to three in 2018. This broad objective rallied our organization around how we could use the Cloud to simplify our infrastructure, and drive savings back into the business.

Accomplishing a task this size requires a broad effort, one that continued to leverage the talent being cultivated by our Cloud Center of Excellence. At this point we have trained thousands of engineers in how to use AWS, and our number of AWS Certified Architects and Developers numbers in the hundreds.

As part of application migration, we've continued to work with AWS and their partners to assist on establishing processes and patterns for handling migration at scale. We are actively using the migration patterns described by AWS allocating applications into the 6 Rs (Chapter 6). This includes "Rehosting" when only minor changes are required, and more of a lift and shift strategy is appropriate vs. "Replatforming" or "Rearchitecting" when more significant investment is needed. Common drivers for this include performing kernel and JVM upgrades with the move, or using more native offerings within the applications like Amazon SQS or Amazon RDS.

Stage 4—Optimization

As our AWS footprint grows, we continually look for ways to optimize the cost and improve speed by automating reoccurring deployment activities. Some of the optimization efforts are "tuning" the infrastructure that's allocated for each application. Gradual reduction of EC2 instance sizes where unused capacity is detected, and changing Linux distribution versions can yield major reductions in the compute portion of your bill. This can improve business value for moving to the Cloud, as well as justify other infrastructure advances in automation and tooling.

Other optimization efforts have been bolder, refactoring traditional platforms to use a serverless model. We currently have several key applications that are currently converting over to this pattern, and we have staffed an Agile team to enable our software engineers to use these new services similar to what was done initially with a CCoE. For more insight into the value of serverless, check out some insights here: https://medium.com/capital-one-developers/serverless-is-the-paas-i-always-wanted-9e9c7d925539.

Given the robust growth of AWS services, we expect that optimization will be an ongoing effort, requiring engineering resources to validate new services as they are released and map to our application portfolio. It's also one where we can allocate more resources to once we have closed more datacenters, and moved a greater footprint to AWS.

CHAPTER 36

Cox Automotive's Road Trip: Speeding to the Cloud by Bryan Landerman, Chief Technology Officer, Cox Automotive

◆ ◆ ◆

Before I dive into my experience, the journey, and our learnings, let me provide some context about who we are and where we started.

Where We Came From

At Cox Automotive,[80] we're the leading provider of software and services to the automotive industry—from Manheim's physical and online auctions to Autotrader[81] and Kelley Blue Book,[82] and from dealership websites and service scheduling to all aspects of operational software like ERP, CRM, BI, and parts. We're comprised of 40+ acquisitions, with more than 15 Engineering locations and 52 data centers in North America in a company with a global footprint in 90 countries and 34,000 team members.

Growth by acquisition can lead to a lot of interesting dynamics. For Engineering, it means we have IBM Report Program Generator (RPG) on the iSeries, Oracle DBs, Oracle Exadata, and IBM DataPower, .Net, Java, and Python and we've even had some Massachusetts General Hospital Utility

80 https://www.coxautoinc.com/future-cox-automotive/

81 https://www.autotrader.com/

82 https://www.kbb.com/

Multi-Programming System (MUMPS) in the mix. Sadly, that's just to name a few. Put simply, we have a diverse set of cultures, technologies, and techniques. While we're one big, happy family, our journey to the cloud is complex and much like many other enterprises face today.

How We Got Started

As I reflect on where we began and what led us to where we are today, it all seems quite obvious in hindsight. We started small and achieved early wins. The successes came with learnings and created enough confidence to continue adopting. Our footprint and interest grew but began stalling as the migration cost analysis for certain solutions didn't make financial sense. For example, while we had to provision hardware for two times peak Super Bowl traffic with an equal disaster recovery (DR) site for Autotrader.com, the migration cost outweighed the gains. We paused work in those kinds of situations as approaches and pricing models evolved, but we knew that the cloud was our future. So, we continued investing in tooling and building out a Cloud Center of Excellence so we would be ready.

In late 2015 and early 2016, we explored Microsoft Azure, AWS, Google Cloud, and Pivotal Cloud Foundry. We decided to prioritize integration of our skills, conversations, technologies, and products, which led to selecting a single cloud provider—at least for now—for all but exceptionally specialized workloads. We decided AWS was our path forward and started by asking our teams, "Why not AWS?" We weren't ready for mass adoption, but we knew preventing divergence would give time for our strategy to emerge. We asked our teams to assume AWS was the right choice and requested that they prove it couldn't work before going down an alternate path.

At AWS re:Invent that year, everything clicked, and I mean EVERYTHING. My leadership team and I left knowing what we had to do, and our head of architecture and I set out to make it happen.

What unfolded in the subsequent 10 months started with the AWS team and centered around some of the concepts outlined throughout Stephen's book, namely Best Practice One: Provide Executive Support (Chapters 11-14) and Considering a Mass Migration to the Cloud? (Chapter 4) rooted in the 6 R's (Chapter 6). With the diversity I mentioned above, figuring out the plan was difficult but we knew where we had to start, both for ourselves and the company: What is cloud, and why does it matter?

Now, you might be asking yourself, "Doesn't every enterprise and technology company already know that?" I can't answer that for your organization, but I can tell you that most people at Cox Automotive hadn't taken a step back to think about what was really happening in the technology industry. We had to help them grasp the macro transformation and get comfortable with the cloud and, more important, get comfortable with making such a large commitment to adopt and migrate.

Simple, right? Well, getting to where we are today was definitely painful at times but as Andy Jassy has said, and Stephen and many of us have repeated, "There's no compression algorithm for experience." The experience has been worthwhile, despite taking longer than we wanted. And, we learned a LOT along the way!

We're still learning and refining. While I don't have regrets, there are things I would do differently if given a second chance and things I'd do again that made a huge difference. The following details our approach and the lessons we learned along the way.

Establishing the What and Why

I used the history of the energy industry to provide the much-needed macro perspective on the shift in computing. (I read *The Big Switch* by Nicholas Carr, thanks to a recommendation from Drew Firment when we met at re:Invent. Read it!). The presentation articulated—for everyone from our executives to product leaders to engineers—why giving up control of our infrastructure and adopting PaaS was the right thing to do. The presentation really resonated, and I knew the message landed when a senior product leader said, "I saw the topic and thought, I already know about the cloud. But, this opened my eyes and is making me think differently about why it's so important, especially to me in product management. Thank you."

Learning: Don't assume everyone is on the same page. Spend the time to make sure cloud is a companywide, company-owned initiative. If it's viewed as a pure cost savings play or simply a technology initiative, you're setting up for failure. There is a lot more value than cost savings, and there's a bigger shift happening that must be understood!

Building the Business Case

Our business case is rooted in a sophisticated model that considers many factors and risks to create a balanced point of view on cost and value. We put in a significant amount of time gathering data (refresh rates, licensing agreements, and data center and hardware reuse) and vetting it with our teams, including mapping our applications to the 6 R's, which is a solid framework for reasoning about your migration and simplifies how you articulate the complexity that exists in your environment. This allowed us to develop a business case with confidence.

Learning: It's important that this isn't simply viewed as a data center move because it's more complex and involved than that. Spend the time thinking it through! Being able to sign a deal with AWS that allows your teams to execute against the plan that's right for the business versus constantly having the CapEx to OpEx and cost bubble conversation is worth the extra legwork at the beginning!

Planning the Approach

We decided to eat the data center elephant one bite at a time. This allowed us to build up our Cloud Business Office (a single owner for both execution and enablement) and prove our migration capabilities and skills as each migration progressed, learning and adjusting as we went.

1. We're starting by picking data centers that allow us to focus, minimize politics, and reduce the number of people involved. They are occupied by a single business unit, which typically means a single Engineering team in a single physical location. This allows us to increase support, simplify training, and rally our teams.
2. We aggressively migrate out of the given data center based on the 6 R's and then close that data center.
3. Rinse and repeat!

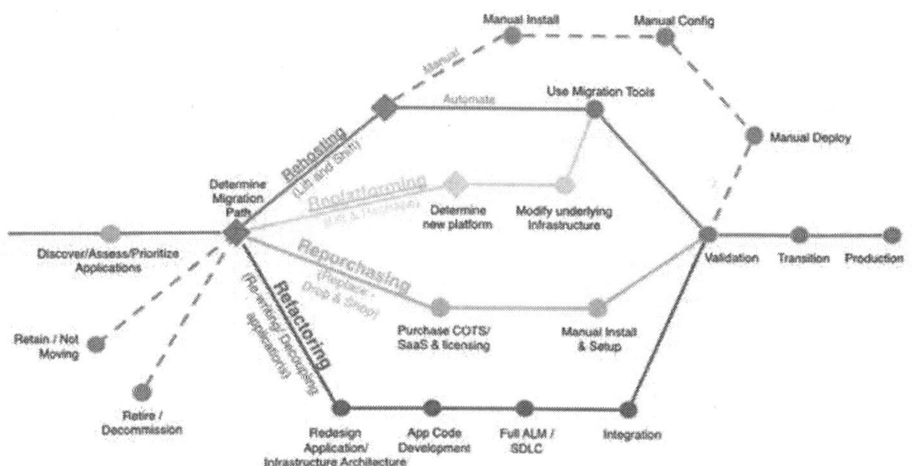

Source: http://amzn.to/migration-strategies

We're doing this data center consolidation in parallel with cloud migration and attacking multiple data centers at the same time. By combining the workstreams, we're reducing unnecessary data center to data center to cloud migrations. This approach helps minimize the cost bubble while maximizing cost avoidance and long-term savings.

Learning: AWS has some great resources available to push your thinking and evolve your point of view; take advantage of them. The discussions we had with our AWS contacts helped us land on this approach and articulate key concepts like the cost bubble as we built our business case. Capturing value early and often is critical, and as you know, cost savings resonates with everyone! That said, some migrations were cost-neutral or costlier than existing on-prem architecture and infrastructure. Taking a holistic approach created balance in our migration portfolio and resulted in a favorable business case.

Harnessing Momentum

We had a lot of momentum toward cloud in the Engineering organization. We focused that energy by asking our teams to justify why AWS wouldn't work for them, whereas AWS was pre-approved.

Learning: Momentum is critical, so find ways to embrace it. There is a significant amount of change that will need to take place in the daily lives of your team; how you build software and the tools you use will change overnight. Having momentum will increase your rate of change and accelerate the building of your cloud community. Our momentum crystalized our internal conversations about the cost bubble because it was clear that without offsetting activities and a coordinated program, our momentum would create runaway cost growth and very likely reduce our ability to accelerate value delivery.

Finding a Partner

You'll have the choice of many partners to help you with your migration and strategy. For us, it made sense to work directly with AWS. We wanted a partner who also had skin in the game, and we felt like AWS would be incented to help us succeed. Our migration was—and is!—a major undertaking that ultimately benefits AWS too.

During our 10-month expedition, I found that we weren't sure what we needed and therefore didn't know how to ask for help. There were periods of confusion and a non-linear path. I've watched our partnership with AWS evolve as we collectively learn more about this journey.

Learning: Having the right partner is crucial. While partnering with AWS was right for us, I'm not sure that it's right for everyone. Find someone you can trust to guide you toward what is best for your business. In general, I look to avoid situations where others may benefit from dysfunction or inexperience.

Also, spend time talking to those who have done this before. Ask AWS, or whoever your partner is, to connect you with other clients. Learn early and often; we didn't do enough of that.

Investing in the Foundation

We have significant momentum, but are still missing some key ingredients to ensure long-term success. With 52 data centers, I'm extremely sensitive about executing a migration that takes us from snowflake applications in snowflake datacenters to snowflake applications in AWS.

Learning: Invest early on the foundation, including:

1. Establish your landing zone
2. Train your team
3. Transform your security practices
4. Simplify your CI/CD practices and operational tooling
5. Establish an API approach including a micro-services POV, tooling, and reference architectures, especially if you have monoliths to decompose!

Communicating Early and Often

This is a complex process with many factors. Having buy in from all levels of the system is critical to the execution of this transformation.

Learning: Keep your stakeholders in the loop by communicating early and often. Transitioning ownership and accountability from the core group developing the business case to those that will ultimately own the execution is critical. Include it in your plan—timing is everything!

In closing, we still have many data centers and at least one more business case to put together—there are many bites left in this elephant.

Stephen has outlined strategies and techniques in Part I, The Stages of Adoption, and Part II, 7 Best Practices, that will guide you through this journey. I think you'll find that those of us who have been through some phase of this movement can easily relate to Stephen's learnings and that helps to unify us. We're happy to help so don't be shy, reach out and learn. Our collective adoption of the cloud will lead to the next big shift in technology!

CHAPTER 37

AQR Capital's Cloud Journey: The First Production Application By Neal Pawar, CTO and Michael Raposa, VP, Cloud Services, AQR Capital

◆ ◆ ◆

As companies start making their journey into the cloud, many firms get stuck on the first step. We thought it would be helpful to provide detailed prescriptive guidance on this crucial step by describing the journey that our firm, AQR Capital Management, a global, quantitative investment manager, took from having a zero AWS footprint to deploying our first production workloads.

Making the Cloud Business Case

When it comes to making the business case for cloud, our first recommendation is to not limit the business case to Total Cost of Ownership (TCO). In fact, if at all possible, we recommend removing TCO from the discussion completely.

It's a catchy headline to say how much you can save from a TCO perspective if you move to the cloud, but in truth it's not quite as simple as that. What is included in a TCO calculation can make a big difference. For example, simply comparing the purchase and vendor support cost of a physical server vs the comparable EC2 instance is not fair. In this simple comparison the physical server can be significantly cheaper. This comparison fails because it does not accurately include all the peripheral costs that go into maintaining a server on-premises over its lifetime. To accurately compare total costs, additional expenses for people, rack space, electrical, networking, cooling, etc. need to be included in the on-premises analysis. To be clear, we're not suggesting one *shouldn't* look at the costs involved before and after, we're saying that moving to the cloud should not be looked at as an "apples to apples" cost play.

We took a different approach in building our cloud business case. First, we focused on use cases where an on-premises implementation would be time consuming and expensive, like deploying a GPU fleet or developing a map-reduce cluster. Second, we believe that the cloud has also become the "New Normal". Roughly 10 years ago virtualization transitioned to a best practice in the datacenter. We believe that cloud is making a similar transition. With some of the largest and most well-known financial services firms operating production workloads on AWS, there are numerous indicators that cloud has become a more acceptable solution for running IT services.

We're also fortunate that our firm has an established culture of innovation. As researchers, we embrace experimentation. Cloud allows us to experiment in a way that is not easily possible on-premises. Financial research consumes large amounts of data and computation. Our researchers have a never-ending appetite for data, only exacerbated by this era of "big data" and new interesting, non-obvious data sets. By embracing cloud, we have been able to start satiating this appetite. Additionally, researchers can also experiment with technologies like Deep Learning and Big Data Analytics without making big upfront investments.

Starting with a Proof-of-Concept

As Stephen suggests throughout the Stages of Adoption, we recommend that you start with a proof-of-concept. At AQR, we engaged with a small group of researchers and engineers who had some excellent use cases; the implementation of which could be accelerated by adopting a cloud-first approach. The project, which we will describe in a bit more detail below, was a wonderful opportunity to prove both the technical feasibility as well as the business benefit for running on AWS. In particular, we made sure the proof of concept was not throw-away, but solved a specific real-world problem that we came to rely on once it had been stress tested, passed QA, and completed acceptance testing.

Running our proof-of-concept was our newly organized Cloud Services team. Similar to the Cloud Center of Excellence mentioned by Stephen, the CS team is focused on delivering cloud value to the engineering teams at AQR. This team oversees AQR's cloud initiative and works in conjunction with the CISO and AQR's Engineering department heads. The team ensures that the cloud architecture is designed for agility with high levels of security, operational robustness, operational control, and auditability. Finally the team works with key business stakeholders to explain cloud risks and the mitigating controls designed into our cloud environment.

Once you've got a good proof-of-concept in place, you need to start building a coalition to help drive this across your organization. Do not think of the cloud as just another Engineering project. In order to get the benefits of the cloud, many of your processes and even organizational structure will need to change to achieve the full benefits of an adaptable infrastructure, experimentation & innovation, and DevOps. We recommend you get buy-in from senior stakeholders outside of Engineering. If you don't get this buy-in, you may be opening the door later for AWS initiatives to lose momentum at the first "bump in the road". By getting support at the start, these teams have a vested interest in a successful adoption of cloud computing.

Writing a Cloud Policy

Part of building consensus across the organization on adopting cloud is to develop a Cloud Policy. In simple, easy-to-understand language, this document lays down the rules for operating in the cloud. This document will be used across the senior leadership team to get buy-in on the operational processes for running workloads in AWS. The leadership of these teams should be included in the document's development as it is key to making sure they have "skin in the game" for your cloud strategy. Make this document a "living document" by tracking changes or highlighting exceptions as they occur, helping auditors to follow along. Many organizations refer to this as the "Thou shalt" document, i.e. unbreakable rules for operating in AWS. The CIS AWS Foundations Benchmark provides many example policies that you can incorporate into your policy document, which include:

- All root accounts will protected with an MFA
- Internet gateways will not be used
- AWS IAM Password Policy will match Corporate Password Policy.
- Encryption at Rest and In Flight is required for all AWS services

Once the document is finished the Cloud Services (CS) team can then proceed to develop the governance and operational guidelines and processes used to implement the policy. This way the CS team has clear direction on what needs to be implemented operationally and from a security perspective in order to operate "correctly" on AWS. The policy is used to provide clear direction from all senior stakeholders on how the company should operate in the cloud.

We recommend using a consulting firm to develop this document if you don't have the internal expertise to do so. A consultant firm would have generic versions of this policy document that you can build off of and tailor to your company. In addition, it's important that this policy document is independently verified and validated as you don't want to make any mistakes in this part of the process.

Without this document and these guidelines, it will be too easy for the CS team to make simple mistakes or worse diverge from a corporate standard accidentally. If this occurs, the AWS project will be put in jeopardy. All it takes is a simple governance mistake — even in a development environment — to derail the AWS project. For example, assigning a public IP to an EC2 instance even in development can have serious project and reputational repercussions for the security and risk teams.

Multi-Cloud?

For us, the multi-cloud debate began right after we decided to go to the cloud.

From a technology perspective, we viewed multi-cloud as a strategic hindrance. We felt that a multi-cloud approach would limit us to the lowest-common-denominator of features across clouds. This feature reduction takes away many of the managed service type offerings that make the cloud proposition so compelling. In a full multi-cloud strategy, we are effectively not embracing the many new design patterns, e.g. serverless, that can further enable our developers.

However, there were concerns from the risk and compliance teams around the single vendor risk associated with such an important part of the firm's operations. We created a strategy to mitigate this risk.

First, we developed a multi-region strategy with a HOT/WARM failover scenario. AWS has made this process significantly easier with the release of both more North American regions and Direct Connect Gateway. By being multi-region, we have not alleviated the single vendor risk, but we have removed the risk associated with a geographic outage at a single AWS region.

Next, we abstracted away the operating system using containers (specifically Docker). One of the primary benefits is that it separates the underlying platform from the application. This makes it easier to migrate from on-premises to AWS and to another cloud if need be.

Third, we have completely automated our cloud deployments. This has two benefits to mitigate single vendor risk:

1. The entire environment is in code so we can easily audit what needs to be changed if we need to change cloud providers. Essentially we could transform this code to the configuration of a different provider.

2. With automated deployments, changing providers is just a matter of changing the automation. It is certainly a difficult task, but still orders of magnitude easier than doing this by hand.

Additionally, we use simple low-cost abstraction layers where appropriate. For example, we have written a simple wrapper around Amazon Simple Queue Service (SQS) as it has a simple application interface that is common across many messaging platforms. Developers integrate with the wrapper and we can easily swap out the underlining SQS component without changing the developer facing API. Please note that we try to avoid writing abstraction layer as much as possible. We believe that adding these layers forces us to keep up with AWS's pace of innovation in areas that aren't core to our business, which can negatively impact our investments in software engineering. We avoid these layers except in those cases where he layer is obviously needed and easy to implement without compromising functionality of the underlying service.

Discussions around being able to negotiate better prices with the vendor when using multi-cloud were dismissed. While price negotiation is a common argument made for multi-cloud, we found that argument lacked depth. Amazon has an established history of lowering costs for AWS. Additionally, the cloud market is very cost competitive and we didn't see that changing any time soon. Competitive pressures would continue to drive costs down. Therefore, the expense associated with a multi-cloud strategy will likely exceed any cost savings associated with price negotiations.

Finally, there's a slightly different way to think about multi-cloud. While our philosophy is not to dumb-down the environment to the lowest common denominator across the major cloud providers, we also don't put all our eggs in one basket. We have found that between Software-as-a-Service (SaaS) and other Cloud Infrastructure providers, there are distinct areas where we might prefer one over the other. For example, we make use of a popular ticketing system that is hosted in the cloud — and we're very happy with it. Similarly some of our more Windows centric workloads run elsewhere. Obviously we try to do this when there are little to no requirements to cross pollinate workloads, i.e. where there is little communication between cloud hosted applications — which is quite possible, especially with the SaaS solutions.

Find the Right Consulting Partner

As Stephen describes as a best practice, one of the first steps in your cloud journey should include partnering with an AWS consultant. By using a partner you can speed cloud adoption by using additional contract staff to augment existing staff. But more importantly, you can leverage a partner's prior knowledge, learning from past mistakes and gaining insight into best practices — so you don't have to make these same mistakes yourself.

Be sure to properly vet consultants at the start of the engagement. We've had experience at where these partners have not delivered consultants that meet our standards. You should confirm that consultants not only have the technical skills that you need, but also make sure that they are a cultural fit for the organization. We like to hold consultants to a hiring bar as high as internal staff hires – which sometimes might mean waiting until you get the right person. It can be frustrating, but it is worth it – you don't get too many chances to get this right.

Engage with a consultant that has "pre-canned" templates and processes for cloud migrations. These building block components are used to set up the foundational AWS pieces, (e.g. Amazon Virtual Private Cloud (VPC), AWS Direct Connect) and are key to accelerating adoption. It is much easier to modify an existing template then build a new one. Again you are learning from their mistakes and using their best practices that they know already work. Ask to see the consultant's templates and documented processes. Consultants who have done this work before will have deliverables from other customers available for your review. This document review is a great way to ensure that you are working with a partner that meets your standards.

At AQR, we engaged with several partners. We leveraged a "fail fast" approach and experimented by engaging with several partners simultaneously.

Our goal was to learn the best ways to migrate and operate on AWS from as many partners as possible.

Migrating Your First Application

Choosing your first application to migrate is a key decision in the AWS adoption. A failure with the first application can be a setback to the entire migration effort.

We recommend that you focus on an application that is "Cloud Obvious". You are looking for an application that is a clear fit for operating on AWS. Your goal in selecting this application is to ensure that no reasonable person will disagree to moving this application to AWS.

Here are some things to look for in a "Cloud Obvious" application:

- There should be clear business benefit that can be unlocked by moving the application to the cloud.
- The application should be low risk. How your organization defines that risk will vary. For example, an application that uses only publicly available datasets could be a good low risk use case.
- The application can and should leverage cloud benefits (e.g. scale-up/down, serverless)
- Lastly the application should be well "contained", meaning the application has few downstream dependencies. The more "stand-alone" the app is, the easier it will be to migrate as their will be fewer dependencies with on-premises applications.

At AQR, we focused on the research workloads (on non-proprietary data) as the first application group to migrate.

AQR is a quantitative asset management firm, and as such our investment decisions are fully encapsulated in our numerical models and systematic trading processes. Our researchers innovate by developing new investment signals and trading strategies through rigorously testing ideas against many years of data (known as back testing). Access to elastic compute with the ability to auto-scale to the demands of our research teams enables AQR to innovate with maximum effectiveness.

This HPC cluster was our first application to migrate to AWS. The application met all of the criteria for a "Cloud Obvious" application. First, the POC successfully proved without any doubts that AWS was a technological feasible solution. Second, the cluster fits perfectly into the scale-up/down model. AWS instances automatically scale based on demand and we only pay for what we need. Third, our research jobs are idempotent, which means we can run the jobs on AWS Spot instances with significant savings off the on demand price. In addition, cost effective and highly scalable data structures and storage are available on AWS. All the AWS data solutions scale to levels that can support the compute requirements as the cluster scales. Finally, the idempotent and stateless nature of the research application allows us to easily leverage several cloud benefits including multi-AZ design, scale up/down, and immutable architectures.

But most important of all, researchers can now experiment with new technologies and methods. On-premises, the "toolkit" for experimentation is limited. In the cloud, researchers can not only experiment faster, but they can also experiment with new technologies and techniques without making significant financial and time investments. This allows our firm to develop models faster and innovate further.

Conclusions

Here are our key takeaways for your cloud adoption and digital transformation:

- Your first application should be "Cloud Obvious"
- Try to ignore TCO as a primary cloud driver
- Build a policy document that describes your rules for operating on AWS
- Get support from senior leadership outside of IT on your cloud and digital transformation journey

- Develop a multi-cloud strategy which may not include multiple cloud providers
- Engage with a Partner to help build-out your initial Cloud platform and practices

CHAPTER 38

New York Public Library's Cloud Journey by Jay Haque, Information Technology Executive, The New York Public Library

Originally posted on 6/21/16: http://amzn.to/NYPL-cloud-journey

"A library is the delivery room for the birth of ideas, a place where history comes to life."

—Norman Cousins

I had the pleasure to meet Jay Haque a few years ago when he started leading the New York Public Library's (NYPL) cloud journey. I was on a similar journey at Dow Jones, and we had the opportunity to share our stories. A couple years ago, I was delighted to see Jay comment on one of my posts, and after hearing a bit more about how his journey at NYPL had progressed, I thought his perspective on best practice would benefit the broader market.

It turns out that I wasn't alone, and Jay and his team were named the winners of the 2016 AWS City on a Cloud Innovation Challenge.[83] Thank you, Jay—I'm looking forward to seeing you and the NYPL continue to transform the way you deliver technology for your customers! Here is a recounting of Jay's cloud journey with NYPL.

83 https://aws.amazon.com/stateandlocal/cityonacloud/

When Stephen asked me to write about my experience with incubating a Cloud Center of Excellence, I revisited his "7 Best Practices for Your Enterprise's Journey to the Cloud" post and found that my company's experience aligns with these practices.

The New York Public Library's journey speaks directly to the concept of scale. A large team or a big project is not necessary to start the enterprise cloud journey, you can start with a small, focused effort, geared at establishing your practice and poising it to scale. Significant top-down support with overwhelmingly strong vision and air cover—along with financial backing—are any technologists' dream come true, but we know that doesn't always happen. In absence of this, start somewhere, no matter how small.

Our journey started with the simple idea of building a configuration management platform in the cloud to prove the redesign of our primary website[84] and the release of our famed Digital Collections[85] site would benefit tremendously from it. We realized quickly that the cloud, and specifically AWS, accelerated project completion times through increased automation, reduced costs with right-sizing, provided redundancies, and enabled seamless scaling capabilities that would otherwise be cost prohibitive. Our journey had humble beginnings and the resulting success has been extraordinary; the use of AWS by our world-class development, product, project and DevOps teams won us the honor of being named the winner of the 2016 AWS City on a Cloud Innovation Challenge in the Best Practice category.

Working with Control Group, an AWS partner, we devised a plan that not only delivered the necessary infrastructure for a web property but also a configuration management platform, which would accelerate future projects. The core idea here is that, while the web property will one day be retired, the management platform will scale as needed and will automate the infrastructure builds for a limitless number of sites. The project would be completed in no more than 12 weeks with less than 50 percent allocation of the team time.

84 http://www.nypl.org/

85 http://digitalcollections.nypl.org/

To give the clearest sense of how our project aligned with Stephen's seven best practices, I present our experience in the same format.

1. Provide Executive Support

Top-down executive support gives your initiative purpose and weight. In terms of scale, start with what you can get, even if it's only one executive or one project. Stay focused on building further executive support as you rack up wins. This will help you garner support organically.

When we first discussed the journey, the Library had two major SaaS projects underway, a newly appointed CTO, limited human resources, and faced potential budget cuts. As you might imagine, the appetite to start a large-scale, focused cloud initiative was low.

Still, we knew we had to start somewhere or risk falling behind industry trends. Our CTO backed building a configuration management system in the cloud as a low-risk, low-resource utilization project that would be completed quickly. Once that project illustrated the value of the cloud, interest from the CTO and other executives grew considerably and would be the foundation of support for the rest of our journey.

To obtain the necessary support of the project, I focused on the following five factors:

1. **Leverage an existing project.** We positioned the configuration management platform as a means of accelerating future, high-priority projects. By building the proposed platform, we would increase execution velocity on future projects requiring infrastructure.
2. **Start small.** This enabled the remaining three factors to play in our favor:
3. **Maximize the probability of success and minimize risk.** The project was small enough that failure was unlikely. In the event that it did fail, the cost and business impact would have been low.

4. **Execute fast.** Small projects that drag on can be a nuisance. The spotlight was on showing immediate results and moving progressively towards larger projects.
5. **Talk scalability.** Though the project was small, we highlighted how various components of it would scale for future successes.

2. Educate Staff

Technologist are always learning—it's the very nature of what we do. In terms of scale, be mindful of the capacity, or available time, to learn. Then, motivate your team and provide any resources you can. Focus on learning the core elements that are going to provide the greatest immediate return. For us, orchestration, configuration management, and code became the centerpiece of everything, so we focused on learning these things first.

At the start of the configuration management platform project, the team was well aware of our ambitious goals. The weeks leading up to kicking off our first AWS project were filled with discussions about the service: how and where we might leverage it, partner presentations, and learning about what other organization were doing. This built a sense of excitement and strong willingness to learn. As the project began, sufficient air cover was garnered by the allocation of resource time through our PMO practice and CTO level support. Finally, in absence of AWS offered courses, we partook in partner-provided workshops.

3. Create a Culture of Experimentation

In leveraging a partner to help kick start our journey, we focused on fostering a culture of experimentation.

The partner presented technical ideas well in advance of implementation, giving the systems engineering team sufficient time to explore and test-drive the technology in our AWS sandbox environment. The sandbox provided a flexible environment that allowed the systems engineers to quickly build and tear down stacks and experiment with various solutions to complex problems. We explored instantiation of our web infrastructure using various methods including using AMIs, complete orchestration using Puppet, and syncing code from external repositories or S3. This level of experimentation, along with deep-dive discussion with our partner, provided a forum to meld our ideas with emerging best practices, ensuring we effectively weighed competing technologies.

The culture of experimentation seeded in those early days of our journey is still very much in place now. Engineers and developers with varying specialties are encouraged to experiment with all aspects of the cloud. We architected and incubated a media-transcoding pipeline using Elastic Transcoder during a one-day internal hackathon. We could not have realized this level of autonomy in experimentation without AWS, which provides a means for organizations to experiment without a significant financial investment.

4. Pick the Right Partners

We could not have made ground as quickly as we did without Control Group. In terms of scale, staff augmentation infused our small systems engineering team with proven AWS expertise. Control Group offers customers established best practices for automating system builds and deployments in the cloud that they also use within their own software development operation. Their practical experience with the AWS, both as a service provider and a user, helped accelerate our journey by drastically reducing our learning curve.

Partner involvement in the early stages of our journey supported efforts to educate our team, internal experimentation, and the application of best practices in the work we did. This close relationship enabled continued success.

5. Create a Cloud Center of Excellence

As our initial AWS project was nearing completion, we focused on the "what's next" element. In terms of scale, we focused on going BIG. This would require substantial support.

The development and systems engineering teams discussed how to build future projects on AWS. This was the beginning of understanding how roles would change, how we would work together, and realizing how much this way of working would impact overall velocity. We maintained partner support as we moved our primary website into AWS and followed by independently working on the release of the highly anticipated Digital Collections site on the platform. The Digital Collections site was large and complex enough to truly test our ability to operate in the cloud. Our systems engineering and development teams had amassed sufficient expertise in the months leading up to the release and having Control Group at arm's reach gave us full confidence in our ability to architect the right solution for the high-demand web site.

We're still very much working on our CCoE, and even on the concept of DevOps. We're learning what the competing forces are and asking hard questions about how to balance them. For example, we want velocity, but don't want to sacrifice integrity of our systems. We want standardization, but not too much overhead. These questions are all asked in terms of optimization: we've gone from months to deliver infrastructure to just days, and yet we're continually asking, "How can we do this better and faster?"

6. Implement a Hybrid Architecture

This was an absolute necessity for the New York Public Library, as we have a significant on-premises infrastructure that we must continue to operate. Our primary focus is on the building new products in AWS and moving those sites that we can (easily) onto the platform. The organization's appetite to move legacy content to the cloud is growing; however, the resources necessary to execute a move are at times better utilized towards moving new products forward. In terms of scale, we must pick our migration targets wisely, and consider all our options with legacy systems. Migration is one; deprecation is another. In the meantime, we actively support a hybrid architecture.

7. Implement a Cloud-First Policy

We are partially here. We are very good at building web-centric systems on AWS, and these are almost always built in the cloud. In fact, there must be compelling technical reason for us to deploy a new web solution on-premises. We've still got some learning to do on how to deploy other types of business applications in the cloud, and even these cases, we tend to ask if a SaaS product is a viable alternative. The road to a cloud-first policy is paved with wins from the journey; the cost and efficiency benefits speak for themselves and enable the realization that cloud-first is the optimal strategy.

Summary

NYPL was just starting its cloud journey when Stephen and I first met to share our stories. We've come a long way since then and the model for success has become clearer in that time. Stephen's masterful articulation of this in the seven best practices is beneficial to any organization, at any stage, of its journey. I hope this piece was helpful to those considering how and where to start their journey. I would love to hear about your own experience as it will add to the collective *library* of success stories, and every story is a learning opportunity.

CHAPTER 39

Channel 4 Builds Retention, Revenue, and Reach by Making the Move to AWS by Barry O'Reilly, founder of ExecCamp and co-author *Lean Enterprise*

◆ ◆ ◆

CHANNEL 4 ARE ONE OF the UK's largest television networks. In 2012, like most other television networks at the time, they recognized they were losing viewers, advertising revenue was on the downswing, and they lacked new avenues to reach new customers. As a result, they urgently needed to come up with new ways to leverage their content, innovate their products and services, and generate future growth and sustainability for their business. At the same time, Channel 4 was very challenged with the technology capability in their organization. There had been a history of difficulties and delays for a number of the key initiatives the organization had tried to deliver—regularly going down under high demand and stress loads.

For a variety of reasons, there was a fractious relationship between the business side of the organization and the technology department. While the business group was housed in beautiful offices, the technology team was down the road—stuffed into dusty gray cubicles in a building that was from the 1940s. There was a checkered past of poor collaboration and low trust between the two parts of the organization.

One of the most popular on-air talents was the chef Jamie Oliver, whose show was watched by about 10 percent of the UK population every week. At the end of the show, Jamie would tell viewers to get recipes for that episode on the Channel 4 website, and you can imagine what would happen next. The Channel 4 website would go from just a few thousand visitors, to an instant crush of 5 million visitors. The website would crash and the opportunity to capitalize on all that viewer interest evaporated. Not only that, it meant Channel 4 was forced to organize the show schedule around this technology challenge, avoiding running certain shows at certain times to ensure the main website wouldn't crash.

The challenge from a technology perspective was, how could Channel 4 scale their technologies capabilities to meet all that demand, delight customers, and make the most of their content? They didn't want to invest loads and loads of money in expensive infrastructure that would only be necessary a few times a week at most. But there was mounting pressure to build much greater capacity for future initiatives. The business had, for example, come up with a new service called the Scrapbook that would provide opportunities for Channel 4 to monetize their content while innovating their products and services. The idea was similar to what now has become Pinterest, where the television station would create partnerships with different companies to advertise their products that the on-air talent would talk about on the show. So, for example, Jamie Oliver might say, "Well look at these great new knives I've bought from Henckels." Then, after the show ran, viewers could go to Jamie's scrapbook and there would be links to the knives he used on the show, or to the grocers who sold the food he used in his recipes.

To further complicate the situation, delivering the new Scrapbook would require the involvement of several stakeholder groups. These groups included the Channel 4 leadership team, the business product and technology division, a design agency that was trying to come up with interesting ideas to create the product, the Channel 4 operations team, and the delivery team which was responsible for actually building the software.

But that wasn't all. There were new partners including the company I worked with ThoughtWorks, Amazon Web Services, which was chosen to host the Channel 4's infrastructure in the cloud, and they were tasked with integrating the infrastructure with a new NoSQL database technology called MongoDB from 10gen. So, there were up to eight different entities, each trying to come together as one to achieve Channel 4's goals. The icing on the cake was that this particular configuration had never been tested together at scale—the team was truly breaking new ground.

Stephen often jokes that, "Culture eats strategy for breakfast." But when you've got multiple cultures in an organization, how do you create one culture in order to succeed? This was the challenge we faced, and was one of the guiding principles we had on this team. When you have multiple different companies trying to deliver, the tendency is if things go wrong, everybody blames the other person. Because we had such a short timeframe to deliver, and with such a challenging outcome to achieve, we really worked hard to create a one-team mindset, behaviors, and culture across all these different entities of the business, the technology, and the various different suppliers all contributing to deliver this product.

Our guiding principle was that we could only be successful if *all* of us were successful. Individually being successful for any of these entities didn't amount to anything. To achieve the desired outcomes we had to achieve in the timeframe we had, this meant creating a culture of collective accountability over individual blame. And for a lot of the technologies we were using, we were finding the thresholds for what they were capable of doing. For instance, pairing MongoDB with AWS to handle loads of 2,500 pages per second had not been done before. The uncertainty was high, and the constraints were challenging.

We rented an office space near Channel 4's main building and set ourselves up in a room where we were working and collaborating together all the time. At the top of the door, we had a statement called the retrospective prime directive. The primer for running a continuous improvement activity like a retrospective is a statement called the prime directive. It says, *"Regardless of what we discover, we understand and truly believe that everyone did the best job they could, given what they knew at the time, their skills and abilities, the resources available, and the situation at hand."*

The purpose of a retrospective is to explore successes and failures related to product delivery—and why they occurred and how we can improve them—and not to use it as a blaming exercise. We had that statement up on the wall, and it was something we all adopted. Steve Jobs used to talk about this approach when they were building Macintosh. They constantly integrated and tested their ideas daily, unearthing their next constraint, iterating the product based on what they learned, and kept moving forward.

Amazon Web Services had never done a deployment of this scale at the time in the UK, and no company had ever done anything that had to rapidly scale from zero to five million people in seconds. 10gen were improving the drivers to support the MongoDB database to cope with this level of performance, and they had never done that before. We were all outside our knowledge thresholds, but we were all figuring it out together. What we worked really hard on was creating a culture of rapid experimentation, testing, and learning iterations that we would, almost on a daily basis, come together to integrate all the work that we had done. We would then run all our performance tests to make sure that the site could cope with the level of loads that we needed to address.

Invariably, through that process, we would find bugs, or issues, or things would break, but we didn't spend time blaming or assigning whose fault it was. What was really magical about that process is that people spent less time focusing on whose fault it was, and instead saw issues or failures as learning opportunities to keep improving the system. Then, whatever we learned, we fed forward to the next iteration of the product, and then integrated our changes as quickly as possible and ran the tests again.

We knew the Scrapbook product provided an opportunity to demonstrate how technology could become a strategic capability of the Channel 4 organization, rather than the old model of IT as a cost center, or always late, or never delivering. It was a catalyst for change in the company. We launched the Scrapbook within a very challenging timeframe of 19 weeks, and the product and content were really well received by the customers of the network. They loved this new concept of the Scrapbook, and how people could interact with the different content that the on-air talent was creating.

In turn, this provided a new revenue stream for the organization as they monetized their content in new and interesting ways. There were no further outages with the site, and this was the first time in their history that Channel

4 had achieved this. They even won an innovation award for technology excellence in their industry. The real outcome for Channel 4 was a team coming together with a one-team mentality, using technology as a strategic capability to innovate their business model and also deliver great outcomes for their customers.

A lot of great things came out of this project in addition to the successful outcomes achieved by Channel 4. The project provided the impetus for me to co-write my book, *Lean Enterprise.* A lot of the concepts we used during the products development were principles that were fed directly into the book. In addition, Kief Morris—the lead of cloud and infrastructure for the team—wrote a book titled *Infrastructure as Code*, which was seeded from the Channel 4 Scrapbook mission.

CHAPTER 40

The Future Waits for Nobody—My Capital One Journey to the AWS Cloud by Jonathan Allen, EMEA Enterprise Strategist and Evangelist at AWS

Originally posted on 6/16/17: http://amzn.to/capital-one-journey-aws

"If you spend too much time thinking about a thing, you'll never get it done."
—Bruce Lee

There's a quote that's always stuck in my mind, and Marvel Comic fans will know it well—"With great power, comes great responsibility." For me, that great responsibility was making sure that millions of our customers at Capital One UK could use the company's technology services 24x7x365, every time, without fail.

But, unfortunately, like most technology leaders, there were many times, perhaps too many times, when I contemplated the possibility of a service failure. And when this happened, I found myself becoming slightly more risk-focused, even a bit risk-averse. It's only natural. But when you let this fear grab hold of you, you tend to reduce your appetite for change.

Of course, if we're totally rational, the flaws in this thinking quickly surface, because the only constant in life is change—and wow, is it getting faster each day! I believe that the Digital Disruption and the Fourth Industrial Revolution[86] we are now experiencing needs to be embraced, and embraced fully, or it will just consume your business. That's why the choice for all of us, for every technology leader, is fairly simple—do nothing and fade away, or embrace the cloud change to survive and thrive. Ask yourself which choice holds the greater risk.

It's against this big-stakes backdrop that I joined AWS. April 2017 marked the end of my tenure at Capital One UK. And I had an unbelievable 17-year run there. I learned more than I could have imagined about leadership, change, technology, and banking at Capital One. In particular, I learned that as a leader you can have all the intent and ideas you want, but without the trust and respect of your team, which is earned by listening, caring, and promoting their ideas, you're nothing. Fortunately, I had an amazing team, a wonderful manager and super-supportive colleagues whilst at Capital One.

Significant Rewards from Change

My last three years there were the most exciting, however. As UK CTO, I had the privilege of leading the people, process, and technology change as Capital One adopted AWS as its predominant platform. It was a career- and life-changing experience for me, although I'll admit that at the start, when it was all new, it was a little scary, especially when we didn't have much of a roadmap to guide us (AWS has now built one by partnering with companies like Capital One).[87] We got through it, and, in the end, like so many of my peers, I learned that it's only by accomplishing the difficult things that we find reward.

This helps explain my recent decision to join AWS as an EMEA Enterprise Strategist and Evangelist, and it also helps explain why I now want to share my AWS learnings and experience with companies all over the world.

---

86 https://www.weforum.org/agenda/2016/01/digital-disruption-has-only-just-begun/

87 https://aws.amazon.com/map/

The AWS Cloud Changed Everything

I've benefited tremendously by leading teams in nearly every area of infrastructure, application development, and support. And, at Capital One, I gained unique insight into how teams and technology operate in the traditional skill and matrixed on-premises world, which is quite constrained, as well as the thoroughly transformative world of the cloud.

I remember quite vividly, for example, when we reached a tipping point with skilled AWS engineers; there was palpable excitement in the room with multiple engineers and teams sparking ideas off one another because of the potential of using the common cloud building blocks that they all now understood. Contrast this with the siloed and—sometimes unfortunately self-interested—matrixed skill sets of on-premises engineering, and it's hard to imagine ever leading teams the old on-premises way again.

Now, back in 2014, I *thought* we had a good setup after we'd just finished building a converged on-premises infrastructure. Things were a bit faster, and there was some benefit. I *thought* we had bought some breathing space to grow. But, in fact, we hadn't. The age-old truisms of running your own data center were still as rampant as ever. We were still dealing with—siloed technology, reliability challenges, forlorn automation dreams, hard-to-scale systems and little appetite to experiment when hardware was so capex-intensive and time-bound to procure.

Add to this list, my most vexing problem at this point in time—never-ending hardware upgrades. The cycle was so predictable, repetitive, and draining; we'd work hard to complete a storage array/big system upgrade project, and then immediately start in on the next one. And this just went on and on, over and over again.

Surely there was a better way, I thought. And there was. Our US colleagues at Capital One had been experimenting in our innovation labs, testing AWS cloud technology and operating models. The ability to provision infrastructure on the fly, as well as the security and the elasticity, were all extremely compelling, because—finally—those old truisms were being vanquished, one by one. Our founder and CEO, along with the leadership of our global and divisional CIO's, gave us the green light to change. And so we began.

At that time in the UK, we were heavily outsourced, and we were running waterfall processes and had engineers predominantly skilled in legacy technology. So, it would have been so easy to attempt to *boil the ocean* and over-think the "how"—how we could migrate with AWS to the cloud.

Instead, with a natural bias for action, we just started. And we started with a small multi-skilled (two-pizza)[88] team of talented engineers who were given the space, support, and focus to build a cloud production environment that could support the first product.

Over time, one team became two, and then many teams. We built different areas of our AWS cloud infrastructure as it was needed to solve customer problems. And some amazing things happened along the way. Engineers moved out of their silos; a common and unifying technical skill and language emerged; and, instead of having two or three engineers in one legacy data center skill, suddenly, we had many AWS Infrastructure Developers, who did more than just patching, installing, and upgrading hardware in the data center. Even better, we were now part of development teams solving customer problems, utilizing many elements of the AWS building blocks that were appropriate for the customer challenge at hand.

The benefits of our first production instance, established transformational patterns. Including Blue/Green deployments, fast and more frequent deployments, end-to-end logging and monitoring, and everything deployable via pipeline code. All able to leverage the inherent elasticity and availability by design that the platform can provide.

Don't Overthink It, Just Start

The pace of technology is not slowing down. You need to be able to stand on the shoulders of giants to compete in this Fourth Industrial Revolution. Using AWS really does give you the superpowers you need to compete. And, for the

88 http://whatis.techtarget.com/definition/two-pizza-rule

first time, the long- promised, yet never delivered, ability to build transformational customer solutions using technology building blocks is only a few lines of code away.

In the meantime, embrace change, and, whenever you think you've hit a wall, remember—"All of your assumed constraints are debatable."

CHAPTER 41

The Devolution of IT: How SGN, A Major Utility Provider in Europe, Is Modernizing IT Using the Cloud by Paul Hannan, CTO, SGN

Originally posted 5/9/17: http://amzn.to/sgn-cloud-journey

◆ ◆ ◆

"Many people believe that decentralization means loss of control. That's simply not true. You can improve control if you look at control as the control of events and not people."
—Wilbur Creech

In my role as Head of Enterprise Strategy for Amazon Web Services (AWS), I'm very fortunate to have the opportunity to learn how the most forward-thinking and innovative executives from the largest companies around the world are transforming their business using modern technologies. Meaningful transformation requires strong leadership, and in my recent conversations with Paul Hannan, CTO of SGN, I've found his drive, passion, and perspective on leadership, transformation, and organizational change infectious. I thought that others would agree, which is why I'm grateful that Paul agreed to write about his experience below!

◆ ◆ ◆

Utilities, just like many industries, are undergoing a huge amount of disruption, driven by a wide variety of sources, such as changes in the make-up of energy (natural gas continues to expand its role while the shares of coal and oil decline), renewable energy sources become more economically viable, dramatic increases in electric vehicles, new market entrants, evolving cyber threats, and new operating models, among others. As a result, the way that Utility companies use technology needs to change to keep pace. The use of 'smart' grids, real-time network monitoring, robotics, artificial intelligence, and analytics are becoming the norm. The increasing dependence modern-day Utilities and other organizations have on technology is often described as the fourth industrial revolution (see *World Economic Forum).*[89]

Expectations of our users, stakeholders, and regulators have rightly soared. For IT to respond to this expectation, we have had to take a very different path to our traditional approach of providing technology.

I'm a great believer in the importance of devolution. As a CTO for a major utility, I've adopted a technology strategy centered around the devolution of IT out to the business—enabled by the wholesale adoption of cloud services.... utilizing standardization, infrastructure patterns, automation, and orchestration.

Whilst this may be at odds of with the traditional *command-and-control* approach of some CTOs, I believe it's essential to ensure we offer our business the shortest possible path to achieving value through use of technology, and to ensure that the IT function remains relevant in our future organization.

Eighteen months ago, SGN decided that the right thing for our business's future was to drive a wholesale adoption of cloud technology. Rather than being driven by the IT department, this was driven solely by our corporate strategy and cold, hard economics. The only way we could achieve the challenges our board had set out for the business was to adopt a far more agile, secure, cost effective, and durable way of delivering IT services—Cloud.

The associated costs and complexity of trying to build our own bespoke capabilities with these characteristics was simply not viable—from an

89 https://www.weforum.org/focus/the-fourth-industrial-revolution

economics or a time-to-market standpoint. We focused on the wholesale, *all-in* migration to avoid a hybrid model, running two different operational, commercial, and security models was too big a risk for us!

Stephen Orban, Head of Enterprise Strategy for AWS, recently described how Cloud is helping IT organizations give greater autonomy to the business rather than control them, which I wholeheartedly agree with.

However, I also think the level of change that the wholesale adoption of cloud services drives is far wider reaching within the business and offers us a 1-in-25-year opportunity to drive far wider business transformation. Recently, a good friend of mine described the need to consider that the "cloud enables you to sort out IT while also shining a light on all of the other process inefficiencies that have been masked for years."

Don't let anyone tell you that the adoption of cloud services is solely a technology project. Cloud is a catalyst for a wider transformation program, both within IT and beyond—as such, its essential that the program is driven and supported from board-level downwards, rather than from IT upwards.

I've referred to our cloud program as "pulling the thread of transformation," let me explain…

The principle here is that a single change will cause a wider reaching knock on impact, changing one element will cause other legacy processes to unravel. Our experience has been that if you are committing to Cloud technology and adopting best practices around automation, consumption of standardized services, buy don't build, commercial and technical portability, etc. it will have a massive impact to the IT organization. Everybody's role will be impacted to a lesser or (more likely) greater degree, as well as much wider areas such as legal, procurement, finance, accounts payable, audit, corporate risk, and business program delivery.

For example, within our own organization, the areas of change that cloud has directly or indirectly made possible include:

- A reorganization of the entire IT department—new target operating models have changed to focus away from build and run towards direct business engagement and consultancy. Adoption of SIAM—Service

Integration and Management or MSI—Multi-supplier Integration operational models.

- A move toward significantly improved security—adoption of best practice security models such as zero-touch, zero-trust, zero-patch, and no-fix.
- New ways of working with our business—the ability for the business to deliver IT solutions without the need for engagement or ownership by IT has totally changed the balance of the relationship. Business-led programs are ideal for ensuring continued business sponsorship, engagement and accountability.
- With lower barriers-to-entry, new commercial ventures and projects become more economically viable for our business to trial and adopt, driving operational and commercial innovation.
- A change in the focus of legal and procurement—away from bespoke, lengthy contracts to acceptance of standardized, often non-negotiable terms and conditions.
- A focus on the full lifecycle of procure-to-pay delays in payment of suppliers in a utility computing, cloud environment poses a risk for service availability. If you don't pay your bills in time you will get cut off!
- New financial models—a move away from capitalization of IT spend and a move towards operational expense—need to be understood by your finance and tax teams.
- New corporate risks which are tracked at board level, for example, data residency.

These are only a set of the wider changes an adoption of cloud-based services will help to drive within your business. Each business is unique, however if I can share one piece of advice from our cloud adoption journey so far it would be to ***align your cloud program to the corporate strategy...it is the only irrefutable document in the company***. Any initiative which will positively impact the delivery of this strategy will have the attention of your executives, if it is clearly defined and well thought out.

I would also urge you to invest in the partnership with your cloud service providers—develop a mutually beneficial relationship. It's fundamental to de-risking the adoption of new technology and really getting the most out of your investment. The old, confrontational Customer/Supplier model just won't work moving forward.

The adoption of cloud services can be a real agent of change within an organization to drive new ways of working, new business models and the adoption of best practice processes—I wish you the best on your journey, just don't let anyone tell you it's just an IT project!!

CHAPTER 42

Cloud-Based Agility in Responding to Disasters: An American Red Cross Story by Mark Schwartz, Enterprise Strategist, AWS

Original posted on 12/19/17: http://amzn.to/red-cross-disaster-agility

◆ ◆ ◆

When we talk about enterprise agility in the cloud, we're often talking about achieving it through DevOps or other Agile software delivery approaches—about the ability to quickly provision infrastructure, load it up with deployed software, receive fast feedback from users, and scale up and scale down instantaneously. But software agility is only one type of enterprise agility that the cloud can enable.

Starting on August 25, 2017, Hurricane Harvey hit the coast of Texas, pouring almost 52 inches of rain on the Houston area and causing $180 billion of damage.[90] The American Red Cross jumped in by deploying hundreds of volunteers to open shelters and provide food, comfort, and support to people frantically looking for help. Ultimately, the Red Cross worked alongside partners to provide 414,000 overnight stays in emergency shelters, serve 4.5 million meals and snacks, and distribute 1.6 million relief items. Thanks to the generosity of the public, the Red Cross was also able to provide $229 million in direct financial assistance to some 573,000 of the most severely affected households in the first two months.[91] Harvey wasn't the only large

90 Kimberly Amadeo, "Hurricane Harvey Facts, Damage, Costs," *The Balance* (website), September 30, 2017, https://www.thebalance.com/hurricane-harvey-facts-damage-costs-4150087.

91 American Red Cross (blog), "Hurricane Harvey Response: At the 2 Month Mark," http://www.redcross.org/news/article/local/texas/gulf-coast/Hurricane-Harvey-Response-At-2-Month-Mark,

disaster to hit the United States in the fall of 2017. In fact, in just the 45 days after Harvey made landfall in Texas, the Red Cross responded to five additional large and complex disasters, including back-to-back hurricanes—Irma, Maria and Nate.

Because it must respond quickly to unpredictable disasters, the Red Cross mission always requires agility. But, in the case of Harvey, even its adaptive abilities were challenged: the scale of the damage and the amount of assistance available combined to cause a flood of phone calls that quickly overwhelmed the Red Cross call center. As a result, the Red Cross engaged the services of an AWS Partner Network (APN)[92] partner, Voice Foundry,[93] an expert in the implementation of Amazon Connect.[94] Amazon Connect is a self-service, cloud-based contact center service that's based on the same technology used globally by Amazon customer service associates. Within 48 hours, a new call center was in operation, and Amazon employees were taking calls for three of the hurricanes and geographical areas. This helped supplement the usual Red Cross volunteer call centers. When the peak volume of calls subsided two weeks later, the Amazon call center was de-provisioned.

This triumph of enterprise agility was made possible by the Red Cross culture of rapid response, its ability to mobilize and focus efforts at the time of a disaster, and the deep experience of an APN partner who knew just how to respond. As with Agile software delivery, this victory was also achieved through the actions of a small, cross-functional team that worked across organizational silos.

In this case, the team consisted of three Voice Foundry specialists who were supported by twice-daily calls that included leaders of the Red Cross, Voice Foundry, and Amazon. The team was assembled overnight and, early the next morning, it began analyzing and reworking the call routing rules while training the Amazon operators to handle what were often highly emotional phone calls. Their focus was on creating a minimal viable solution that

---

November 2, 2017.

92 https://aws.amazon.com/partners/

93 https://voicefoundry.com/

94 https://aws.amazon.com/connect/

could begin adding value quickly. And, as in any good DevOps process with continuous integration at its core, the team rapidly integrated the various volunteer call centers into a single call routing system. In the 48 hours that it took to provision the new phone lines, the team had set up an entirely new call center, established the routing rules, and trained the new operators—a process that would normally have taken 4 to 5 months for a call center of equivalent size.

To me, one of the most interesting things about this event was not just the speed at which the call center was assembled, but the speed with which it was disassembled as well. When it was needed, it appeared; when it had served its purpose, it was gone. This is precisely the kind of elasticity that makes cloud infrastructure such a powerful driver of agility—but how interesting that this elasticity could exist, and be deployed, for an entire business function! This, I think, is typical of today's cloud, where even pre-trained machine-learning models can be made available to support new ways of doing business within moments.

When I think about true organizational agility, I also think about Hess,[95] which found itself with a need to rapidly divest a number of its businesses. By migrating to the cloud and the AWS platform, the energy company was able to prepare its IT assets to move to the acquiring companies in just six months.

Or the Centers for Medicare and Medicaid (CMS),[96] which developed three new products on AWS after the original challenging launch of healthcare.gov, with no further problems in scalability or responsiveness.

Or, perhaps, the Louisiana Department of Corrections,[97] which faced the challenge of getting inmates heavily controlled access to the Internet, so they could prepare to get jobs when released from prison. The solution here centered on virtual desktops provided by Amazon Workspaces.[98]

---

95 https://aws.amazon.com/solutions/case-studies/hess-corporation/

96 https://aws.amazon.com/solutions/case-studies/healthcare-gov/

97 https://aws.amazon.com/solutions/case-studies/louisiana-doc/

98 https://aws.amazon.com/workspaces/

Each of these cases illustrates how organizations can achieve new kinds of agility under demanding circumstances by using the cloud. But the story of how the Red Cross rapidly scaled up and scaled down its disaster relief efforts in response to the unique circumstances surrounding Hurricane Harvey is an unmatched, dramatic example of using the cloud to achieve organizational agility.

CHAPTER 43

Never Let the Future Disturb You—My Journey to the Cloud by Thomas Blood, EMEA Enterprise Strategist, AWS

Originally posted on 11/14/16: http://amzn.to/embrace-cloud-future

◆ ◆ ◆

"Never let the future disturb you. You will meet it with the same weapons of reason which today arm you against the present."
—Marcus Aurelius

How do you stop the bleeding? That was the question we had to ask ourselves.

One of our business units had experienced a decline in revenue for many months and something had to be done. Membership numbers weren't where we wanted them to be. Our customer experience needed improvement. Our site wasn't as reliable as we would have liked. Releasing new features and products simply took too long.

This is the situation I experienced while leading global marketing technology and web development at a FTSE 100 company. I have been a technologist for more than 20 years (since before the World Wide Web) and felt that I had to do something, even if only to offer advice. I teamed up with a business executive and we began to research the root causes of these challenges.

Several things became clear:

1. While the business model had evolved over more than 10 years, the technology had not kept pace and was being used for things for which it had not originally been intended.
2. Business priorities precluded work to address mounting technical debt and growing technical drift.
3. Complexities in the platform and technical debt caused unexpected problems during development and resulted in bugs, outages, and unplanned work.
4. To combat these mounting pressures, the business invested in a large QA effort, which added days or weeks to the already extended release schedule.
5. In combination, these realities severely hampered the business's ability to deliver. New products required months of development and testing and limited the business to making two or three product bets per year.

The system had been very profitable for years and was highly optimized in many areas. We considered refactoring the existing platform, though we quickly realized that it would take several years of concerted effort to effectively evolve the legacy systems. Given competing priorities and budget limitations, this was simply unrealistic.

Instead, we proposed a greenfield project to develop a cloud-native platform leveraging Amazon Web Services (AWS). This would provide faster time-to-market for new products and features while meeting existing requirements. Initially, the business unit executive team and the global CISO received our proposal with trepidation. So, we took great care to clarify assumptions, to explain capabilities, and to mitigate risks. Our leadership paid off and the project was approved.

To limit the risk to the business, we created a small cross-functional team to develop a functional prototype that would demonstrate the effectiveness of this new approach. We received funding for 90 days and a (mostly) free hand to make rapid decisions within the constraints of compliance and security.

90 days later, the 13 members of our team demonstrated the prototype. Not only had we met the business requirements, but we could now make and release simple feature changes and bug fixes within minutes. We had developed self-service capabilities for the business that previously required IT involvement, and we had demonstrated that we could conceive, develop, and release new product features within days or weeks, instead of the typical weeks or months. We could also scale on demand without having to rely on over-provisioned data centers for the first time.

After this initial success, we received additional funding and an aggressive timeline to expand our services and capabilities. Our roadmap primarily focused on user stories for customer acquisition, fulfillment, customer support, and sustained engagement. We also wanted to create additional self-service capabilities that would enable the business to directly manage the product experience. And, finally, we wanted to expand the platform based on DevOps principles to enable developers to better develop, maintain, and enhance products and features.

We learned by doing—none of us had had significant prior experience with AWS. Members of the original team eventually formed a permanent platform team with the objective of creating self-service infrastructure tools that included systems to build, test, deploy, scale, and maintain applications. Within months of deploying the prototype, this team was getting requests for help from other business units in multiple geographic regions, and it's now well on its way to becoming a Cloud Center of Excellence.

We also gained ancillary benefits that addressed internal needs. We realized, for instance, that we now had a more fine-grained understanding of the cost of developing and operating our product than had previously been possible. We could use metrics to independently optimize each service for performance and cost. We made improvements to security operations, so that findings identified by the InfoSec team could be remedied in a more repeatable automated form. Business operations, too, could be optimized using an extensible framework that made it easy to instrument and automate processes. Finally, technology changes created an opportunity to explore ways to improve communications, gain greater engagement in our agile practice, and invigorate the culture by emphasizing innovation and experimentation.

Our foray into the cloud was a success and established a navigational chart loosely based on four Stages of Adoption for other teams and business units to follow and improve upon. The journey was not easy and there are many things I wish we had known beforehand. However, over the course of those two years, I became thoroughly convinced of the strategic importance of the journey to the cloud. I consider Amazon Web Services to be *the* force-multiplier that gave us the ability to accomplish our "overly aggressive" or "impossible" goals, as some stakeholders had called them.

Which is why I jumped on the opportunity to join Amazon Web Services as Enterprise Evangelist for Europe, the Middle East, and Africa. I grew up in Germany, where I attended high school, and now, more than a quarter century later, I look forward to returning to my European roots. What gets me most fired up is how to evolve processes and technology to unlock unrealized potential—whether that's to grow the bottom line or make life easier for customers and employees. In the past, we were locked into IT decisions and investments for years before we'd get an opportunity to revisit a solution and make it better and/or cheaper; but, today, with the emergence of cloud services, we have an opportunity to constantly improve, or even re-invent, our businesses. AWS was transformational in helping us provide superior services to our customers. Now, I would like to help you do the same.

So, check in from time to time and let me know how your journey is unfolding. What can AWS do to help you realize your vision? What would have to be true for you to take your enterprise to the cloud?

CHAPTER 44

Why the Commercial Sector Should Learn from Government IT (and Not Vice Versa) by Mark Schwartz, Enterprise Strategist, AWS

Originally posted on 10/26/17: http://amzn.to/commercial-sector-learn-from-government-IT

BEFORE I JOINED AWS, I was the CIO of US Citizenship and Immigration Services (USCIS),[99] one of the 15 operational component agencies of the Department of Homeland Security (DHS).[100] It was my first and only foray into government—prior to that role, I had been a CIO and CEO of commercial-sector companies. How did I suddenly find myself in the public sector? One day, when I was trying to decide where to go next with my career, I happened to read an article about the IT challenges Homeland Security was facing, given its nature as a merger of formerly independent agencies. Something clicked, and it engaged the problem solver in me. I wanted to see if I could help fix government IT. I like hard problems.

It was, actually, a hard problem. Homeland Security had inherited all the challenges of federal bureaucracy, and had added to them layers of policy and process meant to control the sub-agencies that operated under its umbrella.

99 https://www.uscis.gov/

100 https://www.dhs.gov/

The result was a kind of organizational sludge that resisted change and (perhaps inadvertently) mandated outdated approaches to IT.

Nevertheless, over the course of my time there, we were able to move USCIS to the cloud and to DevOps practices, and to institute a user-centered design approach where we worked backwards from customer needs to capability design. We went from releasing code to users every 6-12 months, to deploying new functionality several times a week, or as much as several times a day. In the process, we reduced our infrastructure costs 75% by moving to the cloud, transformed the culture, and developed new skills for our employees.

To do all this, we had to innovate on many fronts, creating new approaches to QA, security, project oversight, and procurement. We even unleashed the Netflix Chaos Monkey[101] in the DHS production environment to make sure our systems were always resilient.

The more I work with AWS customers, and the more I present at conferences and speak to audience members, the more I realize that the challenges we faced in transforming a US government agency are similar—or identical—to those faced by every private-sector organization trying to pull off an IT transformation. Indeed, the very nature of a transformation means that it will face organizational impediments. Change agents in both the government and commercial sector need to deal with bureaucracy, organizational politics, conflicting demands from stakeholders, oversight mechanisms that were set up for a different world, budget constraints, constraining compliance requirements, general inertia, lack of skills in the new technologies, and the need for cultural change where employees are fearful and perhaps confused.

Think of the government agency as a laboratory where all these problems exist in their extreme form. Then add the fact that everything one does is in the public eye—IT change leaders are second-guessed by the press, Congress, GAO (Government Accountability Office), OMB (Office of Management and Budget), various inspectors general, ombudspeople, and, well, ultimately the public. For problem solvers, this is, in many ways, the quintessential challenging environment: any solution you devise for cultural transformation must be virtually foolproof, withstand scrutiny, and overcome the mountains

101 https://netflix.github.io/chaosmonkey/

of constraints. On the other hand, any impact you make will be magnified and obvious.

Put another way, if an idea works in the government, it is almost certainly widely applicable to commercial organizations. Government is a place to experiment, fail fast, and learn (only don't describe it this way to Congress).

In my blog posts I discuss some of what we learned, as a team, trying to transform The Big Bureaucracy. You can also read about some of these ideas in my two books: The Art of Business Value[102] and A Seat at the Table: IT Leadership in the Age of Agility.[103] For this post, though, I'll just touch on a few high-level ideas for causing change in an environment where change is extremely hard.

Setting the vision. In an environment where change is hard, there will always be fits and starts, setbacks, and unfortunate compromises. One of the big dangers is that, as these setbacks accumulate, employees may lose their way—the transformation becomes just a jumbled set of incomplete initiatives. It's critical for leaders to avoid this by setting and maintaining a strong, vivid, and compelling vision for where the transformation is heading. My choice of the word "maintaining" is deliberate: it's not enough to set a vision once, at the beginning of the effort. As Stephen Orban, Global Head of Enterprise Strategy at AWS, points out in Chapter 13, What Makes Good Leaders Great?, vision must be reinforced as often as possible.

Moving incrementally. To balance that strong and uncompromising vision, the organization must drive for small, incremental wins. No matter how severe the obstacles, the transformation must start moving in the right direction on Day One. And moving in the right direction does not mean having meetings or preparing presentation decks. It means concrete changes that affect outcomes. We always asked, "What is the smallest thing we can do immediately that will move us toward the vision?" Big vision, small execution.

Provoke and observe. I love this term, which I borrowed from an article by Christopher Avery (he says he borrowed it from somewhere as well). Just

102 https://www.amazon.com/Art-Business-Value-Mark-Schwartz/dp/1942788045

103 https://www.amazon.com/Seat-Table-Leadership-Age-Agility/dp/1942788118

as Agile approaches promote inspecting and adapting, transformation in a difficult environment requires provoking and observing. You don't know all the impediments you'll face until you try something and see what the reaction is. And you don't know which changes will turn out to be easier than you expect until you try experiments. The important thing is to provoke in a considered, deliberate way—you want to provoke in a way that will yield the maximum learning.

I hope that these high-level techniques will help you get started on your transformation journey. They might very well—they've been tried and tested in the government!

CHAPTER 45

Don't Fly Solo on Your Migration—Use the Cloud Buddy System by Philip Potloff, Enterprise Strategist, AWS

Originally posted on 8/22/17: http://amzn.to/dont-fly-solo-cloud

◆ ◆ ◆

Lessons from the Edmunds.com All-in Migration to AWS

The notion of a buddy system has been used for decades in many facets of life, including school, work, and adventure. Whether it's a college freshman being paired with an upperclassman at orientation, an Air Force pilot and his or her wingman, or your weekend scuba diving partner, most buddy systems serve one of two purposes. The first is safety, usually in sports or dangerous activities where you watch each other's backs. And the second is to provide new students or workers with training and guidance when they're paired with a more experienced buddy in order to avoid common, first-time pitfalls, and thus, progress more quickly with confidence.

Speaking personally, having a "cloud buddy" would have eliminated much of the excessive anxiety and experimentation in 2012, when I began the all-in journey to the cloud as CIO at Edmunds.com, one of the largest car shopping websites in North America.

But, unlike today, it was difficult back then to find extensive buddy system resources from other companies that were successfully migrating. All-in reference cases at scale (besides Netflix), managed migration programs, or a mature consulting partner ecosystem would have made life much easier. Fortunately, the current abundance of people, process, and technology now focused on cloud migrations means that an organization never has to go it alone like we did at Edmunds.com; it also means that the level of expertise in accelerating cloud adoption and maximizing cost savings makes all-in strategies more viable than ever.

As a lifelong surfer, I can tell you that the notion of a buddy system when surfing is not a thing—even in dangerous conditions. Going it alone is considered the ultimate soulful pursuit. However, these days, I prefer to take a more practical approach when I'm traveling to a new part of the world to surf. I try to find a buddy who has been there and can tell me everything I need to know about the waves before I paddle out. How shallow is the reef? Is it sharky? What tide is best? Hearing this advice, and benefiting from this experience, reduces my anxiety (usually) and just makes for a more quality experience.

I recently joined a group of former CIOs who make up the Enterprise Strategy team at AWS. Our objective is to help technology executives think through and craft their cloud-first strategies, and one of the ways we do this is by inventing and simplifying new migration acceleration programs that take advantage of our accumulated knowledge (there's no compression algorithm for experience). As former CIOs and AWS customers, we've led our own cloud migrations and helped transform businesses of all shapes and sizes in the process, and our stories are much like the tips and advice I get from my surf buddies when tackling a new wave.

In retrospect, there were three major revelations for me from the Edmunds.com migration story; and, as you'll see, even though we shut down the last Edmunds.com data center in early 2016, the process we went through still tracks closely with the cloud Stages of Adoption that most enterprise migrations are experiencing today.

We're Going to Completely Abandon This High-Performing Data Center Operation

Actually, that's not the precise thought. As CIO at the time, my primary objective was to deliver technology capabilities that stayed ahead of business demand. For the seven years leading up to the cloud migration, we had worked tirelessly to develop what was considered a highly efficient infrastructure operation and DevOps practices. But that efficiency came at a cost to the business, even though it provided daily automated releases and unprecedented reliability. The cost stemmed from allocating more and more of the company's finite resources to support code (private clouds and DevOps toolsets) and not enough to customer-facing application code (new customer features and services). We needed a new paradigm to keep the support code-to-customer code ratio in check without sacrificing any capabilities.

The emerging cloud momentum in 2011/2012 offered an alternative with claims that the public cloud—and, in particular, AWS's scale—could provide better infrastructure and higher-level services at a more competitive price point than you could achieve as an individual company. However, the actual picture was much more "cloudy," and there was no shortage of press declaring the cloud to be more expensive and less reliable than proven on-premises installations. The early adoption of AWS by Netflix gave substantial credibility to the argument that larger, more established businesses could run critical operations in the cloud; but, at the time, we were unable to identify a more apples-to-apples reference implementation for the Edmunds.com business.

A peer reference seemed vitally important back then because there were no buddy system migration resources to speak of that would help us leverage proven cloud adoption patterns.

Lacking any of this knowledge, we built our business case in two steps that have, in time, become standard practice for any company's cloud migration:

1. A proof of concept project that demonstrated the viability of running our critical operations in the cloud.
2. A realistic financial model of an all-in cloud operation that would stand the scrutiny of time and show at least cost parity (or less) with the current infrastructure spend profile.

In hindsight, deciding to stand up a full version of the core Edmunds.com website to demonstrate cloud viability wasn't the quickest or easiest choice for a proof of concept. But, after nearly six months of trial and error by a couple of dedicated engineers, we had incontrovertible proof for even the biggest naysayers that the cloud was a real option for Edmunds.com. Today, AWS and good system integrators have developed buddy system approaches, such as landing zones,[104] a component of the AWS Cloud Adoption Framework,[105] to get migration business cases ramped up much quicker than the route we took.

We felt good enough about the results to take the next step with a deep dive into cloud economics. At this point, we hadn't yet discovered the massive leaps in productivity made possible through cloud native architecture adoption, but we were confident that moving to the cloud probably wouldn't destroy the company.

Developing the financial model seemed like an equally daunting hurdle. The model had to be real, and it had to refrain from aggressive optimization assumptions. We were already efficient and frugal, and I honestly didn't know if we would end up with an operating expense increase or decrease. So, I was a little surprised—after more than a month of analysis—that we had a conservative model demonstrating modest operating expense savings once we completed a two-year migration plan to AWS (synchronized with a primary data center lease expiration). This was in addition to the millions that would be saved each year on capital equipment expenditures. The plan was also a bit of a sandbag, because it was based on pure lift-and-shift assumptions, and we were confident that we could deliver substantially more OpEx savings during the migration, but we didn't know how to prove it upfront.

The favorable financial model and a strong proof of concept result led to an exciting and warmly received presentation to the CEO, who promptly approved our AWS migration recommendation.

One stylistic error I'll point out was my overemphasis on free cash flow savings. I almost entirely ignored the favorable OpEx position, assuming that was a prerequisite for approval; instead, I chose to focus on the bigger

---

104 https://www.slideshare.net/AmazonWebServices/aws-enterprise-summit-netherlands-creating-a-landing-zone

105 https://aws.amazon.com/professional-services/CAF/

combined cash savings figure. It turned out, though, that backing up the OpEx forecast assumptions was more important to the CEO.

Sharpening the business case messaging and the ability to forecast deeper cloud savings is now the specialized focus of the AWS Cloud Economics group.[106] But that team, which assists customers with migration and TCO modeling using proven techniques, wasn't fully formed at the time. Today, the Cloud Economics group at AWS offers some of the best buddy system resources early-on in a cloud journey because it has data on thousands of migrations, and these numbers help predict and quantify the savings from maximizing server utilization and workforce productivity as part of a business case.

I Think We're Actually Going to Pull This Off

It really wasn't that tenuous. But any project touching every single application and system carries a fair amount of risk, and there's never any grace for delays or disruptions due to back-end enhancements. Once applications and data are being migrated, however, you begin to realize that the biggest organizational risk has nothing to do with outages or performance issues. It's finishing. Getting stuck mid-migration not only impacts your cloud TCO model, but it can become a prolonged distraction from the company's priorities.

As I mentioned earlier, it's really critical to "buddy up" as early as possible in your cloud migration. Programs like the AWS Migration Acceleration Program (MAP)[107] or tools such as AWS Database Migration Service (DMS)[108] are both broad and targeted examples of the vast amount of buddy system resources that have been created to avoid many of the challenges we faced during the Edmunds.com migration. These resources have been developed with input and experience derived from thousands of customer migrations, and the programs and tools include an extensive list of proven migration patterns, such as moving from Oracle to Amazon's RDS managed database service.[109]

106 https://aws.amazon.com/economics/

107 https://aws.amazon.com/migration-acceleration-program/

108 https://aws.amazon.com/dms/

109 https://aws.amazon.com/rds/

That said, we did learn a few valuable things as we felt our way through a solo migration. And I believe these learnings are key for any cloud-driven organization wanting to glide past the finish line with vigor instead of crawling out of a nightmare.

1. **Adjusting your initial migration principles is NOT a slippery slope to compromised architecture or failure.** Your cloud migration strategy needs to have principles that are flexible enough to adapt to cloud agility as well as your newfound experience of working in the cloud. We actually started the Edmunds.com migration with a principle to only leverage core compute (EC2) and storage (S3, EBS). But this was due to a lack of familiarity with higher-level AWS services like Amazon RDS, Amazon CloudWatch[110] and Amazon DynamoDB.[111] We very quickly realized the integration and cost benefits of these new cloud native services, including the ability to spend more time on customer code. Today, Edmunds.com is leveraging more than three dozen AWS services.
2. **Use the two-week rule for refactoring decisions.** We started our two-year migration plan with a flexible principle that allowed us to be opportunistic about refactoring; but nothing could delay the two-year target due to the data center lease expiration, so lift-and-shift often became the default. Once the migration was more fully underway, however, the team developed a specific two-week rule of thumb that it still uses today. If we could refactor a sub-optimal component or service in our stack within two weeks, we would refactor versus lift-and-shift. For example, the NFS-based shared storage architecture was high on the refactor list, but it didn't comply with the two-week rule, so it got scheduled at the end of the migration window. On the other hand, many things—like load-balancing, caching, OS distribution, and DNS—were refactored during the migration using the new two-week rule. Depending on your migration timeline, or

110 https://aws.amazon.com/cloudwatch

111 https://aws.amazon.com/dynamodb

development cycle, you might want to use a different time period, but two weeks, or one development sprint, was the optimal constraint for Edmunds.com. A good buddy system resource here is the AWS Application Discovery Service,[112] which systems integrators use to help companies identify and map the dependencies of applications before determining the best candidates for simple lift-and-shift or opportunistic refactoring. And now you can track your migration status in the recently released AWS Migration Hub.[113] Be sure to read "6 Strategies for Migrating Applications to the Cloud" (Chapter 6) by Stephen Orban, Global Head of Enterprise Strategy at AWS. This illuminating post provides a very useful construct.

3. **You don't need to dump your current team and hire a group of cloud all-stars.** Edmunds.com didn't hire a single employee specifically for the cloud migration, let alone a "cloud specialist." The lesson here was establishing clear leadership and the equivalent of a Cloud Center of Excellence with well-defined objectives and key results. The head of our cloud migration team, Ajit Zadgaonkar, was originally hired to lead our automated testing team (SDETs). His team already had experience collaborating with the traditional Ops team on automated provisioning and Continuous Integration and Delivery. Again, Stephen Orban has written on this topic, in Chapter 15: "You Already Have the People You Need to Succeed With the Cloud." The other important consideration here is that you are making a choice between new cloud/devops engineers who know nothing about your environment and your existing team that has years of tribal knowledge on the dependencies, flows, and business requirements of your critical applications. My AWS colleague, Jonathan Allen, has detailed the process he went through at Capital One to train and prepare his existing team for the cloud.

112 https://aws.amazon.com/application-discovery/

113 https://aws.amazon.com/migration-hub/

Getting the people and culture components right are as important as the technology decisions you make because they enable the internal buddy system that will ensure consistency across the organization as a migration accelerates and touches more applications.

I'm Glad I Didn't Screw My Future Self

This third—and final—revelation was more of an epilogue to the migration from my new position and perspective in the organization. Shortly after we completed the move to AWS, I transitioned from COO/CIO and became Edmunds's first Chief Digital Officer. In this role, I focused on developing a next-generation advertising platform and bringing new business models to market, such as online auto retailing and messaging applications. So, I went from providing cloud services to consuming them. And, looking back, I was definitely a demanding customer!

After all of its applications and data had migrated to AWS on schedule, Edmunds.com was able to cut IT expenditures by 30 percent.[114] The team achieved even greater savings by starting to optimize or rethink every component of the stack with a cloud native architecture (auto-scaling, microservices, ad hoc compute), or by simply replacing components outright with an AWS service. Many of the initiatives that my new teams were working on had a technology profile that looked nothing like what was initially migrated to AWS, and, in some cases, they were entirely serverless. There is already a burgeoning buddy ecosystem for serverless architectures, and it's changing the math on comparisons between cloud and on-premises installations.

These new AWS services, like AWS Lambda,[115] AWS Elastic Beanstalk,[116] Amazon Kinesis,[117] and AWS Glue,[118] could never have been rationally developed internally by Edmunds.com, but they delivered new capabilities for customers at a previously unimaginable rate. And, looking forward, the gap

114 https://aws.amazon.com/solutions/case-studies/edmunds/
115 https://aws.amazon.com/lambda
116 https://aws.amazon.com/elasticbeanstalk/
117 https://aws.amazon.com/kinesis/
118 https://aws.amazon.com/glue/

in what can be accomplished in your data center versus cloud native services is only increasing. For example, the mainstreaming of machine learning and artificial intelligence requires very different technology profiles than your run-of-the-mill web application. Maintaining those distinct skill sets and specialized compute capacity in house is far from the best option for most organizations.

The goal, of course, is to help get you on the path so you can reinvent your own technology and business.

In the meantime, try using the buddy system to start or finish your migration as quickly as possible. Then you'll be able to reduce your support code obligations for maintaining infrastructure and deliver more customer code using cloud native services.

The biggest changes start with simple steps.

CHAPTER 46

Culture Eats Strategy for Breakfast: Friedkin's Journey Toward XOIT & High-Multiple Cultures by Natty Gur, CIO, The Friedkin Group

Originally posted on 3/16/17: http://amzn.to/friedkin-xiot

I HAVE LONG SINCE FELT that the role of the CIO and central IT is moving away from command and control, and toward line-of-business enablement. I'm also seeing some organizations, like Amazon, which have taken this one step further in a move toward complete decentralization, where culture and best practice serve as the forcing function that allows teams to operate independently. This trend—trading off consistency for time-to-market—is an important one.

I have been engaged in a fascinating discussion with Natty Gur, the CIO of The Friedkin Group,[119] about their cultural transformation. Natty's background in fighting terrorism has given him some interesting, and from my perspective unique, perspectives on this trend, which he graciously agreed to offer below.

One of the main reasons for public cloud transformation is to be more agile, and as a business to provide faster and more reliable services for your customer.

119 https://www.linkedin.com/company-beta/46754/?pathWildcard=46754

But is that enough? Is it just technological transformation that is needed, or do you need to transform your culture as a business as well?

In a previous life, I found myself providing IT services to one of the leading counter-terrorism organizations in the world. Just as I began my work with this organization, they began experiencing a wave of suicide bombers which they couldn't stop, or even minimize. It took this organization considerable time before it realized the reason for their failure was a change within their enemy; their enemy's structure had changed from a single, centralized group to thousands of unconnected terror cells, each with the same purpose: Destroy the organization's country. Once this was understood, they made a unique decision: adopt the same structure and operation of their rivals; break the classical organizational silos down into small hybrid groups, each with the needed expertise from the old structure, in order to reach a clear purpose. These groups were also created to run with complete autonomy and full authorization to do what needs to be done in order to reach the whole group's purpose. This change proved successful and the organization won the war, and while I was there, I learned a very important lesson.

Silos are IT's worst enemy. I have seen it while working for IT organizations as well as working as an Enterprise Architecture consultant to organizations all over the world. No one will argue that silos prevent IT groups from reaching their full potential and fully contributing to their companies.

Today, most large companies' main competitors are the thousands of unconnected startups who all share the same purpose of disrupting and taking over an industry. So, if countries, when faced with this problem, can change the way their defense organizations are structured to help win the war, why are companies are not changing the way their IT organizations are structured and how they operate?

While terror cells and startups are obviously very different, they do share some fundamental organizational characteristics. For instance, as small groups with limited resources, they tend to push their members to take responsibility for many aspects within the group, and are empowering group members to manage themselves. Another similarity between those two groups is the environment of trust between members. Members can make mistakes or bring crazy ideas with the knowledge that no one is going to penalized them. While you may feel that this thinking is too extreme, but empowerment and trust are the two main principles behind the Toyota Production System, which has had such profound influence worldwide.

The world is in a constant flux of change, with new generations entering the workplace. Each new generation has different expectations for work, and are each driven by different values from the previous generations. As leaders, it is our responsibility to ensure that our organization is attractive to the next generation in order to sustain continued success. To that end, have you given thought to your current organization's structure, and asked whether it is attractive to the next generation?

The success of hybrid teams, and the fact that IT silos are actually damaging to organizations, along with the understanding that trust and empowerment, and finally, the need to attract new generations—all these factors pushed me to look for a new way to structure and organize our IT group.

It was clear to me early in that Scientific Management and hierarchies are not going to work for us, however it took me a lot of time, and some embarrassing mistakes, to formulate an alternative. The breakthrough was the discovery of Holacracy. Yet, while this management philosophy held a lot of potential and could lead us down the right path, there were too many aspects that simply wouldn't fit within our corporate culture. Therefore, we made significant adjustments to Holacracy and developed what we call XOIT (Exponentially growing IT).

What follows are the main principles that have helped XOIT be successful for us:

First, we broke down the silos by defining a clear IT purpose. Then we thought about the main functions needed to reach our purpose. From there we turned each function into a group by defining the group's purpose, the group's domains (what the group owns), and the group's accountabilities. The next step was to break each group into sub-groups and roles which are needed to reach that group's purpose. For every sub-group and role, we defined their purpose, domains and accountabilities, and so on. When we finished, we had a clustering of groups containing all roles needed to reach our IT purpose.

Once the structure was in place, we assigned all of our associates to roles based on their knowledge, experience, and preferences. In XOIT we have one golden rule: each role and each group that has accountability or is responsible for a domain must have full autonomy and authority to decide how it will reach its purpose (whether group or role).

To ensure each group has full autonomy and authority, we have taken the classical manager role and broken it down into three distinct roles filled by three different associates. The first role is responsible for the day-to-day operations of the group. This role is filled by an associate designated by the lead of the super-group. The second role is responsible for the way the group is structured and operates. In other words, this role defines the group's other roles, its purpose, its domains, and its accountabilities within the group, as well as establishes group policies. This role is elected by all team members. The third role is responsible for all the administrative personnel that would typically fall onto a classical manager.

While self-management is at the core of this philosophy, it is important that the groups and roles maintain accountability. Therefore, each group has simple and measurable metrics defined for it, which give a clear indication to anyone whether the group is moving forward, backward, or standing still.

Finally, we have adopted a process which enables any associate to bring new proposals of how the group should operate and be organized based on tensions the associate felt as they filled roles within the group. A core tenet of these proposals is that unless a group member can prove that the proposal will take the group backward, they must be tested in reality. This encourages a spirit of experimentation.

Our metrics, and our customer and stakeholder feedback—even our associate engagement surveys—all point to a positive, significant change in IT. It's not that we are perfect, there is still a long way to go and we are in a beginning of long journey. But the evidence shows that this new way to organize and operate is yielding positive results.

For additional information and tracking XOIT, feel free to visit https://friedkingroupcio.com/

CHAPTER 47

The Fast and the Furious: How the Evolution of Cloud Computing Is Accelerating Builder Velocity by Ilya Epshteyn, Enterprise Solutions Architect – AWS Solution Architecture at AWS

Originally posted on 5/15/17: http://amzn.to/cloud-builder-velocity

In my role as Head of Enterprise Strategy for AWS, I have a lot to be grateful for. After having led a large-scale business transformation using the cloud as the CIO of Dow Jones, I now have a front-row seat to watch some of the largest companies in the world (News Corp, Capital One, GE) transform their business using the cloud. This seat affords me the opportunity to learn from some of the brightest and most innovative minds in the industry—both from our customers and from within AWS. As often happens in life, I sometimes run into ideas from others that "if I only knew then," I would have done things a lot differently. One such set of ideas was recently gifted to me by Ilya Epshteyn, one of AWS' well-tenured Solution Architects.

In a world of unprecedented market disruption, where barriers to entry are crumbling and a great user experience means more than a hundred-year-old brand name, CEOs are coming to expect a different conversation with IT. CIOs and CTOs are trying to change the conversation from that of an *IT*

Supplier to that of a *Business Partner.* An *IT Supplier* conversation (Business waiting on IT) sounds familiar: "when will the infrastructure be ready, when will you deliver X capability, how can you reduce my budget by X?" By contrast, a *Business Partner* conversation (IT waits on Business) sounds very different: "Feel free to start building what you need when you need to by provisioning on demand; here is a new security API you can leverage; here are the results of a pilot we ran; and by the way, we cut your costs by X this month." The latter is initiated by IT with a single goal in mind: bringing products to market. And accelerating innovation and product development hinges on increasing the velocity of your builders.

To make this happen, IT needs to focus on the tasks that differentiate the business and enable builders to move faster. IT tasks that do not differentiate the business should be automated and offloaded to a platform that provides as much of that functionality as possible out-of-the-box. This paradigm shift requires a transformation, and as Stephen often points out, it's often more about the people and your organization than the underlying technology. For many of our customers, this is a multi-year journey, one that began long before cloud came along—whether they realize it or not.

Pre-Virtualization Era

In the pre-virtualization era, infrastructure deployment was manual. Infrastructure took months to be provisioned, racked, stacked, wired, installed, and configured. Most applications were monolithic, with tight interdependencies and manual deployment. Installation and configuration guides commonly ran dozens, if not hundreds, of pages long. Data center efficiency was also a challenge. With such long provisioning cycles, businesses would often provision 25-40 percent *more than what was needed during peak usage.* With so much wasted capacity, utilization rates were often less than 10 percent. In this model, the development, infrastructure and operations teams all operated in silos, requiring weeks or months of planning for every change. Operations itself became a major challenge since everything was managed and operated manually, with little standardization across environments.

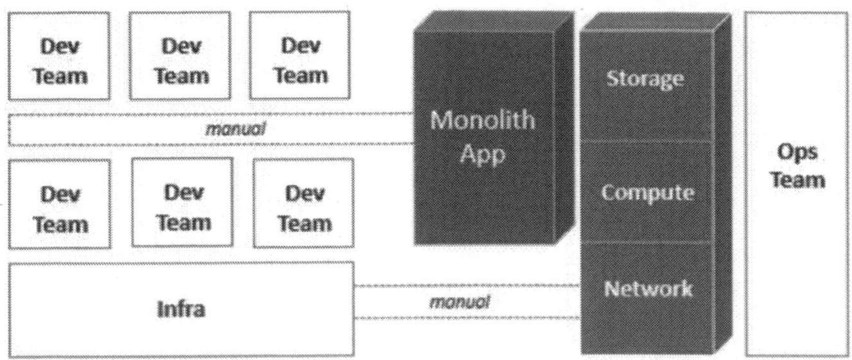

Pre-Virtualization Era Development Structure

Promises of Virtualization/Private Cloud

Virtualization and private cloud promised a better way. They sought to improve server efficiency, shrink infrastructure footprint, enable automation and new service delivery models, and, most important, bring agility to business.

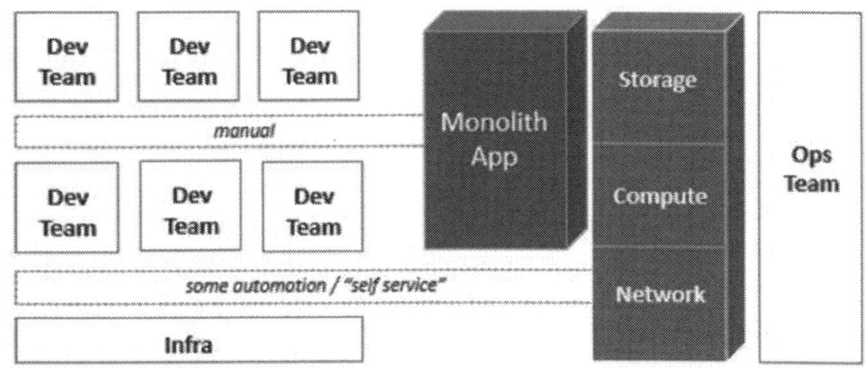

Virtualization Era Development Structure

In reality, while server virtualization had positive impacts on power and cooling consumption and even allowed organizations to consolidate and/or rationalize some data centers, many of the promised benefits have not been fully achieved. Server provisioning time has decreased and servers can often be spun up in minutes, but the reality is that provisioning and capacity planning has not significantly improved. Builders are still forced to procure capacity required for peak based on anticipated (and elusive) usage patterns of their product. In some cases, builders then have to double that to accommodate for disaster recovery (DR, or n-1) scenarios. Business cases to spread this across multiple business units are developed three to five years out to justify the capital expenditure, and in most cases, we've found that they don't end up paying off.

The infrastructure teams have started to take advantage of the automation that virtualization enables, but for the most part this capability has not been extended to the development teams. *Self-service* delivery models are still mostly manual, often requiring days or weeks of approvals using limited automation. Changes are hard since teams are still operating in silos, and orchestrating changes across these silos often comes with a lot of bureaucratic overhead that is rarely managed well. Ultimately, very little has been achieved in terms of builder velocity. Builders are still frustrated by limited automation, which impacts their productivity. It still takes too long to get things done for the business.

The good news is that organizations that have taken steps to virtualize their environments or pursue a private cloud strategy are able to move to the next phase of this evolution at a faster pace than customers that have not already made that shift. Virtualization not only simplifies the actual migration of VMs, but it's also a reflection of an organization's ability to transform, adapt to business needs, and upskill its IT workforce.

Journey to the Cloud

Completing the shift to the cloud helps customers realize the unfulfilled promises of virtualization. The on-demand provisioning of network, compute, storage, database, and other resources in a pay-as-you-go model provides unprecedented agility and helps accelerate the velocity of the development teams. But even in the cloud, this transformation is not instantaneous. Rather, the velocity of the development teams accelerates as the customer journeys through various Stages of Adoption.

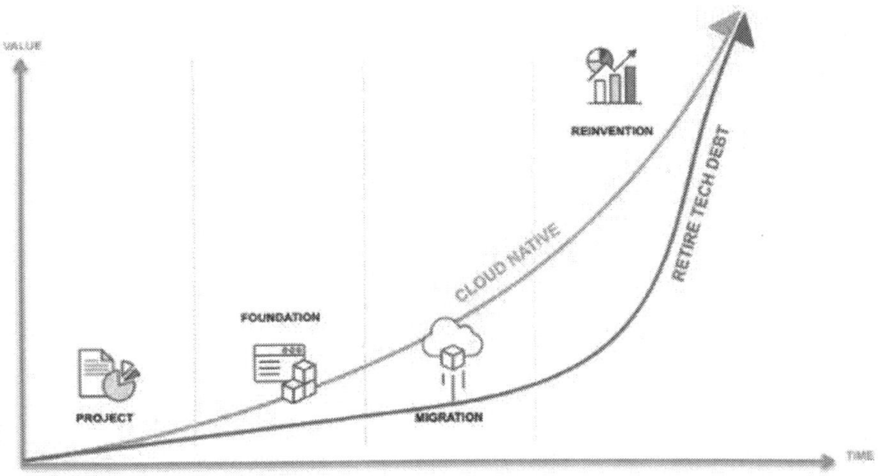

Cloud Adoption—Project Through Migration Stages

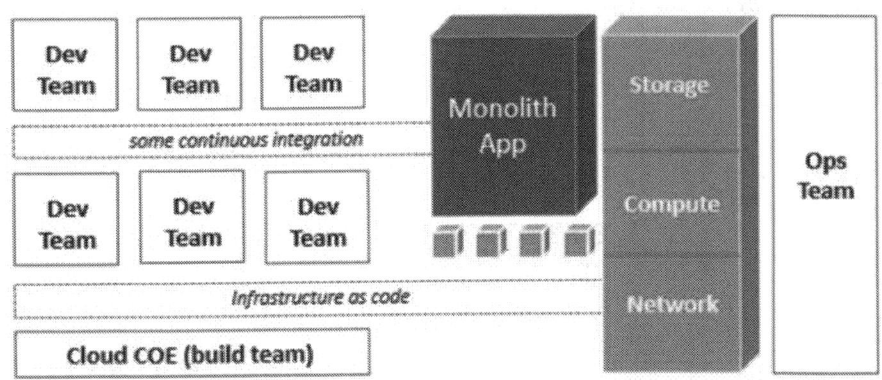

Early Cloud Adoption Development Structure

During the first three stages of cloud adoption, where organizations (1) start with a few projects to learn the benefits, (2) lay the foundation for organizational transformation through a Cloud Center of Excellence team, and (3) execute mass migrations, we start to see realization of several key factors that directly accelerate the velocity of your builders.

- **Infrastructure as Code.** Early in the Project stage, customers may do certain things manually. As they move to Foundation and Migration stages, however, they embrace Infrastructure as Code. This means that all infrastructure is not simply automated with scripts, but is developed and maintained as code (i.e. CloudFormation). These templates can be reused to deploy entire environments and stacks within minutes.
- **Cloud Center of Excellence.** The CCoE team develops and maintains the core infrastructure templates, designs reference architectures, educates the dev teams and helps them migrate applications to the cloud. The development teams leverage infrastructure as code pipelines and are starting to develop continuous integration pipelines for their applications.
- **Adoption of AWS services.** During these early stages, we see a high degree of adoption of AWS foundational services, including Amazon Elastic Compute Cloud (EC2),[120] Amazon Elastic Block Store (EBS),[121] Amazon Elastic Load Balancing (ELB),[122] Amazon Simple Storage Service (S3),[123] AWS Identity and Access Management (IAM),[124] AWS Key Management Service (KMS),[125] AWS CloudFormation,[126] and Amazon CloudWatch.[127] Customers are also starting to decouple

120 https://aws.amazon.com/ec2/
121 https://aws.amazon.com/ebs/
122 https://aws.amazon.com/elasticloadbalancing/
123 https://aws.amazon.com/s3/
124 https://aws.amazon.com/iam/
125 https://aws.amazon.com/kms/
126 https://aws.amazon.com/cloudformation/
127 https://aws.amazon.com/cloudwatch/

their monolithic applications and take advantage of AWS managed services when possible. The degree of adoption of higher level services at these stages usually depends on the customer's migration strategy and what percentage of applications is cloud native and what percentage is being re-hosted, re-platformed, or re-factored to take advantage of the full breadth of the AWS platform.

- **Security.** Although security can traditionally be a big obstacle to agility, when implemented properly in AWS it can bring a level of transparency, auditability, and automation far greater than what can be achieved on premise.

Cloud Adoption—Reinvention Phase

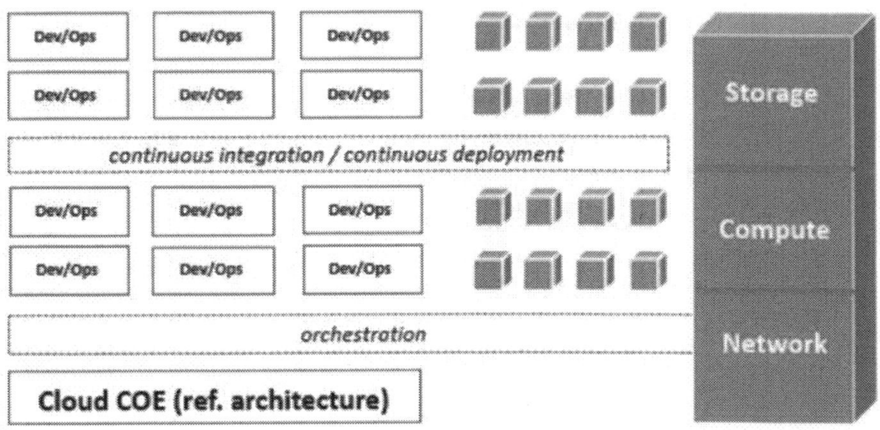

Reinvented Development Structure

There is no doubt that the velocity of the dev teams is greatly improved once the customer moves through the initial Stages of Adoption. But, in most cases, the opportunity to optimize does not end with the Migration stage. Rarely do customers have the opportunity or resources to re-architect all of their applications to be cloud native as part of the migration (see Chapter 7:

Cloud-Native vs. Lift-and-Shift). This creates an opportunity for constant reinvention to further accelerate builder velocity. Re-architecting the applications often entails decoupling and decomposing the monolith into smaller services with APIs while maximizing reusability. As part of this process, customers are looking to offload the undifferentiated portions of the application to the AWS platform and laser focus on the business logic instead.

During the Reinvention phase, organizations typically opt for more fully managed services such as Amazon Kinesis[128] for ingestion of data, AWS Lambda[129] for real time processing, Amazon Aurora[130] and Amazon DynamoDB[131] for relational and NoSQL databases, and Amazon Redshift[132] for data warehousing, so that builders can spend maximum amount of time on the business differentiators. Developing the best queuing, messaging or API management solution is unlikely to move the needle for your business. Rather, it's your algorithms, business workflows, and real-time analytics that will delight your customers and help grow your business. At this stage, we also see a more focused effort to transform Operations to a true DevOps model. The Cloud COE also focuses more on developing reference architectures, governance, and compliance frameworks and allowing the development team more autonomy to deploy both infrastructure and applications through a unified CI/CD pipeline. And the security teams are accelerating their velocity by embracing DevSecOps methodologies and exposing security capabilities via APIs.

Evolution of Compute and Big Data

To put this into perspective, let's look at how this evolution has played out in the areas of compute and big data in the cloud.

The first major compute evolution in recent times was from physical servers to virtual servers in data centers. This stage brought about higher utilization, uniformed environments, hardware independence, and new DR

128 https://aws.amazon.com/kinesis/

129 https://aws.amazon.com/lambda/

130 https://aws.amazon.com/rds/aurora/

131 https://aws.amazon.com/dynamodb/

132 https://aws.amazon.com/redshift/

capabilities. The next phase was virtual servers in the cloud. This brought about on-demand resources, greater scalability and agility, and improved availability and fault tolerance. But from a builder velocity perspective, there is still room for improvement. You still need to worry about high availability and DR, need to manage golden images and patch the servers, and need to right size the instances to your workload. From a builder perspective, all you want to do is focus on the business logic and have it run on schedule or in response to an event.

This is where AWS Lambda and the transition to serverless computing come in. With AWS Lambda, there are no servers to manage or patch. The builder simply writes his or her function while the Lambda service automatically manages execution, high availability, and scalability. VidRoll, for example, uses AWS Lambda to power its business logic for real time ad bidding and to transcode videos in real time.[133] With AWS Lambda, VidRoll can have 2-3 engineers doing the work of 8-10 engineers, a direct result of code reusability and not having to understand or worry about the infrastructure.

Another similar example is in the evolution of big data services on AWS. Customers may run a self-managed Hadoop cluster on Amazon EC2 and Amazon EBS. In fact, they may see some initial benefits in terms of on-demand provision of resources, pay-as-you-go model, many different instance types, and more. But many of the challenges with such architectures on premise may continue to persist in the cloud. For example, because of the coupled nature of compute and storage, your cluster will be over-utilized during peak hours and underutilized at other times. You can't shut down the cluster easily during off peak since you need to persist the data in HDFS, and you constantly need to move large amounts of data to local HDFS before you can even run a query.

Amazon EMR[134] addresses these issues by decoupling your compute and storage and leveraging S3 as your persisted data lake. FINRA, for example, is able to launch a new HBase cluster on EMR and accept queries in less than 30 minutes because the data stays on S3, as compared to two days on

---

133 https://aws.amazon.com/solutions/case-studies/vidroll/

134 https://aws.amazon.com/emr/

FINRA's self-managed EC2 cluster.[135] Leveraging S3 for data storage has also reduced FINRA's cost and enabled FINRA to right-size the cluster for the workload. The builders and data engineers are also no longer locked into long-term technology decisions, but can evolve the analytics platform and experiment with new tools as business demands. And what if the data scientists don't want to manage any cluster at all? Amazon Athena[136] offers a completely Serverless option. With zero spin time and transparent upgrades, the data scientist can simply write an SQL query and have Presto engine execute it immediately.

With any transformation, it can be hard to know how to measure success and keep the end goal in sight. Focusing on the velocity of your dev teams provides a great yardstick for cloud success, and can help guide your decisions as you become a *Business Partner* and continue to evolve and reinvent with AWS.

135 https://aws.amazon.com/blogs/big-data/low-latency-access-on-trillions-of-records-finras-architecture-using-apache-hbase-on-amazon-emr-with-amazon-s3/

136 https://aws.amazon.com/athena/

CHAPTER 48

Tenets Provide Essential Guidance on Your Cloud Journey by Joe Chung, Enterprise Strategist & Evangelist at AWS

Originally posted on 3/8/17: http://amzn.to/cloud-tenets

> *"**Tenet:** a principle, belief, or doctrine generally held to be true; especially: one held in common by members of an organization, movement, or profession."*
>
> —Merriam-Webster

Making a large-scale transition to the cloud means that many development, operations, and security processes are no longer applicable—or, they're dramatically altered in the cloud. For example, AWS provides programmatic access to provision and manage your IT infrastructure (aka infrastructure as code) while many companies still rely on manual processes (e.g. ITIL) to manage their IT services.

Adopting this type of significant change is just the beginning, however; enterprises on a cloud journey or looking to transform the way they deliver value to the business must also find ways to embrace a host of sweeping new paradigms. And fully embracing these new models requires organizations to make a series of decisions about how they'll modify their approach and processes. Having said this, though, we know that there are many areas that are unique to each customer. We also know that confronting so many decisions can be overwhelming—especially when there's no best answer.

At Amazon, our Leadership Principles[137] guide and shape our behavior and culture, and they're at the heart of our ability to innovate at a rapid pace to serve our customers. But what you may not know is that our programs and teams have a culture that establishes tenets to help guide decisions and provide focus and priorities specific to their area. My recommendation is to define a set of cloud tenets to help guide you to the decisions that make the most sense for your organization. As one of my colleagues at AWS says, "Tenets get everyone in agreement about critical questions that can't be verified factually."

For example—

Do you want application teams to have full reign and control over all the services available in AWS, or should you enforce service standards or provide additional control planes on top of AWS?

There's no absolute right or wrong answer to this question, and it's likely that your environment or industry will push you in one direction or the other. But defining a tenet that encapsulates your philosophy on the control or freedom you want to give your application teams should be worked out up front.

Here are some other questions to help define your organization's cloud tenets.

What type of developer experience do you want to create? Do you want to preserve the experience of a startup developer? Or perhaps all interactions will be handled through code. Do you want allowances for people to manually provision or change services?

What are your security tenets? Your existing policies will probably be oriented to an on-premises world. So maybe this is an opportunity to refine your policies; for example, do you want to use intrusion detection technology or allow full transparency to all events, with the ability to act when necessary?

How do you want to operate in AWS? Full automation? Consistency with existing operations processes?

And do you want centralized decision making when it comes to which cloud services will be leveraged? Or do you want to give full autonomy to your development teams and move to a DevOps model?

137 https://www.amazon.jobs/principles

To better assist you in defining your cloud tenets, I've picked out six of the most relevant suggestions from guidance provided to Amazon teams and programs. But, before I list them, I want to be sure to give a shout out to the many authors at Amazon who have helped contribute to the thinking below.

The charter or mission states the what; the tenets state the how. Tenets are principles and core values that the program or team uses to fulfill the mission or charter. Exceptional tenets explain what the program is about better than the charter.

Be memorable. Being memorable is correlated with effective teaching. Experience shows that the best tenets are memorable. Two attributes of memorable tenets are challenging the reader, and being concise.

Each tenet has only one main idea. Chiseling a tenet down to a single essential idea makes the tenet memorable and clear.

Be program specific. Good tenets will get people excited about the cloud program. People outside the cloud program should find that the tenets give them insight about the program. Don't make a common tenet-writing mistake—creating a tenet that applies to many projects and communicates virtually no information, such as, "We will have world-class cloud capabilities."

Counsel. Tenets help individuals make hard choices and trade-offs. A tenet takes a stand by declaring that a program cares more about one thing than another. Tenets guide rather than prescribe detailed actions. There will also be tension between tenets, and that's okay (e.g. tenets around agility versus enforcement of policies or control).

Tenets keep you honest. It's easy to get caught up in group-think or distracted by the nuances of a specific project and lose sight of the overall goals. Stepping back, setting tenets, and then considering those tenets along the way (only changing them when you step back again) will help you keep track of the wider strategy.

I'll leave you with two of my favorite cloud program tenets that I helped defined for Accenture's journey to the cloud.

We need the ability to provision and manage cloud services as fast as consuming the "native" platform directly—"Provision as fast as with a credit card."

Give app teams the control / ability to consume cloud services without artificial barriers—"If AWS deployed to the public, why can't we use it?"

I'd love to hear your cloud tenets, so please send them to me for the benefit of those making a cloud journey with AWS.

CHAPTER 49

Building a Center of Excellence (CoE) team to transform your Tech Organization Milin Patel, Principal Architect and Co-Founder, Rearc

◆ ◆ ◆

I HAVE BEEN VERY FORTUNATE to be involved in a few enterprise IT transformations over the past five years. It all started under the leadership of Stephen Orban at Dow Jones where I was tasked to figure out the new way to build and run software in the cloud so that we could stay relevant and cater to constantly changing customer demand. Stephen talks about our journey in this book and I can only add that the 3 years I was leading Dow Jones' DevOps movement were the most fulfilling and rewarding years of my career. So much so, that I have partnered with some of the others from this journey (Mahesh Varma and Chad Wintzer) to found Rearc, a business that helps other companies unleash the potential of DevOps and the cloud.

Our success at Dow Jones and Rearc can largely be attributed to making developers the focal point of the journey, and treating them as paying customers. My goal with this story is to inspire leaders looking to transform their organization with my experiences building and running a successful Center of Excellence (CoE) team at Dow Jones. As Stephen describes, the CoE team at Dow Jones enabled the transformation of our Software Development and

Operations practices. While this CoE story is more geared towards Cloud and DevOps adoption, the 6-step approach I outline can be applied to solve other problems across your organization as well.

From my perspective, *the goal of a Center of Excellence team is to take a large, widespread, deep-rooted organizational problem and solve it in a smaller scope with an open-minded approach and then leverage the small wins to scale it across the organization.*

The specific problem we were tasked with at Dow Jones was **accelerating software delivery**. In 2013, we were seeing a big shift in consumer behavior around consumption of news and media content. The Wall Street Journal (part of Dow Jones) has traditionally been a newspaper company, but our readers were looking to consume news information on their phones, tablets, and other connected devices. They expected us to provide a seamless digital experience across devices and platforms.

In order to meet our readers' needs, we had to deliver new features and experiences at a very fast pace, but *we were just too slow.* Our current waterfall approach (see diagram below) to building and running software was just not meeting our growing business and customer needs.

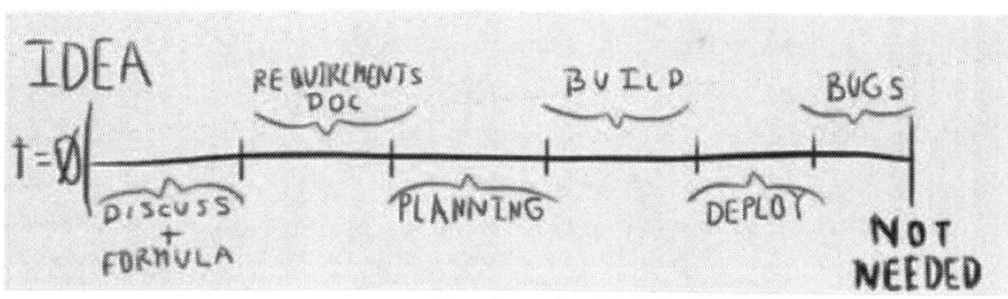

Simply too slow

The only way to solve this problem was to fundamentally change our approach to software development and delivery.

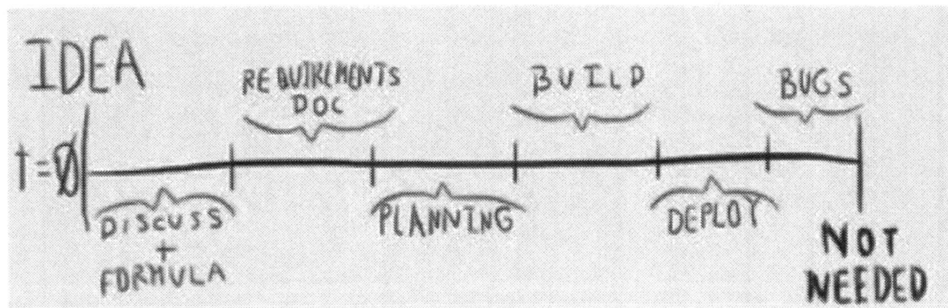

Software is never done

We had to move away from infrastructure-driven projects with huge capital costs and slow delivery cycles to a nimble, software engineering-driven cloud-first approach that would allow us to iterate quickly without the fear of failure and financial risk.

Given this problem and some initial experience working with cloud, Stephen was confident that Cloud based technologies and DevOps practices were necessary ingredients to the solution. But how do we take a large organization accustomed to working in a specific way and change everything it knows about infrastructure, operations, and software delivery? At the time, there wasn't much industry knowledge for us to draw from. All of this led to the formation of our **Center of Excellence** team at Dow Jones (internally referred to as the DevOps team). I am still very honored to be given the opportunity to be one of the 3 founding members of our CoE team.

Our ***mission statement*** *was to figure out the right tooling and practices that would empower our development teams to deliver awesome digital experiences for our customers with agility and confidence.*

Cloud was implicitly included in the solution since our primary goal was to *deliver software development agility* which required us to experiment, fail fast, and move on to the next experiment until we found the right answer. It required us to use cloud services that abstracted away the undifferentiated heavy-lifting so that we can focus on the customer.

The target end state was clear, but the approach on how to get there was built over time. I am hoping that sharing my 6-Step approach will provide a path for you to consider within your organization.

Step-1 Forming the team

The CoE team should start small. After having done it at Dow Jones, I have realized how important it was to have the right people be part of the founding team. A few important traits to look out for members of the founding team:

- Experimentation-driven: possesses ability to learn from failures and iterate quickly
- Bold: not afraid to challenge the status-quo
- Can take an idea from its ideation phase to successful implementation
- Appreciates the impact of developer productivity and operational excellence
- Can scale his/her skills through others

Our CoE comprised of engineers with strong technical skills and diverse backgrounds. Your top-notch tier-1 engineering talent usually has a good amount of trust built within the organization which makes it easy for them to have a positive influence across rest of the organization. I personally think internal hires work best but having a mix of internal talent with new hires or strategic partners can also jump-start your CoE efforts. In our case, we needed engineers that understood networks, storage, systems administration, and software development. While our founding team comprised of internal hires, we subsequently added external hires and college graduates.

Step-2 Deliver some quick wins

With the larger vision of an organizational transformation, it is necessary to narrow the initial focus to deliver a single, relatively small, but important project successfully. In our case, as Stephen describes in Chapter 1, one of our early projects was to migrate out of a datacenter in Hong Kong.

Lift n' Shift Application Migration

Within six weeks, we migrated the WSJ Asia datacenter (in a lift n' shift manner) to AWS' Tokyo region. It was a perfect start for the CoE team—we had to figure out the networking (VPCs, load balancing, WAN acceleration, data replication between our US data centers and Tokyo), machine images (AMIs) in AWS, application performance, traffic distribution, change management etc. We were able to do this only because we had the autonomy to make all the necessary decisions to make the migration successful.

The success of our first production cloud deployment allowed us to showcase our work to rest of the organization and get over that initial cusp of running a production app in the cloud. There was lesser fear and uncertainty about operating in the cloud. It opened up a dialogue around what's possible rather than what's unknown.

Step-3 Acquire Leadership support

It is important that the technology leadership delivers a clear message to rest of the organization about the challenges we face and what the plan of action is to address those challenges. In our case, Stephen and his leadership team did not miss any opportunity to talk about the CoE team's work. While you absolutely need to have a grassroots adoption for a new technology, I strongly believe that a clear vision and message delivered from leadership is equally needed. For us, internal blogs and town halls strengthened the message across the entire organization.

Step-4 Build re-usable Patterns and Reference architectures

Once we gained some experience running the first set of applications in the cloud, it was clear we needed a somewhat repeatable process to onboard more applications. In talking with multiple application teams, a few patterns started emerging. We were able to build reference architectures and blueprints that were slightly opinionated but mostly non-objectionable to the app teams.

Our CoE team did an awesome job with not only building the reference architectures but also building the necessary tooling to automate the provisioning and operations of applications leveraging these reference architectures. It was a carrot for the application teams to get their apps up and running quickly while we got to standardize patterns across the organization and reduce the operational overhead.

Step-6 Engage and Evangelize

Riding on the success of our initial wins and leadership support, the rest of the organization began to engage and be part of the transition. The CoE team has to capitalize on this. We started engaging with rest of the organization by doing DevOps Days, Lunch Workshops, Training sessions (via a DevOps University program) and showcased case studies of successful cloud projects. Our internal customers (development teams) presented their work in the DevOps Days and workshops which was a much more powerful message than just external presentations. Bringing architects and developer evangelists from AWS and Chef brought in a good deal of excitement and showcased how serious we were in our transformation efforts.

Step-6 Scale and Re-organize

Once you have a few initial projects delivered successfully using the newer approaches and practices, the rest of the organization should become eager to leverage the services, tools, and expertise of the CoE for their specific needs and problems.

You have to carefully plan for this critical last step of scaling the CoE function across the rest of the organization. In our case, we were a little late to find out that the CoE had become a bottleneck for rest of the organization to adopt Cloud and DevOps practices. Eventually, we built federated teams and built DevOps capabilities within each application team to scale out the CoE's function.

Conclusion

The bottoms-up approach to DevOps with strong leadership support allowed us to discover what's possible and implement new experiences for our customers at a pace never seen before at the company. In 2013, a change to WSJ.com required the developer to submit their build artifact to QA by 10am for Tues and Thurs build nights. 10–15 engineers got on a conference bridge that lasted for hours and often didn't succeed. In 2016, and we had 100+ deployments throughout the day across multiple services to production and non-production environments. No one missed the build nights, but perhaps most importantly, the number of production incidents decreased significantly and the confidence level was much higher across all the engineering teams.

CHAPTER 50

Driving Change and Managing Innovation in a Cloud-First Business Reinvention by Joe Chung, Enterprise Strategist & Evangelist at AWS

Originally posted on 12/21/16: http://amzn.to/cloud-driving-change-innovation

◆ ◆ ◆

"Without change there is no innovation, creativity, or incentive for improvement. Those who initiate change will have a better opportunity to manage the change that is inevitable."

—William Pollard

I discovered the future of enterprise computing five years ago, when I attended QCon in San Francisco. And, surrounded by some of the world's leading architects and engineers from companies like Amazon, Facebook, Netflix, and LinkedIn, I kept picking up on two major themes at the conference—the move to micro-services and distributed systems, and the use of AWS to host these micro-services architectures. Coupled with AWS, the new architectures provided unprecedented levels of scale, elasticity, and availability. But even more astounding was the amount of innovation and change that sites like amazon.com and Netflix were able to drive into their platforms without downtime.

This contribution by: Joe Chung

Back in 2011, when I attended QCon, I was a managing director in Accenture's IT organization, responsible for Enterprise Architecture, Agile Delivery, and Innovation. Before that, I spent 15 years driving global, large-scale IT implementations and transformations in many areas of Accenture's business functions. Today, however, I'm an Enterprise Strategist at AWS, and my role is to share experiences and strategies with enterprise technology executives so the cloud can help them increase speed and agility while lowering costs.

Returning to my technological epiphanies at QCon—once the conference ended, I was eager to put my new learning to work. I immediately changed our architecture principles at Accenture so they were services-first and cloud-first. We then looked at ways to apply AWS services to meet our challenges.

There was an application which leveraged a proprietary scanning and imaging technology to ingest millions of documents. But the system took days to scan and process the documents and have them available for the user to see. With low—and unacceptable—levels of customer satisfaction, my team created an architecture component that allowed our custom applications to use AWS S3 as a storage mechanism. The team then created a mobile application that allowed users to take pictures of the receipts and store them in S3. The benefit was quicker storage and retrieval achieved in seconds with no additional load on the legacy application.

But the truly amazing result was cost; what was implemented was actually 100 times cheaper than the proprietary system because of the move away from the need for a physical scanning solution and leveraging S3's low storage costs.

Another example of how the power of AWS was leveraged was in the management of development and test servers. Despite having virtualized over 95 percent of server hardware in our data centers, the elastic usage pattern of development and test environments meant they were only utilized a low percentage of time; even for a well-run operation like this, that was still too much waste. So, the development and test environments were shifted to AWS and put on a schedule that shut servers down during weekends and nights. The benefits of the cloud were clear at this point, but we still had internal debates as to whether the cloud or on-premises machines were cheaper to run. Through these projects, however, we began to invest in training and enabling architecture, engineering and infrastructure resources on cloud technologies.

Three years ago, we had a changing of the guard with a new CIO and new boss—and Accenture IT shifted from an era of consolidation, outsourcing, and cost take-out to an era of digitalization. Like so many organizations, we felt the pressure to quickly adopt cloud, mobile, analytics, and other capabilities to create end-user-focused digital services.

In order to move at speed, and with agility, we launched a cloud mass migration program with the goal of having 90 percent of our workloads in the cloud in three years. A year into the program, all workloads in our data center on the east coast were migrated to the cloud. We also provisioned 90 percent of new infrastructure in the cloud, particularly when it was aligned to new investments. For example, when we re-platformed the accenture.com website, it was provisioned from the get-go on AWS. As a result, we achieved savings of $3.6 million in annualized benefit because the cloud enabled optimized server schedules and server sizes. With our services running in the cloud, we also saw better performance, better uptimes, and lower mean time to resolve when incidents arose. Toward the end of 2016, over 60 percent of workloads were in the cloud. Meanwhile, Accenture was on track to shut down its primary data center by August 2017, and it was also on target to meet the 90 percent goal. This put to rest any debate as to whether the cloud was cheaper.

Despite Accenture's rapid migration to the cloud and AWS services, it still didn't have a Netflix or amazon.com-like story. This changed in 2015, however, when there was direction from the C-suite to implement a critical new capability in less than a year's time.

Once we got to work on this, we decided to build a micro-services-based architecture on AWS because the business had to leverage an iterative design process and we needed the ability to adapt rapidly to changing requirements. Through the development of this capability, new features and changes were continually deployed into production. When I reviewed the final stats with the team, I was blown away by the results, which were pretty awesome and far-reaching. In less than a year, we had —

- Deployed over 12 major releases
- Developed 20 micro-services
- Deployed over 4,000 times to our environments, with zero downtime
- And, delivered a successful service and experience to a global population of almost 400,000 employees

The business was absolutely thrilled with these major breakthroughs. And, during our postmortem, I asked the team if we would have been as successful without the power of AWS. The answer was no.

One last note—as I reflect on Accenture's journey to the cloud, I see a strong alignment with the AWS Stages of Adoption mental model. Accenture started with a few projects so it could begin to leverage and understand AWS services. It then moved to the foundation stage by growing a group of people focused on cloud-centric architecture and engineering. And, once the transformative decision was made to become a digital organization, Accenture implemented a mass migration to the cloud. Finally, with the latest services we developed, Accenture was able to re-invent how it architected and engineered services with new levels of capability, speed, scale, and availability.

I believe every enterprise has the opportunity to deliver stories like this—and stories like those of Netflix and amazon.com, too—and that's why I'm super-excited to be a part of AWS and help enterprises in their journey to the cloud.

CHAPTER 51

3 Benefits of Automating Compliance in the Cloud Thomas Blood, EMEA Enterprise Strategist, AWS

Originally posted on 1/4/17: http://amzn.to/automate-compliance-in-cloud

◆ ◆ ◆

"It takes 20 years to build a reputation and five minutes to ruin it."
—Warren Buffett

I've supported compliance and security requirements throughout my technology career. In some cases, these requirements were extremely burdensome—for example, when my team was preparing for a Department of Defense audit, which consumed more than 50 percent of our time for months on end. But, in almost every case, I was able to promote the use of automated solutions to make our lives easier, while enhancing our security and compliance posture as well. And today, moving to the cloud offers you the potential to significantly improve your compliance efforts without an equally significant increase in personnel and cost.

Let me explain.

Compliance officers are typically charged with assessing and managing risk to the financial, organizational, and reputational standing of an enterprise. This is a tall order in an enterprise setting because of the complexities inherent in people, processes, and technology plus the regulatory variations across industries and geographic regions.

There's also a natural tension between the business and compliance. Businesses must innovate their products and improve the customer experience. The compliance team, on the other hand, is focused on limiting or preventing risk exposure, which can be at odds with introducing new products and features. That's why the compliance team often seeks to maintain the status quo. The bottom line is that the natural tension between business and compliance—while healthy at times—can strain relationships and frequently results in increased costs, and slower time-to-market.

Typically, the compliance team engages in an annual compliance assessment, writes a report, and sets goals for remediation. The business and technology teams are then presented with timelines in which to remediate any findings. Product managers and technology leaders understand the importance of compliance, but they often regard the assessment as an "exercise" and a distraction from generating value. For their part, business leaders dread the findings of the annual compliance report because they believe that these "non-functional" requirements will redirect resources to something that's not on the strategic roadmap for the next few quarters. Furthermore, compliance is frequently addressed as an afterthought in the development process. Unfortunately, however, experience tells us that, left unattended, compliance issues can eventually turn into technical debt.

Even though the compliance process is often perceived as onerous, the outcomes can add meaningful value to the customer. Indeed, informed by legal and ethical considerations, compliance should be seen as a measure of quality that ensures a great customer experience, especially if the review encompasses security, reliability, and responsiveness. Your cloud strategy can play a major role here—by transforming the relationship between business and compliance stakeholders and, thus, improving the outcomes for your enterprise and its customers. More specifically, by including compliance requirements early in the product or service lifecycle, you can ensure that you meet policy and regulations objectives, while improving your value proposition.

Here's how.

First, there's an immediate savings in moving to AWS. During my own journey to the cloud, I realized that the AWS Shared Responsibility

Model[138] was our friend. In the old days, we had to manage the physical infrastructure in order to ensure regulatory compliance. This caused additional delays when we had to procure hardware to support technology initiatives. It also invariably increased our operational burden, because it usually meant more work for the infrastructure team without additional staffing. By moving our workloads into the cloud, we shifted the responsibility for maintaining a secure and compliant physical infrastructure to AWS, bringing to bear resources and expertise that we could never have provided ourselves. Put another way, we were able to grow our capabilities, while decreasing the surface area we had to secure on our own. This freed up time for our operations team to focus on other value-added work, such as creating additional automation.

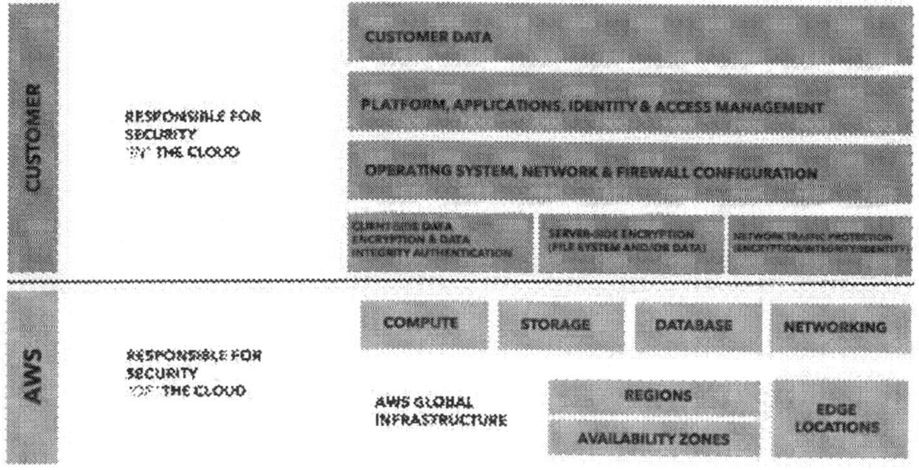

AWS Shared Responsibility Model

Second, shifting workloads to the cloud encourages greater automation. Environments can be deployed based on standardized and approved templates, which can then be version-controlled. This concept is known as *infrastructure-as-code*, and the security and compliance benefits are profound. When infrastructure is managed as code, infrastructure can automatically

138 https://aws.amazon.com/compliance/shared-responsibility-model/

be validated using scripts that ensure security best practices are followed. AWS also supports defining compliance rules in AWS Config[139] that can be automatically verified. As a result, when automation is leveraged, the compliance team can validate legal and security requirements every time the system is changed, rather than relying on a periodic system review. In addition, compliance and security test automation can be pushed into the software development process with the potential to prevent policy violations before they are deployed into production. Lastly, findings can be captured in a daily report and sent to a ticketing system that assigns the problem to a specific individual or even triggers an automated remediation response. Capital One, for instance, has developed a rules engine called Cloud Custodian[140] that it uses to define and programmatically enforce policies in its cloud platform.

And third, when the automated process or manual review identifies a problem, the remediation can be much easier to deploy. In the case of an infrastructure vulnerability, for example, the infrastructure template can be modified in code and will automatically be applied for all future implementations. If the problem exists in an application, the risk might be mitigated either by deploying a fix to the application, or by implementing a compensating control, such as adding a rule to the AWS Web Application Firewall.[141]

Over time, your cloud strategy can foster a proactive culture of compliance that regards compliance and security as value-added customer-centric activities. You'll reach this milestone when your product team includes compliance requirements as user-stories in the product backlog, or when developers routinely add compliance-related tests to their software development process.

---

139 https://aws.amazon.com/config/

140 https://medium.com/capital-one-developers/cloud-custodian-9d90b3160a72#.5cwjzy2ce

141 https://aws.amazon.com/waf/

Let me know if you've automated your compliance process in AWS, or if you'd like to learn more about this topic. In the meantime, here are some links to additional resources that might be helpful:

Automating Governance on AWS:
https://d0.awsstatic.com/whitepapers/compliance/Automating_Governance_on_AWS.pdf

How to Monitor AWS Account Configuration Changes and API Calls to Amazon EC2 Security Groups:
https://aws.amazon.com/blogs/security/how-to-monitor-aws-account-configuration-changes-and-api-calls-to-amazon-ec2-security-groups/

Introduction to DevSecOps on AWS—Slideshare
https://www.slideshare.net/AmazonWebServices/introduction-to-devsecops-on-aws-68522874

AWS re:Invent 2016: Compliance Architecture: How Capital One Automates the Guard Rails:
https://youtu.be/wfzzJj3IiDc

CHAPTER 52

Lowering the Cost of Curiosity by Mark Schwartz, Enterprise Strategist at AWS

Originally posted on 1/3/18: http://amzn.to/Lowering-Cost-of-Curiosity

In his post on the AWS Public Sector blog, John Brady, the CISO of the Financial Industry Regulatory Authority (FINRA), talks about building a data lake in the cloud to reduce the cost of curiosity. The concept is brilliant and consistent with the way I like to think about agility and innovation: that reducing the cost of experimentation with the cloud and DevOps gives enterprises the key to encouraging innovation. The cost of curiosity is essentially this same idea translated into the world of data.

FINRA regulates one critical part of the securities industry—brokerage firms doing business with the public in the United States. Its mission is to protect investors and maintain market integrity by looking for cases of fraud, abuse, and insider trading. Every day, FINRA receives and processes 6 terabytes of data, representing an average of 37 billion new records, although, on peak days, it can receive over 75 billion transactions. FINRA analysts run analytics on this data and also run interactive queries on what is often more than 600 terabytes of data. They can also query years of historical data—petabyte scale—in minutes or hours, rather than weeks or months.

Because they are looking for suspicious patterns—where "suspicious" is not always well-defined in advance—it's important that FINRA analysts be able to be … well, curious. And the speed and low cost that FINRA is able to achieve with its data lake in the cloud make this curiosity actionable.

That, in a sense, is data agility—a state where companies can explore possibilities without defining all their requirements in advance; where they can get fast feedback on results and use that feedback to modify their approach; and where they can adapt rapidly to change and work to confirm or refute hypotheses they may generate. Lowering the cost of curiosity is crucial to achieving this state. It's a necessary enabler that permits organizations to use data in an Agile way.

Of course, security is an important consideration when allowing analysts the freedom to be curious. For most companies, keeping personal information private is a key consideration in analytics; for FINRA, the integrity of its data and compliance with financial industry regulations are especially critical. That's why—consistent with good Agile development practices—FINRA brought security engineering into its process at the very beginning. Indeed, FINRA's DevOps process gives it consistency in deployments to ensure fully compliant environments, and AWS tools help it oversee systems in production by monitoring for continued security. According to Brady:

In the last four years as we transitioned to the cloud, I have come to realize that as a relatively small organization, we can be far more secure in the cloud and achieve a higher level of assurance at a much lower cost, in terms of effort and dollars invested. We determined that security in AWS is superior to our on-premises data center across several dimensions, including patching, encryption, auditing and logging, entitlements, and compliance.

I agree with Brady. In my earlier role as the CIO of US Citizenship and Immigration Services (USCIS), I often made the case that, even as a relatively large organization, we were more secure in the cloud than in the Department of Homeland Security (DHS) data centers, especially when comparing across similar dimensions to those Brady mentions.

The specifics of FINRA's solution, as Brady explains, included the involvement of security, audit, and compliance groups early in the process; micro-segmenting servers with security groups; administering keys with AWS Key Management Service (KMS); using the controls it could inherit from Amazon EC2 and AWS Lambda; and setting up a DevOps automation process to ensure testing and compliance during its development and deployment processes.

With these security controls, FINRA has been able to reduce the cost, as well as the risk, of curiosity. For a look at what it means to make big data Agile, please take a look at Part One[142] and Part Two[143] of Brady's posts. I think you'll agree that this represents a new dimension in enterprise agility.

142 https://aws.amazon.com/blogs/publicsector/analytics-without-limits-finras-scalable-and-secure-big-data-architecture-part-1/

143 https://aws.amazon.com/blogs/publicsector/analytics-without-limits-finras-scalable-and-secure-big-data-architecture-part-2/

CHAPTER 53

12 Steps to Get Started with the Cloud by Jonathan Allen, Enterprise Strategist & Evangelist at AWS

Originally posted on 1/5/18: http://amzn.to/12-Steps-To-Get-Started

"The hardest thing about getting started is getting started."

—Guy Kawasaki

Executives are under increasing pressure to deliver cloud transformation results quickly. Getting fully setup for success should not stop you from getting going, that said, understanding lessons learned from those who have gone before, saves time and money.

As an enterprise strategist for Amazon Web Services, I currently travel around the globe helping the largest companies in the world discover and unlock the power of AWS. Having lived the journey to cloud and worked with countless customers, executives are always keen to understand what journey lessons they can learn from those who have gone before.

With the benefit of hindsight here are 12 steps to get going when starting, that consistently deliver results:

Step 1—Don't Over-Think It; Assign a Developer and start!

Just start. Focus on developing the skills and then delivering. All the help you'll need is available. And all the answers to your questions have already been written. Start with one forward thinking Engineer or Developer and have them start using AWS through the Console, get to know the services and spin up an EC2 test instance. From my own journey we started with a very small team of forward leaning Engineers, the early lessons they harvested, compounded and continually informed our journey.

Step 2—Empower a Single-Threaded Leader

In my experience, it can be fatal if you don't have the support of a single-threaded executive leader during the transition. This leadership function simply can't be delegated. The CIO, or, at the very least, a direct report of the CIO has to lead this effort and be visible each and every day to provide direction and remove roadblocks. And ensure inclusive executive alignment and air cover across the leadership spectrum to reinforce the profound benefits of moving to the public cloud across the spectrums of cost, security, and speed of product development speed.

Put another way, the single-threaded leader must be a rallying point for all change curves. They must listen well and bring a "can-do" attitude to the cloud transition. When I was acting in this capacity at Capital One UK, I used the tenet "All of your assumed constraints are debatable" this served as a forcing function so people looked at each perceived problem as an opportunity instead. Finally, the single-threaded leader must be responsible for establishing Step 3, which is crucial.

Step 3—Create Your 2-Pizza Cloud Business Office

Amazon's 2-pizza team concept means a team of around 8–10 people. And, in this case, I'm referring to the virtual leadership team, which needs to provide strategic oversight and tactical air cover for engineers and developers as you move to the public cloud. It's essential that this cloud leadership team takes into account—and addresses—everybody's fear (of the unknown).

The best Cloud Business Office teams include —

- CIO or Direct Report with Single Threaded Ownership
- Procurement or Vendor Management
- Legal Lead
- Chief Information Security Officer
- Chief Financial Officer or Direct Report
- Head of Infrastructure
- Head of Delivery
- Engineering or Product Manager of the first Cloud Engineering Team
- Risk Leader (needed in most organizations, but especially regulated ones)
- Audit Leader (needed in most organizations, but especially regulated ones)

These folks need to follow the Agile cadence established in your organization and meet at least weekly (if not daily), to review progress and remove roadblocks.

Step 4—Establish Your Tenets (And Be Prepared to Amend Them as You Go)

Tenet—"a principle, belief, or doctrine generally held to be true; especially: one held in common by members of an organization, movement, or profession." Common Tenets provide a common frame of reference for everyone to understand the 'how' questions that can arise. When creating them, seek feedback from a wide source, but strive for a small but powerful list. I've written and read a lot of cloud tenets over the past year; here are some of the best and things you should consider when creating yours:

1. Be Clear on your Business Goal—Are you reducing cost? Transforming to digital native? Reducing your app footprint? Or closing your data

center? It's challenging to do all this at the same time, so my advice is to go cloud first for all new, lift and shift the old, and then optimize and eliminate apps. See Chapter 6 for more details.

2. Choose a Predominant Public Cloud Partner—This provides focus for your organization to get to an expert level with a predominant platform, avoiding the distractions that come with too many platforms, across people, process, and technology paradigms.
3. Agree on Your Security Objectives. I recommend reading these excellent white papers and getting advice on this from AWS ProServe and working backwards from your regulators' compliance bar, this enables wide adoption as engineers and developers will understand the 'Why' things need to be a certain way.
4. Remember That the Team You Have Is the Team You Need. Recruiting new takes a very long time, so invest in the people in your organization. Training, hands-on management, and certification will make a significant difference.
5. You Build It, You Support It—small 2 pizza teams that own what they build can be transformational for a business. Its one of the mechanisms Amazon uses to scale and innovate.
6. Command and Control or Trust, But Verify approaches for your Engineers and Developers. Both have pros and cons, see step 12 for more.

Step 5—Create Your Questions Parking Lot

The leadership team (everyone) will have lots of questions. Unfortunately, many hours will be wasted trying to answer them without the right folks in the room, and your progress could stall. Create a parking lot for these questions, and be sure to respect every single question on the list as you keep moving forward.

Top Tip—The very best way to answer a lot of questions quickly is to arrange an executive briefing centre session with AWS. These sessions, which are always fascinating, enlightening, and exciting, can be best held in Seattle or can potentially be arranged for the country where you are based. Speak to your account manager to arrange a session, and we'll work with you to answer all your questions or ping me.

Step 6—Create Your 2-Pizza Cloud Engineering Team

Creating your holistic cloud engineering team, which will be hands-on with the AWS cloud, is critical. The word holistic is very important here. This team must comprise a cross-section of multiple skills types, including—

- Infrastructure Engineers, who understand the existing IP addresses, boundary security (firewalls), routing, server build standards, and a whole host of things in between.
- Security Engineers, who will ensure that everything is built and coded to meet your company's security objectives.
- Application Engineers, who will ensure that the coding logic of the product you're building gets built.
- Operations Engineers, who will ensure that your ITIL elements can be adapted to benefit from the cloud.
- A Lead Architect, who has deep and broad domain experience. Ideally, this person will also have experience with infrastructure as code.

A solid understanding of how to use AWS services and features in an optimal way will also greatly accelerate your cloud journey. This cloud engineering team should work together in one physical group. Remote working, while possible, isn't optimal. And the team must be fully dedicated to your organization's cloud journey, side of the desk just won't work.

Step 7—Bring in a Partner or AWS ProServe

The cloud engineering team will probably have valid opinions in terms of best approaches and best tools. And it will probably have strong feelings about which practices to keep from your data center and which to discard. To accelerate this process, bring in some experts who have been there and done it before.

Step 8—Work Backwards From Your Security, Compliance and Availability Objectives

First and foremost, the AWS cloud is secure. Taking time to ensure that the Cloud Engineering Team and the Cloud Business Office understand the AWS Shared Responsibility Model is a crucial priority though. (Illustration below) Then, work with your AWS Solutions Architecture/ProServe resource to ensure that you're using the Deep Security tools appropriately to meet your security objectives. There are a number of different configuration possibilities available, but my advice is to work backwards from your company's external regulatory bar (PCIDSS, HIPAA) etc. You should also work with AWS to ensure that you've adopted the best practices that meet your compliance and security objectives. Once you agree on these, write them down, publish them, and make sure there's a direct channel to the leadership team and single-threaded leader so people can cordially challenge them if they want.

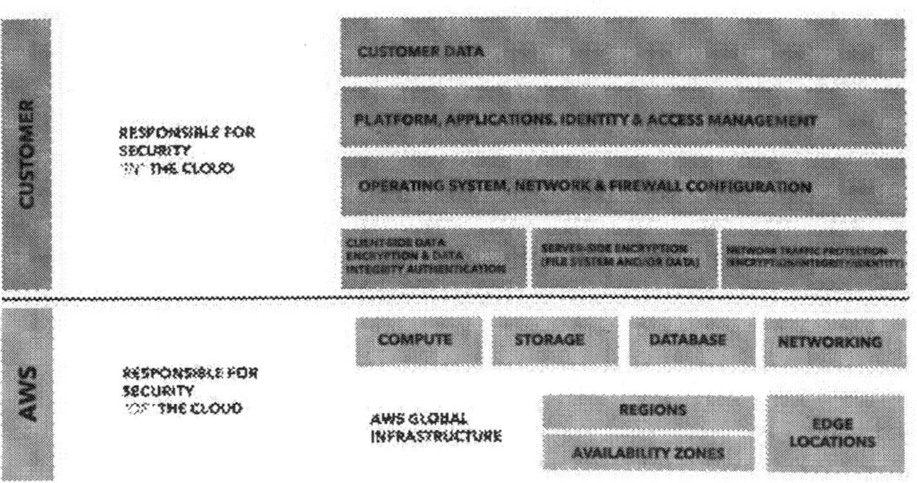

AWS Shared Responsibility Model

Step 9—Ship Something to Production That Is Important, But Not Critical

You need to get something that's meaningful into production. When I was doing this at Capital One, getting the first micro service live was the team's goal. Don't set a deadline; instead, set a Minimum Viable Product (MVP) and have the Cloud Engineering Team stay focused on the product. Experience has shown that shipping something live in this way can take anywhere from a couple of days to 12 weeks. If it's taking longer than 12 weeks, one of the earlier steps isn't working, so have a retrospective and utilize the 5 Why's to understand why.

Step 10—Train, Gain Experience, and Certify Your Teams

The key role of the CCoE is to ensure that the people journey for everyone is managed positively and proactively. It's also crucially important that you put in place the right training and certification programs to enable scaling. I cover this comprehensively here.

Step 11—Start Migrating—"Plans Are Worthless, But Planning Is Everything"—Dwight D. Eisenhower

Once you have multiple teams you can really start thinking about migrating. And, as teams realize how easy it is to build on AWS, building new on Cloud becomes the default. But what about all the incumbent systems that still require a staggering amount of 24x7x365 maintenance and upgrades? This is a good place for the Cloud Business Office to work with AWS on using the AWS Migration Acceleration Program (MAP) which has been shaped by all the customers who have migrated to AWS. To shape your migration journey, use the 6 R's, which is a simple looking, yet comprehensive decision guide on how best to migrate your apps. In its simplest guise, using 6 colours of Sticky Notes I have worked with leaders in a day, and have got to an 80% Straw Man Proposal that can help towards generating a Directional Business Case for MAP. The best programmes are continually planning to make the maximum use of Re-Host, some Re-Platforming and a little Re-Architecting to get there quickly alongside a MAP Partner.

Step 12—Trust, But Verify

Finally, the question that many larger enterprises come back to time and time again is "How do I balance control (especially security) and innovation?" It's a tough question to definitively answer. At Capital One Cloud Custodian, which allows administrators and users to easily define policy rules for a well-managed cloud infrastructure that's both secure and cost-optimized worked incredibly well. My good friend and ex-Capital One colleague Kapil Thangavelu talks here on the this great Open Source project for which he is the Product Manager. It was fascinating to hear 3M talk at re:invent 2017 about how they are leveraging the Cloud Custodian tool to help them with their Governance and get their setup just right.

Remember—"All of your assumed constraints are debatable."

Acknowledgments

◆ ◆ ◆

FIRST AND FOREMOST, THANKS TO my wife Meghan and daughters Harper and Finley for your ongoing love and support. I can't imagine what it must be like to listen to me talk about technology all of the time, and the fact that you put up with my travel schedule is greatly appreciated.

Thanks to my Mom, for putting me on a pedestal that I don't deserve. I couldn't have possibly appreciated what you've done for me until I had my own children, and the learning in this book would not have been possible without your love and support.

Thanks to every leader I had the opportunity to work for, with, or watch along the way. In a strange way, I've learned more from observing how not to lead than I have from observing how to lead.

Thanks to all the people who have put up with me in the trenches—at Bloomberg, Dow Jones, and now AWS. I've never had a job or worked on a team I didn't like, and I've appreciated creating products with all of you.

Thanks to everyone who contributed guest posts to my blog (and this book). I've learned a lot from working with you, and I am glad to be able to call you my colleagues and friends.

Thanks to the many customers who have agreed to spend time with me and the AWS team. You are shaping the products we offer each and every day, and I've learned more about business and how to affect change in large organizations from you in the last three years than I have throughout my entire career. More good things to come.

And thanks to the people who supported me with research and editing of the blog posts that are included in this book, including Jennifer Marsten, Bill Meyers, and Peter Economy.

A special thanks to Jack Levy, Miguel Sancho, and Mark Schwartz, each of whom spent many hours providing feedback on this manuscript as it came together. Readers will be the ultimate judge, but I found your feedback very useful, even if it was hard to accept at times.

Finally, I'd like to dedicate this book to my "Nanny and Gampa." My grandfather began teaching me about the market when I was 8 years old, and taught me how equity options worked before you could find a strike price online. He taught me the importance of hard work and education, and he sparked my strong passion for business at a very young age. My grandfather passed away in 2012, and my grandmother followed a few months after. Not a day goes by that I wish I could call them for advice, but I know they're listening.

Made in the USA
Middletown, DE
12 April 2018